National capital
Provincial Capital
Provincial Boundary
Kankesanturai
Point Pedro
Jaffna Peninsula
Karaitivu I.
Jaffna
Kayts I.
Punkudutivu I.
Jaffna Lagoon
Elephant Pass
Palk Strait
Delft I.
Palk Bay
Devipattinam
INDIA
Rameswaram
Pamban I.
Dhanushkodi
Adam's Bridge
Iranaitivu Is.
Kilinochchi
Puthukkudiyiruppu
Nanthi Kadal
Mullaittivu
Vellankulam
Talaimannar
Mannar Island
Mannar
NORTHERN
Nayaru Lagoon
Kokkilai Lagoon
Gulf of Mannar
Bay of Bengal
Trincomalee
Koddiyar Bay
Karaitivu I.
Anuradhapura
NORTH CENTRAL
Puttalam Lagoon
NORTH WESTERN
Batticaloa
EASTERN
Madura Oya Reservoir
Kurunegala
CENTRAL
Kandy
Uhana
Amparai
Negombo
Victoria Falls Reservoir
Senanayake Samudra
Badulla
Colombo
Sri Jayewardenepura Kotte
Mount Lavinia
Moratuwa
UVA
Laccadive Sea
WESTERN
Ratnapura
SABARAGAMUWA
INDIAN OCEAN
SOUTHERN
Galle
SRI LANKA
SKETCH MAP NOT TO SCALE

# A POWDERKEG IN PARADISE

## Lost Opportunity for Peace in Sri Lanka

# A POWDERKEG IN PARADISE

## Lost Opportunity for Peace in Sri Lanka

Jon Oskar Solnes

KONARK PUBLISHERS PVT LTD

KONARK PUBLISHERS PVT LTD
A-149, Main Vikas Marg, Delhi-110092 (India)
e-mail: konarkpublishers@hotmail.com

ISBN 81-220-0777-5



Typeset by The Laser Printers, New Delhi, and
Printed at ASK Advertising Aids Pvt Ltd, New Delhi.

# Preface

As I visited bookshops in the chaotic metropolis of Colombo in my Sri Lanka years, I often wondered why there was so little written material available on the ethnic conflict in the state. Sri Lanka inherited an excellent education system from the British colonial rule and a very strong academic base in the English language. Yet, few scholars or seasoned journalists seem to have been inclined to document or put into a coherent perspective a conflict that had raged for so many years in this charming tropical island in the Indian Ocean.

Furthermore, for the outsider it seemed that most of the domestic media reporting on the issues of contest and the countless tragic incidents resulting from the conflict was extremely biased both in the south and the north. The tendency to deify political leaders both on the Sinhalese and the Tamil sides did little to bring more reason to the reporting.

There was limited help in the international media, as for years the news stories coming out of Sri Lanka were limited in scope and played the role of a sideshow to the wars in Iraq, Afghanistan and Darfur. There were many knowledgable correspondents residing in

Colombo, however, they seemed to be met with limited interest in their stories when wired back to their agencies. To be sure there was no oil of substance to be found in Sri Lanka as noted by some of the more cynical diplomats residing in Colombo. Nevertheless, it was evident that there were some considerable external interests in the island, its government and its strategic location in the Indian Ocean.

Hundreds of thousands tourists visit Sri Lanka every year for an exquisite tropical holiday far away from home. They come for the warm and stable climate, the clear blue sea with its cozy temperature inviting for a swim all year long, the luxury hotels, the mouthwatering cuisine and the sheer and friendly hospitality. All this is available at relatively affordable prices. However, it appeared to be that most of the visitors had little or limited knowledge of what was going on in the northern part of the island and how the human rights situation had deteriorated to a completely unacceptable level in Sri Lanka. This was a common observation by the international staff of the Sri Lanka Monitoring Mission in countless casual conversations with friendly foreigners in hotels, restaurants or shops. Maybe, the tourists were not interested and avoided being informed on the armed Tamil insurgence.

I thought, nevertheless, as I became deeper informed on a plethora of facets of the conflict, that I should make an effort to write a book that might explain some of the main issues of the war in Sri Lanka. Such a book would be available for visitors who wanted a better picture of what had been going on in the island's north and east in the last three decades. Maybe, there would be some interest in other parts of the world, although I was not sure if there was extensive demand for such a publication. But I did know that I had observed countless amazing occurrences in Sri Lanka that deserved to be chronicled. I felt after what I had learnt through my work as a monitor of a comprehensive ceasefire I would be obliged to have a go at the rather thankless task of writing a book on the ethnic war in Sri Lanka. Simply, I felt it was a story that needed to be told.

It would be a book about lost opportunities to find a way to a negotiated peace acceptable both for the majority Sinhalese and the minority Tamils. Moreover, it would be a text describing the Tamil insurgence that is the armed uprising of the Tamil Tigers or the LTTE, the Government of Sri Lanka and its military operations to counter the Tamil Tigers. It would be a book that would hopefully, to a reasonably correct extent, describe the thinking and the tactics of the adversaries, as I understood the situation. And that could be generally said for all of my writing efforts.

I was not motivated by taking either side in the conflict or passing on judgments or verdicts, although I hope the reader will bear with my occasional expressions of grief or even anger at witnessing appalling incidents of bloodshed. I suspect, however, that at times I may be perceived of describing terrible occurrences in a way that might appear insentient at times. Generally, I have tried to explain what I think are incidents linked together in a quite causal manner, hoping to shed some light on the course of events in the long chain of tit for tat atrocities which were to be the most regular feature of the war in Sri Lanka. I write critically about actions taken by both parties to the conflict and expect no particular thanks from either side, but such is the nature, I suppose, of describing the devastating and horrible effects of ferocious warfare.

I would like to thank my family for showing me enormous patience in the past, both during the time when I went to another end of the world to monitor a brittle ceasefire in a remote jungle war and during the past two years when I have sought considerable isolation for working on my manuscript.

I have gained a lot of insight into the situation in Sri Lanka through long discussions with the national staff of the Sri Lanka Monitoring Mission (SLMM), which was established in 2002 to monitor a comprehensive ceasefire between the Government of Sri Lanka and the Liberation Tigers of Tamil Eelam (LTTE). Without them driving me, translating for me and explaining to me, this book would never have been written. So I have dedicated the book to them, the valiant national staff of the SLMM.

I worked with countless colleagues from the Nordic countries in Sri Lanka and learned a lot from most of them. They were seasoned and resourceful and a pleasure to work with, well at the least by far the most of them. I particularly thank my superiors from whom I benefitted immensely, especially Mr. Trond Furuhovde who has since passed away, Mr. Hagrup Haukland and Mr. Lars Johan Sölvberg. All the three served as Heads of Mission of the SLMM. The other two Heads of Mission in the history of the SLMM were Mr. Tryggve Tellefsen and Mr. Ulf Henricsson, both of whom I was fortunate enough to briefly meet at a conference in Helsinki in 2008.

I would like to extend special thanks to my trusted Public Information Officer and sidekick in my second tour in Sri Lanka, Mr. Þorfinnur Ómarsson, who became a household name in the Sri Lanka media during his two-year stay. Mr. Sverre Waldal Iversen, my former Chief Ops, was a trusted source on aviation and the Mannar area. Mr. Teitur Þorkelsson was the first spokesman of the mission and was present at meetings with the reclusive leader of the LTTE in the early days of the CFA. He was kind enough to share with me vital information from those meetings and also gave me an insight into the sentiment prevailing at the beginning of the ceasefire period. Former Naval Monitor in Trincomalee and later Kilinochchi liaison officer Mr. Kristján Guðmundsson gave me important insight for key chapters in the book. He would later become quite controversial in Sri Lanka as he participated in Tamil-sponsored aid effort for Sri Lanka which the GOSL deemed to be a propaganda stunt. Mr. Roland Nystad who served in multiple capacities in Mannar, Jaffna and as a Naval Monitor was an inspiration for tracking important events and establishing the likely connection between them. Mr. Lars Bleymann, former Naval Monitor in Jaffna, helped in piecing together the records on the naval conflict in the seas off Sri Lanka and provided very useful comments on various chapters. Many other SLMM Monitors have helped me substantially in writing this book, although some have been more aware of it than others. A number of dear colleagues and friends have asked not to be named by me, yet my sincere thanks go out to them as well.

I would also like to take this opportunity to thank the various diplomats with whom I engaged in Colombo during my stay there and my special thanks go to the many representatives of Norway which I learned to know and value as friends and colleagues.

I thank my publishers at Konark, who were swift in inviting me to hand in the manuscript after having received some sample chapters. They were very supportive, especially Mr. KPR Nair and I am grateful for the cooperation which has been faultless. I would also like to thank my literary agent Mr. Pétur Már Ólafsson, who guided me through uncharted terrain in setting up the text in a logical and coherent pattern.

I have hoped to avoid any factual errors in the text. However, given the scope of the manuscript some may have sneaked in. If so, I assure the reader that any misrepresentation of events or persons has been fully unintentional. In the end, I take the sole responsibility for the following text.

**Jon Oskar Solnes**

*Brussels*
February 2010.

# Introduction

Over a quarter of a century ago, civil war erupted in Sri Lanka, turning a tropical island in the Indian ocean, renowned for its beauty, into a theatre for a protracted war of barbaric bloodletting, costing up to ninety thousand inhabitants their lives. Initially, the war in Sri Lanka started as an uprising of armed groups of angry young Tamil men protesting against the complete domination of the state of affairs in the island by the Sinhalese majority.

Since independence from the UK in 1948, the social and political status of the Tamils had declined in Sri Lanka. The Tamils had previously been seen as over-representated in the British colonial administration by the Sinhalese majority in the south. The two dominant Sinhalese parties even appeared to have outbid themselves in consolidating rampant Sinhalese nationalism in order to obtain votes from the simple masses constituting the bulk of the electorate in the south and the west of the island. In the early years of independence, Tamil lost its status as an official language and a "Sinhalese only" legislation was passed by Parliament, elevating the Sinhalese language and Buddhism to supremacy in Sri Lanka's society. The "Sinhalese only" doctrine, was not just seen as a measure to diminish Tamil influence in official administration and cultural affairs, it was also aimed at reducing the influence of English and to cast the cultural shackles of the colonial past, which had led to Christianity gaining a strong foothold in Sri Lanka.

The Tamil minority, mostly Hindu, constituted just under a fifth of the total population in Sri Lanka with around 14 per cent living in the north and the east of the island whereas the so-called Indian Tamils lived mostly in the hill country in the tea growing region of central Sri Lanka. The Indian Tamils were a major bone of contention during this post-colonial spurt in nationalism as they had been brought to Sri Lanka by the British in the nineteenth century from India, to work for subsistence on the tea plantations. They were still considered migrant workers some generations later. Several hundred thousands of them were deported to India following an agreement between the two states, but eventually the remaining hill country Tamils gained their citizenship. They constituted just under 5 per cent of the total population including the few Indian Tamils living in the north.

The Tamils were indeed a distinct minority of the overall population in Sri Lanka. However, they constituted a clear majority in the northern part of the island, which included Jaffna peninsula and the Mannar region. These areas became almost completely homogenously Tamil populated as the conflict developed, not the least as the LTTE forcefully ejected a Muslim minority from the north. The picture was more complex in the eastern region around the towns of Trincomalee and Batticaloa. In those districts, Tamils would constitute a major component of the local population along with Muslims or Moors and to a lesser extent Sinhalese. The Moors were of mixed ethnicity with roots from Arab traders and their native wives. They spoke Tamil in a distinct way with a wealth of Arabic words and terms carried on from the past. Many of the Moors, who constituted 7.2 per cent of the population in the latest available census, also spoke Sinhalese to some extent.

The Sinhalese made up the vast majority of inhabitants of Sri Lanka with about 74 per cent and controlled successive governments led by either the United National Party (UNP) or its main rival, the Sri Lanka Freedom Party (SLFP). The latter was in power during the 1970s. It was a difficult period marred by internal strife and insurgency in the south. The economy of Sri Lanka had been almost shattered by poor economic governance, a succession of disastrous political interventions into the financial and business sectors in the island and a string of external shocks such as the explosion in the price of imported fuel.

In Jaffna, the main Tamil city in the north, the few cars driving around were old relics of the colonial time. As a matter of fact, there had been very little socio-economic progress in the north, whatsoever, and the general infrastructure, which was still the one built by the British, had started decaying due to inadequate upkeep. Jaffna seemed to have been arrested in time, it virtually looked the same as it had at independence. Walking around in Jaffna was like stepping into a time machine and going a few decades back. The grim life of poverty in the Tamil heartland, as the Tamil exponents would fondly call it, provided a perfect hotbed for radical elements. The Government of Sri Lanka was perceived as corrupt and incompetent and had moved the country towards a policy of socialism and Sinhalese nationalism and extreme economic distress. Unemployment was rampant in the island and tens of thousands left every year for jobs abroad.

It was to this backdrop of a rather bleak state of affairs in Sri Lanka that the traditionally strongest party, United National Party, was swept to power in 1977 in a landslide victory. One of its key political promises was to seriously examine proposals for a package of devolution of powers to the Tamils in the north and the east. It was also anticipated that the UNP would be able to increase economic growth and decrease unemployment by turning the country back to a more market-oriented economic system.

The Tamils themselves were encouraged by the fine result of the

Tamil United Liberation Front, TULF, which became the second largest party in Parliament. Tamils had for the first time united under the wing of an alliance rather than scattering their votes on a plethora of small Tamil splinter parties. They had spoken with one voice and were hoping to reap benefits from it. The elections in 1977 would, however, not bring the tangible changes that had been hoped for in Sri Lanka. Moreover, it would be the last elections for twelve years as democracy in Sri Lanka would become temporarily defunct under the UNP. The party would both renege on any devolution proposals for the Tamil minority and also become embroiled in a military campaign against armed Tamil insurgents.

In the wake of the promising election in 1977, optimism would eventually be supplanted by bitter disappointment and radical elements would start to thrive in Jaffna. A dangerous momentum had started to develop as embryonic groups of young Tamil males sought and succeeded in acquiring firearms which were used to harass the local police forces. At first, there were only minor incidents and much of the energy of the emerging sub-groups was spent on fighting each other for supremacy in Jaffna. As the security forces of Sri Lanka got wary of the armed youngsters in Jaffna they initiated a crack-down and tougher measures. Many of the young men fled across the narrow Palk Strait to India where they were welcomed with considerable sympathy for their cause. In the following years they even received guerilla training in rudimentary camps, courtesy of their hosts. The youngsters had left Jaffna in disarray but returned to the north of Sri Lanka in the form of several revitalised paramilitary groups. They all proclaimed to want to fight for an increase in Tamil rights but at first appeared to be mostly interested in slugging it out internally. A remarkably brutal war of Tamil fratricide erupted between the factions. The most ruthless of the groups and the one emerging dominant was the Liberation Tigers of Tamil Eelam or LTTE for short. Following the turbulent years of the mid-eighties the LTTE claimed exclusive representation for the whole of the Tamil population in the northern and eastern provinces of Sri Lanka, even though its sole remaining competitor, the Eelam People's Democratic Party, EPDP, enjoyed considerable support in Jaffna.

As the LTTE stepped up its armed insurgency against the Sri Lankan security forces in the north, the common mood in the Sinhalese south turned more militant, at times resulting in terrible reprisals against the Tamil minority. Increasingly violent acts of revenge against Tamils by the security forces divided the sentiment in Jaffna with many strongly advocating a political dialogue with the south, instead of an armed insurgency. However, the sporadic clashes of Tamil paramilitaries with the police and the army also spurred support for the LTTE which claimed that Tamil interests could only be advanced through a show of force. In the course of the eighties there appeared to be a trend emerging, resulting in the more moderate Tamil voices being marginalised and muted as the ethnic conflict escalated and slowly but surely developed into an outright civil war.

The LTTE or the Tamil Tigers, an organisation branded both in the USA and EU as one of the deadliest terrorist outfits in the world, acquired an aura of both fighting efficiency and enormous brutality. It honed to perfection asymmetric and unconventional warfare skills such as the widespread use of child soldiers and suicide bombings through its venerated Black Tigers.

The Indian intervention in 1987 at first brought great hope to Sri Lanka and the signs were set to bring an end to the armed struggle of the LTTE. However, the Indians did not achieve their objectives. Their efforts were allegedly jointly undermined by the Government of Sri Lanka, deeply wary of the presence of thousands of peacekeeping troops from its giant neighbour on Sri Lankan soil, and the LTTE refusing to be accorded a role of subordinance to its perceived mentors from across the Palk Strait. Shortly after the Indian Peacekeeping Force (IPKF) had finally retreated from Sri Lanka in 1990, having suffered over a thousand casualties at the hands of the LTTE, war erupted again in the island.

Two decades of savage warfare was sporadically interrupted by weak and futile attempts to bring about a cessation of hostilities. A Comprehensive Ceasefire Agreement (CFA), however, brokered by Norway, was co-signed by the Government of Sri Lanka and the LTTE in 2002. The signatories were defined as two distinct parties to a conflict both agreed had to be halted and brought to a formal end through a negotiated peace agreement. The CFA offered a great window of opportunity for finally finding ways to arrive at a lasting peace as the guns were silenced. The CFA was remarkably successful in its first years, but the complementing peace progress was lagging behind. At the end of the year 2004, the CFA had worked astonishingly well and had lasted for longer than any previous attempt to stop the bloodshed. On Boxing Day, Sri Lanka was hit by a devastating Tsunami that crushed almost all settlements on the eastern coast causing widespread death and damage all the way to the island's southern-most towns.

In the aftermath of the horrific catastrophe, Sri Lanka was showered with sympathy and goodwill from the outside world, resulting in a major influx of external aid and foreign investment. However, having suffered tens of thousands of deaths in a catastrophe caused by nature, instead of burying the arms with the dead, Sri Lanka's protracted ethnic conflict was rekindled and the island descended into a chaos of violence leading to the full resumption of war.

This book represents an intimate inside account of the years of the CFA in Sri Lanka which ended with its abrogation in 2008 by the Government of Sri Lanka. It attempts to describe the political and military contemplations of both parties and tries to go behind the scenes to reveal and explain the background of countless devastating incidents of terror and war. The text details the vanity and obsession of different interlocutors in the conflict. It describes terrible incidents and acts that delayed and derailed the peace process. The book also strives to bring insight in the appalling and often cynical lack of concern for civilian casualties, on both sides of the divide, resulting in ever more deadly military operations on land, at sea and in the air.

This is a prolonged visit to an island where, to the external observer, some of the most basic human rights appear to have ceased to exist and where disappearances and extrajudicial killings have become a widely accepted side-effect of the seemingly endless conflict. The contested regions are described in depth where tens of thousands of lives have been extinguished and hundreds of thousands of civilians have been deeply traumatised by the ferocious battles. This is also a journey deep into the tropic jungle to meet directly with the reclusive leadership of the dangerous and demonised Tamil Tigers, so enigmatic to the outside world.

It is a tale of the integral terror of war and the suffering of a desperately poor population in a remote corner of the world. It is a description of a potentially idyllic and beautiful island, blessed with abundant resources, an inviting climate and gentle and friendly people, which has been turned into arguably the most militarised democratic state in Asia. It is an account of one of the most resilient and ruthless fighting groups the world has witnessed, a description of nationalist politics and bigotry, a tale of great opportunities for a lasting peace, glaringly lost by two adversaries, locked into a seemingly endless war, blinded by the hatred of each other.

# Contents

1

# A Lasting Ceasefire Agreement is Brokered by Norway

The last few years of the second millennium witnessed an ever escalating, yet forgotten, war in Sri Lanka. The conflict had raged for over two decades in an island which is about the same size as Bosnia and Kosovo combined or just under 66,000 square kilometres. The two mentioned hotspots above had taken much of the headlines on security and conflict matters in the international media in those years and had also commanded much of the focus of the international community. Relatively little was reported on an obscure jungle war in a remote tropical island in the Indian Ocean.

Although the Sri Lankan Army appeared to be suffering increasing setbacks in the war, politically and economically considerable headway had been made. Sri Lanka was no more spiralling down into economic and political chaos as had seemed to be the case in the 1970s and the 1980s. Democracy had been restored, with an executive President holding vast power, however, with a Parliament that was able to provide significant checks and balances. A young and flamboyant woman, and political heir to Sri Lanka's strongest political dynasty, Mrs. Chandrika Bandaranaike Kumaratunga, had been elected President in 1994. She had pledged to end the war, once in office, through negotiations with the LTTE. However, the head of the LTTE, who was also its founder, Mr. Velupillai Pirapakaran, had been a very difficult interlocutor in a quest for peace. Under his command, the LTTE had stuck to extremely bold demands of establishing a separate Tamil state in the north and the east of Sri Lanka, a separate state that was to be called Tamil Eelam, or Tamil homeland. Going down the path of actually carving up the sovereignty of Sri Lanka was unthinkable for any political leader in Sri Lanka let alone the President. As the LTTE flatly rejected proposals of limited devolution packages differing in scope and generosity there was little hope for halting the hostilities between the LTTE and the security forces of Sri Lanka.

The Government of Sri Lanka, with Mrs. Kumaratunga in the driving seat, lost patience with the LTTE in 1997 and launched a massive and comprehensive military offensive on multiple fronts in order to drive the LTTE out of the Vanni area in the north of Sri Lanka. The ethnic distribution in Sri Lanka saw the Sinhalese in a commanding majority in the south and the west of the island reaching up towards the golden triangle of the ancient kingdom cities of Polonnaruwa in the east and Anuradhapura in the north, just over two-thirds of way up land from the southern-most point of Sri Lanka. Further north, the ethnic mix changed towards becoming almost exclusively Tamil and so did the geography, as the land became flatter and less densely populated. This stretch towards the Jaffna peninsula, which was exclusively populated by Tamils, was called the Vanni and had existed as a buffer zone between the ethnicities for ages.

The Sri Lanka Army (SLA), in a sustained campaign, but surely pushed the LTTE further up to the north, squeezing the Tamil Tigers out of sizeable areas of land in the remote Vanni jungle. It was a hard-fought way to establish government control over the land that the Tamil Tigers had dominated in the past two decades. The military campaign would last for two full years, as the conventional Army of

Sri Lanka was put to its most rigorous test yet in a terrain that suited the LTTE well for its asymmetric guerilla war tactics. The SLA marched on but had to pay a heavy price for its slow advance in the form of casualties and equipment. As the SLA commissioned troops into this epic offensive against the LTTE, it had also to keep an eye on the east, where the LTTE had grown increasingly strong. The Army had also to commit great resources to Jaffna and its defense against a potential offensive by the LTTE from its jungle strongholds just south of the Elephant Pass. It was the narrow land corridor from the island proper into the Jaffna peninsula. After a full year of fighting characterised by a slow rugged retreat of the LTTE, the Tigers launched a surprise attack on the northern-most garrison town of Kilinochchi. The SLA had constructed a heavily fortified camp there which was located strategically on the A9, the main highway from the south towards Jaffna in the north. The LTTE overran the SLA camp in September 1998 leaving the complex littered with bodies of government soldiers as others fled in disarray. A lunge by support units from the giant SLA installation at Elephant Pass, just fifteen kilometres up the road, was also beaten back decisively. The LTTE would hold on to Kilinochchi to make it the seat of their rebel administration.

Following the debacle at Kilinochchi, the SLA increased its efforts in marching north. Just over a year later, the government could proudly proclaim that the security forces had taken control over almost all of Vanni, barring the short stretch of the A9 highway around Kilinochchi and pockets of resistance towards the north-eastern town of Mullativu on the coast. Conceivably, Kilinochchi would be the next tactical objective for the SLA.

However, it was soon clear that the Government of Sri Lanka and the Army command had completely underestimated the Tamil Tigers. In the following month the LTTE attacked the SLA controlled towns in Vanni, taking them one by one in swift and deadly battles. In Colombo, the authorities could only stare at the map with amazement and disbelief as the LTTE knocked out the SLA defenses with uncanny effectiveness day after day. It was to be the most decisive and successful military campaign seen in the war in Sri Lanka to date, as the LTTE effectually pushed the SLA back on all fronts in Vanni. The Tamil Tigers, with their rag tag fighters, many of them only youngsters, managed to grab back control over the land that had taken the SLA more than two years to secure. It took the LTTE some ten days to completely crush SLA in Vanni despite its vast superiority in number of troops and equipment. It was a very heavy punch indeed, and it begged the question in Colombo, if the LTTE could be beaten militarily at all.

A year later, the LTTE had overrun the great military complex in the Elephant Pass. This was an immensely strategic location, as the large military base guarded the only road on land linking Jaffna peninsula with the mainland. The A9 highway was the potentially vibrant artery for transporting goods and people to and from Jaffna. The peninsula was very densely populated with possibly as many as six hundred thousand Tamils living in an area that was about sixty kilometres wide and stretched some twenty kilometres from the inland shores of the Jaffna lagoon in the south to the northern shores at the magnificent Bay of Bengal.

Jaffna had been the cradle of the ethnic conflict in Sri Lanka and had over the many years since the Tamil uprising or insurgency shifted in control in accordance with different phases of the war. The security forces of Sri Lanka had retaken it from the LTTE in 1996 in a massive show of force and held on to it since. This was a deeply unsatisfactory situation for the LTTE who defined Jaffna as its core heartland, now squarely administered by its Sinhalese adversaries. There had been sporadic attempts at dialogue since then with little tangible results.

The LTTE had trained its young recruits for years to form a fighting force which was believed to consist of nearly 10.000 cadres. The LTTE described itself as a liberation army forced to take up an armed struggle for the Tamil population subjugated by the Sinhalese dominated Sri Lanka Army. The methods of the LTTE in building up its fighting force were widely criticised by international agencies such as UNICEF and Amnesty International, as many of its young men and women under arms had been forcibly recruited at a young age and then indoctrinated, or simply brainwashed, and trained for battle. Many of LTTE's child soldiers wore no uniforms and as such could only be identified as combatants by their T-56 Chinese made assault riffles, cheap replicas of the Russian AK-47 original. The higher ranking LTTE fighters who wore distinct camouflage uniforms were assigned military ranks, whereas the bulk of the LTTE combatants were simply called cadres. The LTTE was believed to have built a network of arms merchants in Asia and the former eastern bloc which provided it with firearms and ammunition. They were smuggled ashore by vessels disguised as fishing trawlers. Larger military hardware such as artillery pieces and mortars had to be taken apart before being smuggled on shore and then assembled at arrival. As with many rebel movements around the world, the LTTE also depended on its ability to stage surprise attacks and loot as much weaponry from their opponent as possible.

The ethnic war in the island had been a long and exhausting one, and the Government of Sri Lanka had reluctantly been forced to gradually increase its military budget year after year. The war had to a large extent been contained and confined to the northern and eastern regions and due to limited exposure in the international press, there was still a thriving tourist industry in the far south where affluent visitors from all corners of the world enjoyed their pleasant stay at luxurious resorts by the Indian Ocean. In the south, the war could indeed seem remote at times, but the Sinhalese civilian population was repeatedly alerted to the fact that there was indeed an ongoing conflict in the island, as the LTTE would regularly launch bombing attacks out of the blue. One had taken place a few years before in central Sri Lanka in the town of Kandy, an important tourist destination. In that attack, the LTTE breaking with conventional rules of military conduct detonated explosives close to the most holy Buddhist shrine in the island, in the ancient city, high up in the majestic mountains of Central Province far away from the traditional battlefields. Such acts not only sparked both fear and terror in the Sinhalese population but also instilled a deeply rooted hatred against the LTTE and to some extent against all Tamils. It was an effective way to feed the negative sentiment of distrust between the ethnicities.

Young men in the south were apparently wary of the long lasting conflict and morale in the SLA was considered low. There was a looming discussion on the problem of widespread desertion in the southern media, which regularly published official decrees of amnesty and reintegration for deserters who turned themselves in.

To this backdrop in the conflict, the LTTE had launched the massive ground-attack on the SLA complex at Elephant Pass, unusual for an organisation that preferred guerilla tactics of asymmetric warfare rather than comprehensive and complex conventional operations. Although the LTTE did not possess the firepower of the SLA, its cadres seemed to outweigh that handicap by ruthless determination in battle. The LTTE had managed to cut off the support roads to the Elephant Pass and had then broken through the outer perimeters of the giant camp. The SLA defense seemed simply to implode as a result of the onslaught. Waves of Tamil fighters poured into the complex from different angles and it was impossible to say how many were killed on either side before the LTTE secured control over the base. Hundreds of SLA bodies lay scattered around but further hundreds of soldiers had hastily fled in disarray to the north over the shallow marshes by the Jaffna Lagoon. The LTTE had not only scored a decisive military victory over the SLA, it had shaken its core and badly wounded its pride and morale. The LTTE delighted in showing off some of the bounty they could claim at the Elephant Pass, among them huge long-range artillery pieces that would be able to reach as far as the Air force base at Palali to the north. The LTTE filmed parts of the battle and copies were made and sold under the counter at corner store shops in Jaffna Town, for years to come. The images were quite powerful, a close-up of the battle with cameramen at times falling wounded on the ground only for someone else to step in pick up the camera and continue filming. It also depicted smiling fighters, most in fatigues and hence elite commandos, often only wearing sandals, going with determination into battle. It showed LTTE firing from artillery batteries and also contained shaken and wobbly pictures of incoming impacts. The lighting and soundtrack were poor and looked like an ancient documentary on warfare, only in faded colour rather than black and white. Later on, the LTTE would continue to take particular pride in showing the footage to special visitors in Kilinochchi.

At the same time as the LTTE seemed to go from strength to strength, quiet diplomatic efforts had been undertaken by the Sri Lankan government to seek some other ways of settling the ethnic dispute rather than having the young from the south and the north decimating each other's formations in the killing fields in Vanni.

Norway had earned itself a considerable reputation as an international peace-broker in the wake of highly applauded diplomatic successes in early nineties. Norwegian intermediates had amongst other ventures managed to broker a cessation of hostilities in one of the most contracted conflicts on the planet, the seemingly insolvable conflict between Israel and the Palestinian Liberation Organisation. The international community saluted this splendid diplomatic achievement of Norway, paving a way for a comprehensive peace process. In the wake of this remarkable success story in international diplomacy, Norwegian diplomats would try to offer advice and help in delicate security situations in some of the most remote corners of the world.

Norway had appointed a special envoy for Sri Lanka, Erik Solheim, a tall lanky politician from the left spectre of Norwegian politics. The Government of Sri Lanka had invited him and his team to enquire if there could be some common ground to be found with the LTTE and see if the Tigers could first be persuaded to halt military operations and then possibly brought to the negotiation table. The Norwegian task was no simple matter as it was difficult to reach the LTTE and its leader, the elusive Mr. Pirapaharan, who was believed to be commanding his organisation from a hidden bunker deep in the Vanni Jungle. But, a meeting was indeed managed and moreover the results from it appeared quite promising. Norway established a troika later on for the delicate task of trying to pursue peace in Sri Lanka, consisting of Mr. Solheim, Mrs. Kjersti Tromsdal from the Norwegian Ministry for Foreign Affairs, and led by the Deputy Foreign Minister, Mr. Vidar Helgesen.

The quest for a cessation of hostilities in Sri Lanka appeared to be an elusive one at first. However, there were to be a number of developments in the year 2001 that would provide sound arguments for an end to the fighting. Earlier, the President, Mrs. Kumaratunga had narrowly escaped a LTTE attempt on her life in 1999, which had cost her the sight of one of her eyes, but had probably helped her in securing a second term in the presidential elections a few days later. The assassination attempt had obviously not prodded her to a more conciliatory approach towards the LTTE, quite to the contrary. But in late 2001, the President was forced to call a surprise election to parliament which transformed the political landscape. The previous election had been held only a year earlier, in a climate of increasing discontent within the population as the economy turned for the worse and the SLA was suffering major defeats at the hands of the LTTE. The unpopular coalition government led by the President's own Sri Lanka Freedom Party fell apart and its main rival the United National Party won a landslide victory.

The leader of the UNP, Mr. Ranil Wickremasinghe, had long advocated negotiations with the LTTE and favoured a proposal of a self-administration for the Tamils in the north-east, although the modalities would have to be discussed in depth first. He was quick in engaging with the Norwegian envoys that had temporarily fallen out of favour with the SLFP-led government. The timing was also favourable, as both the LTTE and the SLA had declared unilateral ceasefires that would last for two months.

The LTTE for the first time in many years appeared to be ripe for taking a rest from the fighting. It had won control over most of Vanni and large areas in the east where Tamils and Muslims were the predominant ethnicities south of the magnificent bay of Trincomalee. The LTTE could well do with a time for consolidating its control over these areas, at least for the time being. Moreover, following years of limited progress in sending out feelers to the SLFP, which had to rely on hard line coalition support to govern, the LTTE was now faced with the UNP leader who had officially stated that he was in favour of some sort of self-administration although stopping short of a federal solution.

There was an external pressure also that was pointed out to the LTTE. Following the 9/11 attacks in the US, the Bush administration had declared a worldwide war on terrorism. The LTTE was proscribed as a terrorist organisation in the USA and at home in Sri Lanka. A ceasefire agreement and the prospect of peace talks might fix that predicament.

After Mr. Ranil Wickremasinghe had been sworn in to the office of Prime Minister, the Norwegian efforts gathered momentum. On 22 February 2002, the Foreign Minister of Norway, Mr. Jan Petersen, went public in Oslo and declared that a comprehensive and lasting ceasefire agreement, the CFA, would take effect at midnight. The Norwegian troika had conducted very efficient shuttle diplomacy, meeting with the main political advisor of the LTTE, Mr. Anton Balasingham, in London, Mr. Wickremasinghe in Colombo, and even securing the signature of the LTTE Leader, Mr. Pirapaharan, to the CFA document. Mr. Jon Westborg, Oslo's Ambassador in Colombo, and his staff had also played a significant part in the facilitation of the CFA.

Prime Minister Wickremasinghe signed the CFA on behalf of the sovereign state of Sri Lanka. The President, who felt she had been sidestepped on the whole issue, was furious and came out to condemn the CFA. It was a remarkably vain position taken by a seasoned political leader at a time when the whole of Sri Lanka was cheering an end to the fighting. Nevertheless, she was forced to grudgingly accept the commencement of the CFA faced with the international community which strongly acclaimed this positive watershed in the conflict. However, Mrs. Kumaratunga had not had her last word on the CFA.

2

# A9—The Kandy-Jaffna Highway

One of the keystones to the commencement of the CFA was the reopening of the A9 highway, the main road from the south through Vanni to Jaffna, the most densely populated Tamil area at the northern tip of Sri Lanka. The A9 or the Kandy-Jaffna road had been closed for more than a decade before the CFA. The reopening of the road, in the wake of the Norwegian-brokered CFA, was a major event in the recent history of Sri Lanka. Its importance for the movement of goods and people to and from Jaffna could not be overstated. The opening of the road, which was stipulated quite clearly in the CFA document, was widely celebrated both in the north and the south. It was the single most important step taken towards normalcy in the island for years. This in itself instilled considerable hope for further steps towards a negotiated peace settlement.

From the air, pleasantly humming northwards in a Sri Lanka Air Force Bell Huye helicopter, one could observe the A9 going dead straight through Vanni as if drawn with a ruler. Along the road there was a steady flow of lorries carrying food, merchandise and fuel to Jaffna. There would not be as much cargo to carry back on the return trip however as the Jaffna economy had become very basic and depended on the flow of goods from the south. Nevertheless, some trucks would bring produce from the fertile plains of the flat peninsula, including the famous Jaffna onions and peppers, a culinary delight much appreciated in the south. There would also be a considerable traffic of four-wheel drive trucks on the A9, many of them flying flags of various international aid organisations located in Kilinochchi. The inevitable three-wheeler autorickshaws spurted and fretted as they moved on powered by their noisy and polluting Indian made engines, and then there were quite a few motorbikes and bicycles. Now and then there would be small groups of people walking along the road, apparently enjoying the fact that they could do so in what appeared to be completely secure conditions.

The CFA had also called for an immediate establishment of an international monitoring mission led by Norway. So the Sri Lanka Monitoring Mission was created with staff from the five Nordic countries, Denmark, Finland, Iceland, Norway and Sweden. The head of mission would be from Norway in all but one occasion. It was a small mission by most international comparison with around 65 monitors. However, most of them were very experienced, with the bulk of the SLMM consisting of retired military personnel, police officers, academics and technical specialists. Headquarters were soon established in Colombo following some contemplation as a more forward seated location, say Habarana, simply did not provide the needed technical infrastructure for the mission. The CFA document also specified where the SLMM would be present in the field. The location of offices corresponded to the regional hotspots and were in the districts of Mannar, Jaffna, Vavuniya, Trincomalee, Batticaloa and Ampara. A liaison office was also established in Kilinochchi, the seat of the LTTE. The SLMM would be operational remarkably quickly and in the districts both the commanding officers of the SLA and the LTTE would soon get to know the mission quite well. Visits by the public were welcomed and civilians could drop by at the regional offices at almost any time of the day to turn in complaints against either the security forces or the LTTE which would be evaluated and, if necessary, acted upon. The SLMM monitors stuck out in the remote regions where few westerners had dared to set foot in the past. Now, these Nordic-looking people, often with rather a pale complexion and wearing distinct and dull khaki-coloured clothes, were busy patrolling both the streets and obscure jungle paths visiting stakeholders in remote corners of the island.

Although the occasional helicopter services by the SLAF were both a timesaving and positive gesture towards the SLMM, they were reserved for the SLMM HOM and his entourage for urgent business. The SLMM monitors bound for Vavuniya or Kilinochchi further north would usually drive up from Colombo via Anuradhapura, the ancient seat of the Sinhalese kings. In earlier years, before the clashes with the LTTE became more widespread in Sri Lanka, a substantial tourist industry had been built up in the northern central province, including luxury hotels and lodges for affluent foreign visitors. Tourism had since gone down to a minimum before the commencement of the CFA, due to the proximity to the fighting grounds in Vanni and Tiger-held territory close by. The abandoned hotels and jungle lodges were a melancholic testimony to what could be achieved by ending the conflict.

The delightful town of Dambullah was situated on one of Sri Lanka's busiest junctions, where the A9 to Jaffna and the A6 to Trincomalee met. It was not only a traditional resting place for the tired traveller but has also renowned for its famous rock cave temples dating from 1st century BC. Some forty kilometres north was the cultural triangle, arguably Sri Lanka's most important heritage from the past. It consisted of the majestic remains of the ancient cities of the Sinhalese kingdoms in Anuradhapura and Pollonaruwa with the breathtaking fortress from the 5th century up on the commanding holy Sigirya rock forming the third spectacular leg of the triangle.

Following February 2002, the whole area saw a major push in tourism with numbers of visitors increasing rapidly, injecting desperately-needed foreign currency into the financial system of the island. Confidence increased massively in the wake of the CFA as there were few and only minor incidents to report in the area and the tourist infrastructure was improved with both public and private investments. The trip from Colombo to Anuradhapura would take up to four hours on hectic and congested roads. The traffic was noisy and diverse with the most dangerous and rude vehicles—the innumerable private and public buses, crammed with people and their luggage and goods, roaring along the road. The drivers were usually young men who seemed completely reckless in their erratic actions behind the steering wheel. Their thuggery and carelessness created immense danger in the whole of the road system in Sri Lanka. They were paid primarily by the number of passengers they could get from A to B, the faster they could go the more lucrative the remuneration. This affected the road culture in general. While driving in Sri Lanka, one had to be extremely alert as a bus might appear screaming out of a bend without a warning on, homing in towards one's vehicle at full speed not giving any space to ease the passage. At such a point the wisest thing would be to try to manoeuvre one's own truck as far as to the side of the road you could get without tumbling down from it into the bush.

The mad way of driving by Sri Lanka's many bus conductors was accepted only up to a point by the locals. There were inevitably many traffic incidents as a result, some which ended tragically for pedestrians on the wayside who could only be mourned by their families. Sometimes however, particularly if children were savagely run over by a ruthless bus driver, losing control of his bus in a populated area, an angry mob would form at the site of the accident. In extreme cases, the angry crowd would drag the bus driver from his steering wheel and simply lynch him with stones, sticks or machetes. This was reported every now and then in various parts of the island.

Next in the pecking order after the mostly yellow or red buses were beautifully decorated lorries with wooden sideboards, most of them displaying wonderful paintings and ornaments. The lorries would not go quite as fast as the buses but were extremely cumbersome to overtake as they would share the preference of their colleagues from the buses, sticking invariably to the middle of the road. Four-wheel trucks of the security forces and aid organisations took the next spot of respect in the traffic followed by old and battered 'white vans' of various Asian production that were imported as used cars into the country, having served the best of their years somewhere abroad. Tractors commanded some respect as well as they were not a viable target to hit due to their sturdiness, but the bustling and sputtering three-wheeler rickshaws had to look out for themselves if something larger and heavier was moving in their vicinity. Driving a motorcycle was a considerable challenge and one could only admire the bravery of the young and the old wobbling along the road on run down squeaking bicycles. Of the animal species trespassing on the roads, the elephant was the most feared as hitting one could be mortal both for the beast and the one colliding with it. The danger of driving into a herd of elephants was considerable in some parts of the island, especially towards dusk when these gentle giants would become virtually invisible as they crossed the roads towards a resting place. Cows were also preferably avoided and to the Tamils they were holy as well. Dogs and other animals had to rely on their reaction skills, but at the bottom of the pecking order in the vast roads of Sri Lanka, one would squarely put the pedestrians.

# 3

## Vavuniya—A Garrison Town

At Anuradhapura the visitor could only marvel at the countless and beautifully crafted grand Dagobas, or Buddhist shrines, dotting the horizon along with giant Buddha statues carved out in the hills. North of the city, the traffic waned as the jungle grew thicker around the road which leads towards the garrison town of Vavuniya. Approaching Vavuniya, one could sense the tension increase and the massive presence of security forces would become very evident. This was one of the key locations of the Sri Lanka Army as the entrenched frontline, that had become a *de facto* border between the Government of Sri Lanka-(GOSL) held territory and the LTTE-held Vanni which was only a ten kilometre drive to the north of the town. The official crossing point was at Omanthai on the A9 road. The Sri Lankan Air force had one of its most important bases in Vavuniya, from where it would regularly send drones over Vanni for intelligence gathering. The base was considered vulnerable due to its forward position, so the closest fleet of combat helicopters was kept further south in Anuradhapura but the extremely expensive fighter jets and tactical bombers were kept in the south at Katunayaka airport north of Colombo. Despite a strong SLA garrison, the SLAF airbase and a massive deployment of soldiers and police on the streets of Vavuniya, it was sometimes claimed that the security forces only ruled the town during the day. At night the Tigers could move around more or less freely and go around their business. Vavuniya was certainly not the ideal place for a nice relaxing evening stroll. There had been several attempts by the GOSL to claim Vavuniya as an ethnically mixed town, however, its ethnic composition would strongly support the LTTE claim that this was in essence a Tamil town. Most of the people you would come across in Vavuniya and its small businesses were Tamil and so were the commercial signs, although many official signs would be jointly in Sinhala and Tamil. There were indeed a number of distinct communities within Vavuniya. First, there were the inhabitants of the town proper, who seemed to be doing fairly well, but second, there also was a large colony of internally displaced Tamils. They had fled the fighting in the north years ago and were eking out a humble life of poverty in camps made up of small clay or cardboard huts sometimes draped with plastic sheets handed out by international aid agencies or the Government Agent. It was remarkable that people could live in such conditions for years, in a country where primary education was surprisingly high and socio-economic prospects for the inhabitants had been very good after breaking away from the UK. Although it was disturbing to visit the IDP camps and hear the sad tales of many of these families that had not had a proper home for years, it was also a pleasure to meet with the friendly children with their big innocent eyes and their great white smiles to the strange "white faces" visiting them. The Tamil Tigers had a very strong influence in such camps and would use them for recruitment into their fighting formations.

To be sure there were also Sinhalese in Vavuniya. The latest official census in Sri Lanka had put them just under 17 per cent in the Vavuniya district. However, they tended to live in separate areas slightly outside the town, where the LTTE claimed they were settled by GOSL to render more legitimacy to itself in Vanni. The language barrier between the Tamils and the Sinhalese was strong, although some of the locals, generally a few of the Tamils, could speak both the languages. Inter-group marriages were relatively seldom in this tense part of the island and interaction between the two communities could only be described as strained.

Driving around in Vavuniya could be quite confusing as there were not many distinct hills to form a landscape. There were indeed very few landmarks to guide the traveller. On the outskirts of the town however, the vegetation would subside somewhat and traffic would wane considerably to the north side towards the crossing point into LTTE controlled Vanni. The LTTE had come so close to taking Vavuniya in 1999 that the inhabitants had fled the town moving further south fearing getting caught in crossfire. The LTTE had then asked them to return, strongly indicating that they were content with their current frontline north of the town, at least for the time being.

# 4

## A *de facto* Border Crossing at Omanthai

In the spring of 2002, when the A9 had been opened all the way up to Jaffna, there had been a steady flow of lorries and other vehicles through the entry point at Omanthai, which had constituted a *de facto* border between the south and the north. Security forces guarded the customs clearing infrastructure, and cargo was unloaded and inspected before being released for entry into Vanni. This indeed looked like a formal custom clearing area in any third world border facility. Bus passengers had to step out at Omanthai and walk through the clearing and inspection points showing their identity cards. They would then walk by the road through no-man's land and through the LTTE check point on the other side. Quite frequently the LTTE check points were empty of its guards, but it was well known that there were other observation posts within the bush even though one could not detect much LTTE presence up close to the crossing point. Sometimes, however, the entry point on the northern side would be manned by young LTTE cadres smiling in a polite but reserved manner at the passers-by. There was a lively hustle and bustle at Omanthai in the years when the CFA was functioning properly, and passengers crossing through looked cheerful and relaxed, enjoying their precious freedom of movement that had been guaranteed by the parties.

SLMM vehicles were well marked sporting the SLMM logo in both Sinhalese and Tamil on their sides and the bonnet. They also, as a rule, flew a highly visual banner with the same inscriptions. As the security forces manning the checkpoint became familiar with the SLMM and its work, they would simply wave the monitors through without inspection of identity. The SLA soldiers manning the crossing point were friendly and courteous, obviously well trained and informed on the role of the SLMM and its mandate. On the way through no-man's land, SLMM staff would sometimes stop by and have a cool drink or tea with the representatives of the International Council of the Red Cross (ICRC) who invariably sat by their humble shack seeking shelter from the torrid sun. Their mandate was to facilitate the movement of civilians and displaced people through the crossing point. Sometimes they would also have to engage in the tricky and distressful business of handing over the bodies of fallen combatants, following major incidents when there had been casualties on either side. All in all, the ICRC had found Sri Lanka a tough place to operate. The organisation had played a major role in the Sri Lankan conflict in the nineties and had tried to facilitate cease-fires and peace talks, but in the end the Government of Sri Lanka had turned against them accusing them of being biased towards the LTTE. Furthermore, sentiment in the Sri Lanka Army became very negative towards the Red Cross increasing the inherent danger for its workers in the battle areas. This was a common outcome for scores of international missions, substantial or small, that had tried to alleviate the difficult situation for non-combatants in the long lasting conflict in the island. The ICRC had stressed its neutrality but had had to give up some of its initiatives although it still played a very useful role for both parties, especially regarding the handover of dead fighters. Sitting in no-man's land day in and day out at Omanthai crossing point was not a job for the restless, to be sure. Discussions with the ICRC, who were also still running important aid projects in other parts of the island, representatives of UN agencies and other relief organisations were very important in order to try to get a fair picture of the situation in different locations at all times. This interagency sharing of information and viewpoints helped in construing a fairly balanced and dynamic overview of the situation in the remote regions. When these were combined from the various theatres in the north and the east, a relatively coherent overall situation report could be drawn up at all times.

Following the commencement of the CFA, foreign aid had started pouring into the country and substantial funds, not the least from Japan, Norway, the EU and the US were earmarked for the refurbishment of the run down A9 highway, as it was officially rather grandly called. In the years 2002 and 2003, road maintenance groups would be busy along the A9 repairing potholes, mending the gravel and clay foundation and pouring asphalt. This was welcome activity in a region where the flow of funds for upgrading the infrastructure had been very limited for years if not decades. Both the reconstruction of the A9 and the ensuing flow of goods on the refurbished road were profusely positive and tangible benefits, resulting from the CFA. These were also highly visible steps towards normalcy, for all to see. Following the overhaul of the A9, it would be asphalted in most stretches all the way from Omanthai up towards Jaffna town in the furthest northern corner of the island.

As with many construction and infrastructure projects in Sri Lanka, the quality of the work was rather poor and the A9 would only remain in a proper state for a short period. In 2004, heavy monsoon rains swept away the asphalt in long stretches north of Kilinochchi, towards Elephant Pass. To the south of Kili, as the town was often called for short, some dangerous stretches had developed, with deep potholes and substantial cuts into the road itself. Driving too fast could be extremely perilous, with stray dogs and motorcycles adding an element of surprise to reckon with. Yet, the A9 continued to function well as the main artery for the flow of goods and people to and from previously isolated Jaffna.

# 5

# Kilinochchi—The Seat of the Tigers

From the crossing point at Omanthai, it would take over a good hour's drive to reach Kilinochchi, the seat of the LTTE, a town they had captured from the SLA a few years earlier and clung on to since. The SLMM had permanent representatives in Kilinochchi and the heads of the SLMM would visit there for meetings regularly. It was a posting dreaded by most of the SLMM monitors as Kili was notorious for its isolation and total lack of nightlife or any sort of entertainment. However, a few extraordinary members of the mission cherished the idea of being up close to where the conflict was really being orchestrated. They wanted to make a difference and some of the monitors inhabiting the SLMM house in Kili managed to forge an excellent working relationship with the LTTE representatives over the years.

In the early years of the CFA, life in Kili changed to the better, normalcy was restored up to the point possible as there was a glaring lack of progress in further peace negotiations. There were nevertheless few signs of the conflict visible, when entering the town. Following a rare long bend in the A9, after an hour's drive without much sign of civilisation, one would pass a substantial thicket of trees and all of a sudden one had left the seemingly deserted Vanni plains and was in the southern outskirts of this dreaded town. People were walking around or bicycling, running errands, going to the modest shops along the A9, on their way from or to work, seemingly relaxed in their everyday activities. As further south in Vavuniya, Kilinochchi was built on flat ground, with some larger clearances by the A9 which ran through the town. Further away from the main road, houses appeared to melt into the jungle backdrop. For the visiting guests, this did not look like a haunted place being ruled with an iron fist by a deranged mob of terrorists, as it was more or less perceived to be the case in Colombo.

The myriad of NGOs operating in Vanni had brought desperately needed economic activity to the area and during the first years of the CFA the fundament of the Tamil community was rebuilt once again. Schools were constructed, a rudimentary health provision was established, administrative buildings were refurbished and the LTTE established a functioning state within the Sri Lankan state, with a strong rule of law and a judiciary. The latter of course falling well short of what would be considered acceptable in a Western country. A police force was established which was by and large accepted and respected by the population. The tidy appearance of the LTTE police was in many ways remarkable in such a basic community. Officers would sport their newly designed, rather elegant, blue and powder blue uniform with the red Tiger insignia and somewhat strangely fashioned caps. Police officers obviously took great pride in their positions and rank within the LTTE apparatus. No forms of corruption were accepted and the rule of law was upheld with draconic measures which stamped out most petty crimes. Smaller offences and domestic violence were dealt with in a swift and resolute manner according to the decrees of the LTTE. In reality these were procedures completely lacking transparency where the defendants were commonly sentenced to forced labour for a time deemed suitable at the imposing cemeteries for fallen LTTE cadres. Serious offences were rare and kept behind the scenes; however, it was well known that the LTTE would not hesitate to resort to extreme methods of punishment if it believed that the organisation or its rules had been significantly wronged. In that sense, Vanni was a society run by the rule of fear and obedience.

The LTTE took special pride in keeping its burying grounds spotless even during the difficult months of the north-eastern monsoon. The cemeteries with their long rows of tombstones, honouring the fallen fighters, were a sobering sight for visitors and presented a very visual reminder of the long and bloody conflict. It was believed that the veneration of fallen combatants in this manner had been ordered directly by the LTTE leader Mr. Pirapaharan himself. This was a break with the ancient Hindu tradition of burning corpses rather than burying them. However, the cemeteries were also very useful in many ways. They constituted an ideal background for rallying support for the LTTE cause. Tamils were called upon to hold festive remembrances there on several occasions, the grandest being the weekly festivities around the annual Heroes Day on November 27. This culminated in the yearly and much awaited policy speech given by the LTTE leader transmitted via radio in all LTTE-held territories. On Heroes Day, the cemeteries were decorated with endless banners and red and yellow pennants, the main colours of the LTTE flag and coat of arms, depicting a Tiger's head over two crossing sub-machine guns surrounded by a chain of bullets. This flag was well known in the south where it had the same effect as the red cloth waved in front of a bull in a ring.

The buildings in Kilinochchi were mostly low rise and modest, but in some parts of the town there were nice large houses, some occupied by international NGO staff, others by senior members of the LTTE. If one ventured a bit away from the main A9 road, one could see buildings completely destroyed by fighting, but they had become covered by the vegetation springing up in these fertile plains. The main landmark in Kilinochchi was the rebuilt water tower, and in essence it was the only highly visual sign for orientation on the horizon. One of the most remarkable stops in Kilinochchi for high-level visitors was the spotless Tank View Guesthouse aptly named after the large water tank at the south-eastern fringe of Kili. The guestrooms were squeaky clean and Mr. Puleedevan, the head of the LTTE Peace Secretariat, would offer lunch of the highest culinary level, if sometimes extremely spicy and hot for the western palate. Dishes would invariably include delicious rice-based curries, but would at times also include sea food and exquisite tiger prawns brought in from Mullativu of which the LTTE were quite proud. At these meetings Mr. Puleedevan would recite poems and scripts from ancient Tamil times and would pull out all stops to convince the visitor of the distinct and separate culture of the Tamils in the northern part of Sri Lanka through the ages.

For the visitor to Kilinochchi, almost all economic activity would seem to occur at or in the close vicinity of the A9, which split the town in two. Small shops would sell the most fundamental items such as sandals and clothes and the variety of goods was markedly less than that in Vavuniya's main shopping street on the other side of the demarcation line. There was, however, also some small markets with fundamental sanitary items, simple merchandise and even some toys of sorts, but all of this was very basic. As in most of Sri Lanka the staple food was rice with some sort of curry mixtures and hot and spicy pastries and sandwiches. Small shops along the road sold such food at meagre prices.

Much to the relief of most expat visitors to Kili, who did not qualify for a VIP treatment at the LTTE's Tank View, it did offer two restaurants, in conjunction with a motel of sorts, frequented by lorry drivers on their way south or north. One of the two was a somewhat barren and cheerless place, with acceptable food but no beverages with alcohol content served. It was not doing as well, apparently, as the other one which was called I-9 and looked like an old mini-golf facility. It was an outdoors only, apart from the lodgers in the crammed adjacent motel, as they had a community room to gather in for sandwiches and Arak, the pungent local liquor made from driblets from coconut trees, available and consumed all over Sri Lanka. The dining facility constituted of about ten tables spread around a faulty water fountain and a small concrete canal for an extinguished water stream within a concrete garden. There were still a few lights here and there, remainders of a much more ambitious lighting system that had probably once been colourful and cheerful, welcoming families to this little oasis of dining out. The food was very simple, even by rural Sri Lanka standards. Some rice based curries were on offer and chicken pieces that seemed to have been randomly and somewhat erratically hacked or even crushed with their bones, before being fried on a hot pan. The waiter was quick and apologetic for the lack of luxury and would point to a booth at the end of the complex where drinks with alcoholic content for diners were sold separately. With the heat seldom going much below twenty-five degrees Celsius during the night and well above thirty almost all year round, with scorching sun three out of every four days and humidity levels frequently over 90 per cent, the selection of drinks was somewhat inevitable. Drinks should be extremely cool and refreshing. At the booth, there were a few bottles of red and white wine standing in the window with the labels almost erased from the daily sunlight. So beer it usually was, somewhat ironically named after a formidable feline predator which was the pride of the Sri Lanka coat of arms. Many a cold "Lion" beer was emptied over the years in the town of the Tigers, during contemplations on the state of the conflict and developments leading either to war or peace.

Returning back home to the SLMM house was not always an easy task. The restaurant was five hundred metres down the A9. A small inroad led to the SLMM bungalow tucked away behind one of the local hospitals. Earlier it was easy enough to walk there in daylight. However, after dinner, the whole town was completely blacked out. There was not a single light to be seen in the curtained windows of the houses along the main road. The only light came from the odd three-wheeler spurting along at considerable speed through the darkness. There was some eerie movement in the dark as well, as you could hear and sometimes only sense people on bicycles passing by and a few pedestrians walking around in complete silence. If your spotlight broke down, you would have to feel your way with your feet along the asphalt of the A9 a few hundred metres north, and literally fumble in the dark for the sign guiding the inhabitants of Vanni and visitors towards the SLMM offices. Close to the house itself, one could vaguely see a few stray dogs, sense the rats and snakes moving through the moist growth, hear the relentless clicking of the crickets and feel the aggressiveness of the mosquitoes swirling around. To be sure, the nights in Kilinochchi could be dark beyond imagination.

# 6

# The Tamils in Colombo and the Rule of Law

The LTTE had claimed sole representation of the Tamil cause and had been granted that by Colombo in two fundamental ways. First, as a part of the package involving India as a mediator in the conflict in the late eighties, the northern and eastern regions had been merged into one distinct regional authority at the behest of the LTTE, which based its design for a Tamil Eelam on exactly such a structure. Accordingly, elections were to be held at the same time in the merged regions. Numerous and structural procedures were put in place to streamline the administration of the whole area. Presumably, this would be a first step towards increased self administration by the Tamils, devolving some of the powers of central government in Colombo to those regions.

Furthermore, as a second measure, the Government of Sri Lanka (GOSL) had *de facto* recognised the LTTE as the sole actor representing the Tamil population in the north and east by signing the CFA in February 2002.

However, there were other schools of thought on the Tamil issue contrary to the LTTE view. In the Sinhalese south, it was pointed out that a large segment of the overall Tamil population in Sri Lanka lived within Colombo and that some of the suburbs were markedly Tamil especially to the south of the capital where one could observe Hindu Kovils along the road. It was not clearly known how strong the influence of the LTTE was with these southern Tamils. But it was equally obvious that the LTTE would never be in a position to take on any administrative powers on their behalf, far away from their area of operations. Most of the elder Tamils in Colombo remembered and had been deeply traumatised by the so-called Tamil pogrom in July 1983. That month marked the most significant shift in the relations between Sinhalese and Tamils, when the ethnic problem in Sri Lanka exploded into a vicious orgy of violence, which would transform itself into a self sustained internecine civil war in the island.

The Tamils called it Black July, and would refer to it as the most fundamental reason for demanding a homeland of their own. Be it a sort of a federal structure within Sri Lanka proper or as the LTTE demanded an outright independent Tamil state in the north and the east. The bloodshed in Colombo was a revenge reaction of the outraged Sinhalese population. It seems, according to most accords from the time, to have been spontaneous rather than orchestrated from above. The embryonic LTTE had on 23 July 1983 ambushed a convoy of security forces in Jaffna, killing 13 military and police officers with deadly determination. This was by far the bloodiest action of any of the then plethora of Tamil paramilitary groups. These were at the time battling it out with each other for supremacy within the Tamil heartland. But they sporadically found time to assassinate members of the security forces of Sri Lanka, which were by then being depicted as an occupation force in Jaffna. When the news and details of this lethal ambush, perceived by most Sinhalese as an outrageous and unprovoked attack, reached Colombo the following day, a dismal and dreadful reaction followed. Angry Sinhalese mobs targeted and attacked Tamil shops all over the city, dragged the owners and sometimes the unlucky customers, into the streets and lynched them. It was a dark and horrifying scenario resembling an apocalypse as hundreds of Tamils, maybe more, were slaughtered by the berserk mobs. Shops plundered and smashed, young women were raped and murdered, completely innocent Tamils, were dragged around in the streets and some burnt alive. It was widely claimed by the completely shocked Tamils in Colombo that the police and other security forces had at first more or less turned a blind eye to this appalling and unprecedented outburst of hatred. The relationship between Sinhalese and Tamils in Sri Lanka would not be the same after this tragedy.

Tens of thousands of Tamils emigrated from Sri Lanka after Black July. However, most of the Tamils in Colombo had no other choice than to stay put and try to move on with their simple lives. Among most Tamils, Black July would be commemorated mournfully every year and a deep-rooted atmosphere of distrust among the ethnic groups would prevail and be passed on to the next generation. In light of this, it was not surprising that the LTTE gained substantial support from the young and angry among the Tamils. It was equally logical that the more sombre Tamils would completely and categorically denounce the violent course that the LTTE had chosen to take, given the terrible repercussions by the Sinhalese majority.

The real problem for the security forces of Sri Lanka was that it was almost impossible to single out the elements supporting the LTTE from the other Tamils simply intent on living a quiet life in the Sri Lankan metropolis. There were few Sinhalese who also mastered the Tamil language as it had been relegated to a secondary status in Sri Lanka in a show of nationalistic and populist competition among the major Sinhalese political parties, following the independence of the then Ceylon from British rule. It is extremely difficult to break clandestine networks with only the help of interpreters and paid informers in a society speaking a language completely unintelligible for the officers on the ground.

By the turn of the century, young male Tamils were routinely rounded up in the suburbs of Colombo by the security forces for random interviews and interrogations. Checkpoints had been established at all entrances to the city and Tamils were taken into custody at the train stations entering Colombo. Sri Lanka had by then become a police state for all practical purposes, where some of the young Tamils taken into police vans would simply disappear altogether. In 2002, however, with the CFA, there would be a glimmer of hope for a return to a resemblance of normalcy.

Before the CFA, it had become a routine for the security forces to operate under the sinister "Prevention of Terrorism Act". This legislation had given the GOSL an almost free hand in dealing with LTTE suspects and had virtually rendered the human rights of young adult Tamils meaningless. It was a terrible shame that this had been the development during the half of century in which Sri Lanka had enjoyed its long-sought independence from a succession of imperialist rulers, first the Portuguese, then the Dutch and finally the British Empire. The British had granted Ceylon, as it was known then, independence in 1948, leaving a very distinct British mark on the whole administration of the country. One of the great institutions left behind by the British was the rule of law and the court system. Being a barrister in Sri Lanka was considered a noble and distinct profession and judges in the court systems were regarded as pillars of a society with a strong respect for the judiciary and stringent but fair criminal procedures. By the turn of the century, due procedure had evaporated however, and high-profile criminal cases involving political motives and links to the conflict would almost never be brought to a conclusion. In some parts of the country, the "white vans" were especially feared. These were symbols of a failed state. Suspects would be rounded up at night by groups of armed men who came in unmarked white minibuses, not wearing any uniform but linked in an undisclosed way with the police or the armed forces. Some of the suspects would resurface, most not daring to reveal the nature of the in ordeal, others would simply vanish into thin air. In the papers there would be small reports and bylines on persons being found dead in a ditch by the wayside, be it at the outskirts of Colombo, in Jaffna, in the jungle vicinity of Batticaloa or Ampara. Rarely would there be any substantial follow-up on these cases by trained detectives of the police. A disturbing atmosphere of fear was prevailing in many parts of the country. The situation was no better, of course, in the east, where the LTTE routinely operated with death squads.

The CFA stopped these disappearances almost completely in its first years, as the parties had signed up to a clause stating that both would refrain from abductions. Furthermore, primarily addressing the GOSL judicial procedures, article 2.12 of the CFA stated: "The parties agree that search operations and arrests under the Prevention of Terrorism Act shall not take place. Arrests shall be conducted under due process of law in accordance with the Criminal Procedure Code."

For a number of years normalcy returned to the Tamil residents of Colombo and its suburbs. Shop-owners tended to their businesses and there was considerable migration of young Tamils towards the capital seeking occupation and economic benefits from the relative calm in the country. They were able to integrate into the bustling socio-economic melting pot of Colombo without having to fear reprisals from the security forces, despite a significant string of incidents including assassinations and extortion in the north and east apparently, and in some cases evidently, linked to the LTTE.

However, as the conflict started to escalate towards full and undisguised return of hostilities in 2006, normalcy was eroded yet again, primarily for the Tamils. As it was extremely difficult for the security forces to try to intercept LTTE agents and collaborators in Colombo, the police would have to target a large segment of the Tamils in order to try to unravel the clandestine LTTE activity in the capital. This in itself nurtured more distrust between the police and the Tamil population in the south. The evil cycle of hatred and violence had taken effect again by the end of 2006.

To be sure, GOSL was not to blame, far from it as a matter of fact. The return to more heavy handed search operations was to a large extent sparked by and was a consequence of the tactics of the LTTE, which had stepped up its campaign of suicide bombing attacks against high-ranking military officials in that year. The ghastly work of the Black Tigers, as the suicide cadres were called, was one of the remarkably few facets of the ethnic conflict in Sri Lanka that seemed to catch the eye of the major news networks of the world. What the world audience would and could not understand, however, was that the LTTE claimed that the suicide attacks in Colombo were a desperate reaction to GOSL stepping up its military activities on a broad scale against innocent Tamil civilians in the north and the east. The LTTE, on the other hand, could never understand that the international community would simply not accept the concept of the suicide bomb attack as a legitimate means of warfare, and that the use of such tactics would greatly damage their cause and standing with the outside world.

# 7

# Trincomalee Harbour, the Jewel in the Crown

On the north-eastern shores of Sri Lanka lies Trincomalee town, a deeply ethnically entangled community; Tamils, Sinhalese and Muslims living in an uneasy mix as in few other frontier locations in the island. The Tamils proudly stated that they had always been the main ethnic group in Trinco, as Trincomalee is commonly called for short. However, GOSL claimed the opposite. Large groups of resettled people were living in the Trincomalee area. Several thousand Tamils had relocated southwards from the protracted fighting in Vanni in the nineties, joined by thousands of Sinhalese, which the LTTE claimed that GOSL had strategically relocated there to change the ethnic mix in its favour. There was truth in both, and ancient temples of both religions could testify to this. Sometimes GOSL seemed to deliberately fuel the conflict as was the case when a large Buddha statue was put up in the centre of Trincomalee town, at a square where Tamil three-wheeler drivers traditionally waited for customers. In response, the Tamils would demonstrate against what they called Buddhist chauvinism on important Sinhalese days of worship. The latest census figures available for Trincomalee district indicated roughly a three-way ethnic split with Tamils constituting marginally the largest segment closely followed by Sinhalese and then the Muslims.

A prominent monk in China Bay, to the south-west of Trincomalee proper, was the leader of the militant Buddhists. He would not tire in his efforts to stir up trouble on certain religious days, drumming up mass staged events around the central statue of Buddha, which was on occasions met with counter-demonstrations of Tamils. These gatherings of the two ethnic groups frequently ended with clashes and violence. The police in Trinco had a difficult task in trying to calm things down in volatile circumstances. Following such events there would be the apparently never-ending attempts to tear the statue down at night or damage it and such activity would more often than not result in targeted assassinations and counter-assassinations of leading figures of the two communities. This was a very difficult environment to monitor for the SLMM and a tall order for the security forces to contain. Trincomalee would remain restless for most of the duration of the CFA. Towards the end, it seemed that the security forces had gained an upper hand and were able to eliminate the most radical elements of the Tamils, those with the closest affiliation with the LTTE. That was a natural consequence of the successful military push in the area which saw the SLA retake territory around Muttur and Sampoor south of Trinco bay in its major military offensive, which started in the summer 2006.

Trincomalee town is built around its magnificent harbour, only known internationally by a handful of naval experts but one of the natural wonders of the world. Through a generous gap in the coastline, the Indian Ocean flows into Trinco bay which is well protected by a natural peninsula on which the town is located. North of this large opening to the sea, the waters flow into China bay through a wide strait, constituting a natural harbour of colossal depth. Most of the largest vessels sailing the international sea lines could easily embark there, and naval military experts claim that this could be a perfect and discreet calling port to even the greatest of submarines, silently edging their lonely course beneath the surface of the Indian Ocean. In short, a harbour so faultlessly created by nature that it could only be considered a strategic jewel of enormous importance and potential. It was hard to see how the Government of Sri Lanka would ever consider relinquishing this most important location in the whole of the east of Sri Lanka. Yet, the LTTE claimed it for their future capital in the Tamil Eelam they said they were fighting for.

Trincomalee is as of yet quite underdeveloped due to heavy fighting in the area since the late eighties. The main infrastructure in the harbour is the SLN naval base, home to the Eastern Command, an heirloom from the Royal British Navy. Even though Sri Lanka gained its independence from the crumbling British Empire in 1948 shortly after World War II, the naval base was so strategically important for the British that they remained there, in accordance with a separate protocol, for almost a decade, only handing it over to the SLN in 1957. Not much has changed since then within the heavily guarded naval base. The design of the area is neat and old-fashioned and has been kept very tidy and proper for Sri Lankan standards. The mooring needs of the SLN had also been relatively limited as its naval force was one that had been chronically stretched for resources in the past. It operated mainly with smaller vessels such as Fast Gun Boats, Fast Attack Crafts, and In shore Patrol Crafts, either manufactured in Israel, China or in later years domestically in Sri Lanka. That would change, however, during the CFA as the SLN would acquire a few deep-water ships able to patrol much further out to the Bengal Bay.

Regardless of origin, members of the Fast Attack Crafts (FACs) family would conventionally be called Dora's. They were the reliable beasts of burden of the Sri Lankan Navy faced with the unpredictable Sea Tigers. These boats with a usual length of between twenty and twenty-five metres normally have a crew of eight to twelve men. They can sail extremely fast or up to, and some even over, 40 knots at full speed. Dora's traditionally have a fixed 20 mm cannon on the front deck and usually at least two high caliber fixed multi-purpose machine-guns in the aft and/or to the sides. These are the main patrolling vessels in the north-eastern seas of Sri Lanka, which actually were some of the most dangerous seas in the world. Interestingly, the lack of security in the seas off Sri Lanka did not appear to be fully understood by major shipping companies, as they frequently sent their vulnerable cargo-ships up and down the shipping lanes of the east coast. These ships often came perilously close to waters that witnessed violent sea battles regularly, even under the CFA.

From the old Royal Navy base in Trincomalee harbour, there is a beautiful view over the bay, and on the other side, the main industrial landmark of the harbour rises against the sky, a large cement factory producing cement shipped to other parts of the Island for construction and to a limited extent for exports. The huge tanks in its vicinity were storages for imported wheat, an operation partly managed by Japanese enterprises, which had probably made one handsome donation or two to Colombo. The tanks were not only an eyesore, but also a reminder of the commercial importance of this location and its huge potential. There had been many talks on improving the infrastructure, building an oil refinery, a container central, etc. but that would not happen without massive Foreign Direct Investment from abroad. However, international investors would tend to be reluctant pouring their money into a region which had been scarred by massive military clashes, however sporadically, in the last three decades. With a lasting peace agreement, Trincomalee harbour could become one of the most interesting development sites in the world. This was, of course, reflected by some rather obscure NGOs, occasionally active in the north-east, from Japan and the US. There would also be courtesy visits from small delegations from China and the Arabic world, the latter donating funds for restoration of infrastructure and housing in some of the mainly Muslim communities south of Trinco bay. This was quiet but deliberate interest shown by some of the major manufacturing and trading powers, which could surely be translated into tangible projects would there be a lasting peace. To be sure, there were a number of stakeholders in the background, waiting to make a move when the Sri Lanka security situation had been brought under control.

As in most parts of the island, the whole area is beautiful, with the majestic dark blue ocean flowing into the gradually more azure bay, a lavish and lush vegetation in all possible variations of green pleasing the eye, but for the most intense monsoon months late in the year, clear blue skies and the ever smiling sun prevailed. A gentle breeze from the sea would alleviate the intense heat and burning of the sun, making the coastline with its generous sand beaches a potentially perfect place for high-end international tourism. Archeological wonders, the amazing temples and remnants from the Portuguese and Dutch colonial structures and the Old Fort in Trinco added to this inviting picture, not to speak of the delightful hot springs just north-west of the town. In a world full of overcrowded tourist attraction with ever fewer tranquil, reasonably prized beach locations available to the public, blessed with a warm and clean sea, Trinco could have a run for its money, almost all year round.

A few kilometres north of Trinco town, the first entrepreneurs had started building guest houses and hotels in the eighties, some others being financed by state-owned tourist enterprises. During the lull in the fighting in the late eighties and the beginning of the nineties, a number of sophisticated hotels had been constructed and attracted adventurous tourists from wealthy corners of the world. These were low-rise hotels, offering convenience and luxury which the local population could only dream about, with attractive bungalows scattered from the main building, most with perfect sea views and comfort.

The main problem with the fledgling tourism in new resorts north of Trinco remained, however, the lack of security. Over the years, the security forces would seldom have more control than just over Trincomalee town. They retained some control over the Nilaveli road up behind the resorts which faced outwards to the sea, but soon there was only uncontrolled bush to the west of the road and it was anybody's guess who was lurking around in that area. In the troubled nineties, the LTTE had managed to push south on several fronts and at times staged attacks on Trinco from the north. It must have been a ghastly and terrifying shock for the foreign visitors when some of them involuntarily became eyewitnesses to LTTE fighters battling it out with government soldiers at close range in some of the newly-built hotel gardens. The northern-most hotel complexes were eventually overran by LTTE fighters, killing and destroying what was in their path. Nilaveli, the common name for the cluster of hotels about ten kilometres north of Trinco, saw heavy fighting before the CFA and some of the former hotels would end up as mere ruins and rubble. Other complexes were refurbished, but even the most adventurous tourists shied away from the pristine Trinco beaches as taxi drivers in Colombo advised them to stick to the beach resorts in the west and the south. It was only after establishing of CFA that some visitors from outside the island braved the tales of terror and gloom and returned to the east coast. They were rewarded with unexpected comfort at excellent resorts like the Blue Oceanic in Uppuveli and at the legendary Nilaveli Beach hotel. It had taken its share of the fighting but remained open during most of the conflict. The vast white beaches of Nilaveli offered a clear view over the magnificent Indian Ocean towards Pigeon Island, one of the most exclusive snorkeling paradises in the world.

8

# The Elusive LTTE Camps of the Trinco Jungle

Although, the security forces had Trinco under relatively good control in the first years of the CFA, there was widespread political activity by the LTTE in the town and surrounding areas. The political leader of LTTE in Trinco, Mr. Elilan, was a dominant figure behind the scenes, and had great influence on various occurrences in the area. He was also a man that the SLMM was able to discuss practical issues of the CFA with, and given excellent relations with both the Police, the Sri Lanka Army and the Sri Lanka Navy in Trinco, many potential crises were defused during the CFA years. GOSL was, nevertheless, very wary of the influence LTTE wielded in the whole region and was deeply distrustful of LTTE's military intentions in the area. This was understandable, as there were troubling signs of LTTE activities in the jungle surrounding Trinco, both to the north and the south. This was also one of the areas where the lack of the demarcation lines, as stipulated in the CFA, was most acute. The SLN held some checkpoints north of Nilaveli, along the coastal road, the former main road towards Mullativu but it was not quite clear where its control ended and where the LTTE had *de facto* hold over the land. The conventional wisdom was that the last SLN outpost at Kuchchaveli, about 25 km north of Trinco town, marked the end of the road as far as security was concerned. Moreover, some claimed that the SLN control only pertained to the narrow strip of land east of the coastal road, north of Nilaveli, and that the LTTE could operate at will in the jungle inland, also around the famous hot springs northwest of Trinco.

The complexity of the situation was well illustrated in mid-2004, when two official Home Guards were snatched by the LTTE in the jungle north-west of Trinco. Home Guards, were low ranking officials of the GOSL, mostly self-sufficient, and providing security in Sri Lanka, predominantly in remote and poor villages. They were poorly remunerated and inadequately trained, but were armed with rifles and side arms. As such they were no threat to the LTTE and no match for them either. The LTTE claimed alternatively, and sometimes both, that the two Home Guards had been on a reconnaissance tour well within LTTE controlled area and that they had been poaching for their own benefit. The security forces, however, dismissed this and said that the Home Guards had been carrying on their patrolling duties well within GOSL controlled territory, and that they had been kidnapped by LTTE commandos in a blatant violation of the ceasefire agreement. Such was the effectiveness of the CFA, and such had become the state of normalcy in 2004, that this otherwise minor incident, which would hardly have been noticed before the implementation of the CFA, became a major irritant between the parties and an important news item. The fate of the Home Guards was discussed in the media for weeks and months, and it was taken up at the highest level meetings between the GOSL and SLMM and consequently between SLMM and LTTE. The level of importance given to this episode ironically underscored the massive success of the CFA in its first two years. The Home Guards would remain in custody in Kilinochchi for a year, before being released. Never before had the fate of the two low ranking servicemen in Sri Lanka been so thoroughly documented.

In the course of the year 2004, the GOSL became increasingly nervous about alleged LTTE activities on the ground. Colombo claimed that the LTTE was conducting training and trespassing in the jungle south of China bay in the Trinco area. It maintained that the Tigers had started to increase their presence in the area, building camps and sustaining them with fighters on the move from Vanni to the east and vice-versa. The importance of Trinco harbour and the SLN base were more than enough rational explanation for such covert activity by the LTTE, real or otherwise. The issue worried the Army enough to bring it to the attention of politicians in Colombo, who in turn managed to make it a platform for bickering on the whole peace progress. Indeed, the whole Trinco region was a good example of the complexity of the conflict and the supposedly frozen ground situation following the commencement of the CFA. It was an accepted fact that the security forces controlled the A6 highway fully, which stretched all the way, in a straight line drawn on the map, from Colombo to Trinco. However, it was also noted by the SLMM that there were frequent reports on LTTE fighting groups crossing the highway in spots not completely covered by the SLA. As the A6 was running through jungle areas in long stretches on its last one-third leg from Habarana towards Trinco, it was virtually impossible to stop the trespassing of the LTTE, even with a string of checkpoints dotted like pearls on a necklace. In order to consolidate control over the highway, the bush had been cut away some ten to twenty metres from the road in long stretches. While that would at least deter to some extent ambushes and Claymore mine attacks, it could not fully stop the movement of the LTTE in the most north-eastern part of the road. This was a great nuisance for the security forces.

The SLMM would discuss these alleged movements of LTTE cadres from Vanni to the south, but the LTTE would not be forthcoming regarding this matter. At that point in time, it would have been difficult to understand the magnitude of events which would take place in the eastern theatre south of Trinco and in the Batticaloa area, within the next two years. However, at this point in time it was not widely known that the LTTE was encountering a formidable problem in the whole Batticaloa region, due to a surprising internal split within its organisation. Furthermore, rotating medium ranking personnel from the east to the north and vice-versa at sea was getting increasingly complicated. Rudimentary camps would under these circumstances become essential for the LTTE in order to rest their fighters at relatively secure locations on the march from Vanni to Batticaloa, with Trinco lying in the middle.

GOSL would make much noise publicly and complain bitterly about the alleged LTTE camps deep in the jungle south of Trinco bay in the summer and fall of 2004. Furthermore, the Sri Lankan media would publish countless articles accompanied by some sort of satellite imagery provided by the SLA in order to lend more credibility to its claims. The SLMM was for the first time since the commencement of the CFA criticised quite strongly in the media for not being able to put a stop to an alleged development of LTTE camps in the area. The main problem, however, for the SLMM was that the LTTE would routinely deny them access to the deep jungle and monitors would be turned away at remote checkpoints. The monitors would point out the freedom of movement for the SLMM, stipulated in CFA articles. This made a limited impression, to put it mildly, on the LTTE guards manning their posts. As was so often the case outside of Vanni, one would rarely encounter well trained LTTE cadres donning fighting fatigues. Usually, a checkpoint would be a primitive but an effective affair consisting of a hut fortified with sacks of sand stacked in a few rows and some barbed wire. The first ones on primitive byroads in the jungle would not necessarily be manned, but that did not mean that travellers on the road were not being observed. The lack of guards in some of these empty outposts added an element of suspense to exploring the depth of the contested terrain. However, if the SLMM got close enough, they invariably would be stopped by young men in chequered shirts, wearing sandals, nodding in a non-committed way but carrying very real Chinese-made automatic riffles. Most of these cadres on the ground had never been introduced to the essentials of the CFA document and for them the notion of freedom of movement for the SLMM was absurd. They had received specific orders not to let any intruders through, let alone some "whitefaces" flying a white flag on a white vehicle.

Some of the SLMM monitors would, however, manage to come quite close to a few "camps", but the ones sighted and photographed, sometimes covertly, consisted of little more than huts and some limited facilities for washing and cooking. Following further meetings with LTTE commanders in the region, and at a higher level in Kilinochchi, the SLMM was certain that the so-called camps had not been developed recently. These were merely a part of a very limited LTTE infrastructure in the region, well in place before the commencement of the CFA, supposedly freezing the ground situation in its current military localities in February 2002. Moreover, there was no evidence of substantial improvement of facilities, which could be interpreted as bases for developing offensive tactical means to the detriment of the security of Trincomalee harbour and town.

GOSL was not pleased with the findings of the SLMM, understandably, of course. From the perspective of the Sri Lanka security forces, an increased movement of LTTE cadres through the jungles around Trinco down to the east was worrying and not the least compatible to confidence-building measures as stipulated in the CFA. The need of the LTTE to be able to rotate fresh cadres to the Batticaloa region was equally understandable in tactical terms, as supporters of a LTTE renegade were defecting in droves from the LTTE system. The bottomline was quite familiar, the LTTE were roaming around in some remote corners of the jungle region south of Trinco bay. Nobody knew how many, how well armed or where exactly, which was the classic LTTE signature.

There were also practical reasons for the LTTE choosing to rotate cadres clandestinely through a land corridor. The sea troop transports had proven to be a cumbersome and often humiliating experience for the LTTE with the SLN complicating and sometimes dictating terms.

# 9

# Mutur, Sampoor and the LTTE Strongpoint South of Trinco bay

GOSL would claim that it controlled the land to the west of Trinco bay and to the south all the way to the small town of Mutur, predominantly inhabited by a Muslim population. However, the LTTE would not accept such an interpretation and made it clear that it controlled some secure areas in the jungle where the alleged camps were located. One of the key weaknesses of the CFA had been the fact that clear demarcation lines had not been established fully and agreed upon by the parties in all regions affected by the conflict. This area, thus, would remain ambiguous in terms of control by the SLA and the LTTE fighting formations. There were stipulations for such demarcation lines to be established with the SLMM assisting in the procedure, which should have been finished within 60 days of the commencement of the CFA. This proved to be an impossible task.

It was, nevertheless, a fact that the security forces of Sri Lanka controlled the mainly Muslim town of Mutur on the southern shores of Trinco bay. The Muslim population of Sri Lanka was split in a number of factions, although they had been able to forge a loose alliance of splinter parties representing them at times with a coherent voice in the Sri Lankan Parliament and in the political scene in general. The Muslims were of mixed Moor/Tamil ethnicity and spoke the Tamil language with a considerable lexis of Arabic, but defined themselves as Muslims rather than Tamils. This put them in the awkward position of being caught in the middle in the complicated and entrenched conflict, religiously, politically and militarily. The Muslims had not armed themselves and were as such not a player in the hostilities. This had frequently left them in a very difficult situation in the past. Thousands of Muslims had had to flee the fighting further up north in the several stages of the so-called Eelam wars. Hostilities had flared up again and again after ceasefires and external diplomatic intervention. In the Mutur area, thousands of families had lived for up to fifteen years in a miserly state as IDPs, longing to return to their roots and former townships by the sea north of Trincomalee and up towards Mullatiwu. The Muslim community had refused to take the side of the LTTE in its uprising against the security forces and had at times had to pay dearly for that stance. On the west coast of Sri Lanka, there was in many ways a similar situation, where a segment of thousands of Muslim IDPs had had to flee the rage of the LTTE in Jaffna and on the western coastline of the LTTE-held Vanni. They had been located in makeshift camps close to the city of Puttalam, eking out a life of poverty, far away from their origins in the north of the Island. On both the east and west coast a generation of young adults had grown up in these Muslim settlements, having only heard stories about their former towns and family houses, some of which had been devastated years ago.

Some of these young adults were full of resentment both towards the GOSL and the LTTE. In Mutur there had been some indications of radical groups of young Muslims forming and toying with the idea of taking up arms and entering the conflict on their own premises. However, these were small splinter groups working clandestinely, but most likely not able to manage more than organising a hartal or sit-in demonstrations here and there or maybe even conduct the odd targeted assault or assassination in extreme cases.

Hartals were an effective form of demonstration, and fairly common on the eastern coast, especially in areas predominantly inhabited by Muslims or Tamils. Hartals would routinely be announced a day or two before they took effect but could also happen spontaneously if the Muslims felt that they had been harshly treated or something that outraged them had taken place within their communities. In the volatile east where there was an ever deepening split between the LTTE supporters and an increasing number of assassinations related to the conflict, the hartals would become more frequent and more violent. During a typical hartal, all shops and offices in a town would be ordered to shut down, by the community leaders. The same would be the case for all means of transport. Angry mobs of young men would block the streets, often setting fires to stacks of tyres or trash cans. It was wise not to try to break the hartal as this could result in an orgy of violence extremely difficult to contain. The security forces were vary of the hartals in the east and would usually condone them by laying low during the day. In most cases the commercial life and transport would return to normal the day after. The SLMM was trained in confronting the circumstances of a hartal and on occasions tried to forge a conversation with the local leaders concerning the execution of a hartal. Nevertheless, on occasions, such encounters had gone awry and the monitors at times had to flee hurriedly in their double cabs in order not to be caught amidst an angry and violent mob. Over time, the common parole would be simply to stay away from the hartals and respect them as that, a day lost, but hopefully nothing more than that.

The vicinity of Mutur was controlled to the south and west by the SLA which had a large military camp south of the town, whereas in the town itself and by its most important installation, the ferry jetty, the control was in the hands of SLN infantry. The SLN was deeply suspicious of the Muslims as at times they were seen to have entered an alliance of some sorts with the LTTE in the area. Alternatively, the LTTE was equally distrustful of the Muslims, which in reality loathed both the security forces and the LTTE. As it was very difficult for the SLN to distinguish between Muslim fishermen and general Tamil boats in the southern part of Trinco Bay, draconic regulations were introduced for all fishing boats. As a result, all fishermen on the southern shores of Koddiyar Bay were requested to register their boats and obtain fishing permits. Moreover, fishing would only be allowed during daylight, which went counter to the tradition of fishing in the early hours, before sunlight, when the catch would be the most abundant. As with so many facets of the conflict and its implication on the daily life of the inhabitants in the affected regions, there was a clear logic to the measures the security forces found themselves having to take. For the SLN, it was intolerable that the LTTE could operate with boats at the southern shores of Trinco Bay. Many of the Sea Tigers wore traditional fishermen clothing and it was impossible to differentiate them from the everyday Tamils at sea. The fishermen too were trying with their simple and antiquated fishing techniques to sustain their families and their community. It helped that the Bengal Bay provided a splendid array of catch in its bountiful waters. However, to make security issues even more complicated, the LTTE held the immensely strategic town of Sampoor on the southern coast of Trinco bay. It was situated about ten kilometres to the east of Mutur from where the LTTE held the whole coastline up towards Foul Point, where they had artillery positions and were able to reach the naval base in Trincomalee proper. Furthermore, the LTTE positions to the south of Trincomalee could also seriously disturb the coming and going of vessels at the mouth of the bay, including the transport of troops from Trinco to Kankesanturai (KKS) harbour in Jaffna.

# 10

## The Karuna Split

In spring 2004 a sensational rumour started spreading in the eastern part of Sri Lanka regarding the organisation of the LTTE in the Batticaloa region—heartland of the whole of their campaign for decades—claiming this as an essential eastern part of Tamil Eelam or the Tamil Homeland. The notion of Tamil Eelam stretching far south of Trincomalee, down through Batticaloa and all the way to Ampara, was supported by the LTTE claim that the coastal towns and settlements were predominantly inhabited by Tamils. This notion conveniently disregarded the fact that there were significant Muslim settlements along the coast as well and Muslims outnumbered Tamils in many of the major towns in the Ampara district. This notwithstanding, as would soon be pointed out in Colombo, when the intriguing Karuna rumour reached the Capital, already awash with politico-military gossip, there were indeed ways to differentiate the Tamil minority in Sri Lanka into distinct sub-groups.

As noted, a large community of Tamils was living within Colombo proper and on its outskirts since before the independence of Ceylon. At the time of independence in 1948 it had been widely claimed by Sinhalese opinion-makers of nationalistic leaning that the Tamils had received preferential treatment by the British colonial power and that Tamils had been over-represented within the administration of Ceylon. In other words, Tamils were disproportionally well placed in the Ceylon elite and Sinhalese had been treated worse under the colonial rule, in relative terms. Some of these notions had played the most fundamental role in the beginning of the ethnic conflict in Sri Lanka as in the pristine years of the new independent state. This dangerous habit of competition in Sinhalese nationalism by the main political parties would become the most effective way to increase poll ratings.

If there were critical notions rendered in Colombo on Tamils commanding elite positions within the administration and elitist society of Sri Lanka, there could not be a harsher contrast to another distinct segment of the Tamil population, the highland or hill country Tamils. This section constituted the major segment of the workforce in the tea plantations in the mountainous interior of Sri Lanka. It was a widely accepted historical fact that the bulk of the highland Tamils had emigrated from India starting just before the mid-eighteenth century to work as hired hands in the extremely labour-intensive industry of making world famous Ceylon tea. Wages at the beginning of the twenty-first century were still very niggardly. The highland Tamils had more or less joined hands within one Tamil political party that represented their cause in Colombo, the Ceylon Workers' Congress. There would be the odd strike and demands for more reasonable wages for the desperately poor community of tea leaf pluckers, however, in competing with tea exports from India and China, costs indeed had to be kept down. To be sure, the Ceylon Workers' Congress, or the hill Country Tamil party, was primarily concerned with the socio-economic welfare of the highland Tamils and was as such not active in the ethnic conflict. Its leaders would usually operate on the fringes of the government, sometimes in opposition, but sometimes bagging a nice junior minister post with its convenient benefits and perks. Although the hill country Tamils shared the vernacular of other Tamils in Sri Lanka and some of their grievances, they managed through their political leadership to stay out of Sri Lanka's protracted internal hostilities. Following the independence of Ceylon, successive Sinhalese-led administrations had denied the hill country Tamils citizenship and had through negotiations deported or repatriated, as was the politically correct term at the time, several hundreds of thousands of them to India. Such draconic measures were eased as there was a constant need for the inexpensive labour. However the issue took decades to settle before the remaining highland Tamils were formally recognised as full citizens of Sri Lanka. It was surely a lesson that taught the leaders of the highland Tamils to tread gently and stay out of the ethnic conflict.

The LTTE defined the north and the east of Sri Lanka as the Tamil homeland, where Tamils had been the predominant population for up to two millennia according to their own recording of history. Myths and folklore described the splendours of the rulers of the Tamil kingdom of Jaffna, but as with most ethnic issues in Sri Lanka, history was vehemently disputed, depending on which ethnic group defined its ancient roots. However, much indicated that the Tamils had been the major ethnic group in the north as long as records went back, with the relatively sparsely populated Vanni providing a buffer zone to the rich cultural heritage and dominance of the Sinhalese further south, so evidently displayed at the breath-taking ancient cities of Anuradhapura and Polonnaruwa. The east of Sri Lanka, however, was a very hot potato for all parties concerned. Despite major political concessions to the LTTE on the east, such as the Indo-Lanka accord agreeing a merger of the north and the east administratively, there were significant disclaimers made, as substantial pockets of Sinhalese could be found in the contested eastern regions. Furthermore, it was self-evident that Sinhalese would have had to relocate from villages that had fallen under the control of the LTTE at any time in the conflict. This was disputed by the LTTE, which made contrary claims that many Sinhalese communities were forced settlements, for instance, in Trincomalee.

All the disputes of the LTTE and GOSL notwithstanding, the notion of a marked difference between the northern Tamils from Jaffna and Vanni proper and their eastern brethren in the Batticaloa region came as a surprise for many seasoned observers. It had been a notion rarely aired before the Karuna split in 2004. The sensational shift within the LTTE's structure in the east came as a total surprise more than two years into the CFA, which had brought substantial security to Sri Lanka in general and to the population living in and close to the contested areas in particular.

Mr. Vinayagamoorthy Muralitharan, alias Colonel Karuna Amman, had been the military wing leader of the LTTE in the eastern region, officially carrying the title of Special Commander of Batticaloa–Ampara and as such was an extremely powerful man within the LTTE hierarchy. Karuna had apparently enjoyed the full and unconditional support of Mr. P, as the LTTE leader living as a recluse in the north-eastern Vanni jungle, was sometimes called for short. Karuna had been considered a popular and charismatic figure who enjoyed immense personal support in the east. He had been a member of the LTTE delegation to the first rounds of peace talks in Thailand shortly after the commencement of the CFA. Furthermore, he had been considered as one of the key LTTE participants in the Oslo peace talks in December 2002, when the parties appeared to have reached a breakthrough agreement on internal self-determination for the Tamil communities in the north and the east, within a federal structure of Sri Lanka. Karuna was at the centrestage at the press briefing in Oslo with Mr. Balasingham, the political advisor of the LTTE, when it was announced that the delegation of the UNP-led GOSL had agreed to the LTTE's major points, thus appearing to consolidate the legitimacy of the LTTE as the sole representative of the Tamils in the north and the east. In hindsight this was a massive irony considering events that would unfold in the Tamil fraternity around Batticaloa.

What had caused the split was not evident, but soon after it had been officially confirmed by sources close to Karuna, theories started to amass, with one fundamental but rather simple explanation being put forward as the most plausible. Mr. Pirapaharan had observed the rise of Colonel Karuna and his growing popularity and had apparently become uneasy over the support Karuna was commanding, following two years of relative calm and prosperity in the east. The region was in many ways far away from the main seat of the LTTE in Kilinochchi, and communication and transport of cadres between these two regions could be cumbersome. Karuna himself claimed that the Vanni Tigers had started to show some sort of disrespect for the effort of the eastern cadres who had at times borne the brunt of the fighting with the SLA. However, it could also be plausible that the situation in the Batticaloa region had reached a point of normalcy that was not to the liking of the high command in Kilinochchi. It is indeed more difficult to recruit young fighters willing to be trained to become Black Tigers or suicide bombers, from a region that is enjoying a lull from fighting. In the east many Tamils had turned their focus on sustaining a peaceful if simple life in an underdeveloped region that also happened to be one of the most beautiful and seminal places on earth. The LTTE would, however, try to circulate a story indicting Karuna of having lived lavishly and having enriched himself personally through LTTE funds.

Karuna would claim in countless interviews that the Vanni leadership had simply come to the conclusion that he had become too powerful and that they could not control his command of his men from Vanni and hence he would have to be replaced. He, furthermore, claimed that he had been ordered to go to Vanni to attend high-level meetings, but sources loyal to him in Kilinochchi had indicated that he would not return alive. For some reason he had become a nuisance to the highest leadership of the LTTE, which in reality could only mean Mr. Pirapaharan. Karuna added that the eastern Tamils were sick and tired of being treated as inferior to the northern Tamils and that the fact that the LTTE's roots had been in the Jaffna peninsula had always skewed the balance within the movement to the detriment of the eastern flank.

This surprising and swift turn of tides in the eastern theatre came as a thunderbolt out of nowhere to even informed observers, be it the security forces, GOSL or the SLMM. It was all the more remarkable as the process towards normalcy had worked very well in the east. Attempts to solve disputes, concerning the CFA and alleged violations of it, on the lowest possible level or regionally, had been quite successful in Batticaloa. Smaller disputes were usually dealt with by Local Monitoring Committees, LMCs, consisting of two representatives from each of the two Parties to the CFA and a chairperson from the SLMM. Leading up to the split, there was not much to indicate that such a dramatic change within the Tamil side was imminent. Moreover, the SLMM had managed to defuse many potential sources of irritation between the parties and local incidents by arranging regional meetings between the military commanders of both parties with Karuna present as a key figure. In hindsight, the meetings attended by Karuna and the SLA eastern commanders had been remarkably amicable, sometimes rendering positive results going beyond the most optimistic expectations of the SLMM.

Nevertheless, the Karuna split that was said to have occurred in March 2004, came out of the blue and seemed to take most stakeholders by complete surprise. Initially it did not cause too many ripples, but by mid-year it was out in the open for all sides to acknowledge, despite the initial dementias stemming out of Kilinochchi. There were probably not many at this stage who could predict how dramatic the impact would be on the ground situation in the eastern theatre and for the prospects of peace in general in the coming years.

While contemplating the split, Karuna had expected the lethal wrath of the LTTE and gone into hiding with his followers deep into the jungle, somewhere in the vicinity of Batticaloa. Nevertheless, he and his supporters were seasoned cadres and would know how to take care of themselves in their hideaways, if given the proper means. There were soon strong indications indeed for that being the case.

# 11

# Early Naval Monitoring and the Disputed HOM Ruling on the Sea

The CFA was in many ways a concise document, leaving considerable room for definition on the implementation of the ceasefire. It, moreover, clearly stated that the SLMM Head of Mission would be the final authority in interpreting its various articles. Interestingly, there was not a word in the CFA on the conflict situation at sea. This would become a very complex problem in course of time.

The CFA clearly stated in its articles that the parties should withdraw from the most delicate frontline positions, widening the gap between the fighting formations, with stipulations from drawing up definite demarcation lines that would take effect in most cases within 30 to 90 days of the implementation of the CFA. This was achieved in many important places such as in general across the frontline and *de facto* borderline at the south of LTTE held areas in Vanni, most notably at the Omanthai crossing point, and at the frontline in Nagarkovil just north of Elephant pass at the entrance to the Jaffna peninsula. However, at sea, there obviously were no fixed positions, and no demarcation lines were ever contemplated on naval maps.

The lack of any agreement of spheres of influence at sea, would turn into a severe problem for the continuation of the peace process. The Sea Tigers would bitterly note that they had, as a matter of fact, been in control of areas of sea. Their naval arm, the Sea Tigers claimed, was very much a force that had to be reckoned with, not the least in the waters to the east and west of Vanni. This interpretation of the CFA by Colonel Soosai, the leader of the Sea Tigers, would make life very uncomfortable for the Sri Lankan Navy and the SLMM naval teams. He in turn had a valid point, as he specifically declared at a meeting with the SLMM Head of Mission at the LTTE Peace Secretariat in Kilinochchi that the Sea Tigers were an existing fighting force at sea that could not simply be wished away. Mr. Tamilshelvan, the head of the LTTE political wing, was also present at the meeting and concurred with Colonel Soosai. Hence, there was no room for misinterpretation. The LTTE would reserve its right to operate at sea out of land controlled by them no matter what the SLMM HOM would rule.

In practical terms, the dilemma of the lack of articles on the sea in the CFA was ignored at first by the SLMM, which established a *modus operandi* well known to both Parties. The naval monitors would embark on SLN vessels to monitor activities at sea, and when the monitors were on board the Navy vessels, they would fly a clearly marked SLMM flag to signal their presence. At the beginning of the CFA, the naval monitoring was focused on the safe passage to combatants of both Parties. The LTTE would seek to rotate their cadres from Vanni in the north to their controlled areas in the east and vice-versa. On the first occasions of such transports, SLMM naval monitors would be present on the LTTE boats and verify that the cadres were unarmed. Later on, due to the lack of predictability of the LTTE sea commanders, the SLMM would exclusively board Sri Lanka Navy vessels which observed the LTTE movements from a safe distance, avoiding provocations. Furthermore, in the first year of the CFA, the Sea Tigers duly observed the SLMM flag which would deter them from attacking the SLN vessels. However, as time went on, the Sea Tigers became more aggressive towards the SLN, with or without a SLMM flag. Eventually this lead to SLMM monitors witnessing combat situations at sea at close hand.

The SLMM naval monitoring was conducted out of Trincomalee and Jaffna, where the monitors would join Sri Lanka Navy on numerous patrols to and around the islets of Jaffna proper. Some would include excursions into the Jaffna lagoon which was only possible on Inshore Patrol Crafts as the waters are very shallow. Jaffna lagoon would never be all that safe for any craft, as there could be firing from both the northern Government of Sri Lanka-held shores and the southern shores held by LTTE. Moreover, in the shallow waters south of Jaffna and west of Vanni, the Sea Tigers proved to be a formidable force to engage, sometimes appearing out of nowhere, with their very fast improvised attack crafts and high-powered suicide boats. Generally, however, during daylight the Sri Lanka Navy would hold the upper hand, barring a direct suicide attack, which was otherwise very hard to defend against.

There would be countless incidents at sea, witnessed close up by the naval monitors. A memorable one involved a small trawler in the seas, well south of Jaffna, intercepted by the Sri Lankan Navy and signalled to stop. Following signalling, the crew on the trawler refused an inspection by the Navy, a delicate situation that possibly could lead to a serious incident. In the early years of the CFA, both Parties showed much more constraint than had previously been the case in the long conflict. The Navy asked the SLMM monitors for advice. Following communication with the SLMM naval office in Jaffna and some direct communication with the Tamil crew on the trawler, it was accepted that the SLMM monitors would come on board and they would do an inspection of the vessel. This was stretching the mandate quite considerably, but in one of the CFA articles it was stipulated that the SLMM should "conduct international verification through on-site monitoring of the fulfilment of the commitments entered into (*in the CFA*)", and could with a rather liberal interpretation justify this course of action. The monitors inspected the boat for a while, as the trawler crew was getting restless. After fifteen minutes or so, one of the SLMM monitors found a secret cabin stowaway in the hull and opened it. It appeared to contain dismantled military hardware for a cannon of sorts. The SLN sensed something and began to move in closer. The captain on the trawler was at the radio talking in an agitated way and was obviously receiving some information or orders. As the SLN craft was closing in, the captain gestured wildly to one of the two SLMM monitors, drawing his finger across his throat as in a slitting movement, and nodding his head frantically as to tell them to get out immediately. At that moment there was a first explosion in the aft and the SLMM monitors jumped over the rail into the sea, hearing further detonations. They swam away as fast as they could and were picked up by the SLN vessel some minutes later. From the Dvora they could see the trawler fully ablaze with fire and hovering at a safe distance they observed the trawler burning into the night until there was little tangible left other than the hull mooring in the Palk Strait. The Sea Tigers preferred laying down their lives to being taken prisoners. It was a stark demonstration of the many dangerous facets of the conflict at sea.

Following increased skirmishes, the SLMM tried to clarify its stance on the matter, but as it had been left out of the CFA, it would be impossible to rule in a way that was acceptable to both Parties. The first SLMM Head of Mission, Major-General Trond Furuhovde, had an inclination to rule the whole Sri Lankan seaboard as GOSL controlled area. This was based on international law that clearly stated that no non-state actor could claim any sort of control, not to speak of sovereignty over the sea. The LTTE strongly disputed any such legal basis for an interpretation in favour of the GOSL. Discussions on these matters were conducted with both Parties. However, a clear and mutual understanding was still missing.

The matter would become even more complicated with the second SLMM Head of Mission, Major-General Tryggve Tellefsen, who succeeded Furuhovde in early 2003. He was believed to show an understanding for the deep reluctance of the LTTE to accept full SLN control of the Sri Lankan sea waters as it was tactically of utmost importance for them to continue their own operations at sea. Moreover, the Sea Tigers saw themselves as the protectors of the Tamil fishermen who suffered countless incidents of harassment from the Sri Lanka Navy. Following increased and continuous skirmishes involving the Sea Tigers and the Navy the matter became ever more urgent to resolve. The incumbent SLMM Head of Mission sought to explain to the LTTE that their role at sea would have to be very limited in order for the CFA to survive, but he was also pragmatic enough to acknowledge their tactically fully operational naval fleet of medium-sized armed boats. Furthermore, there was a potent portion of realism in this notion, as the Sea Tigers claimed that the CFA had never been signed in order to diminish their *de facto* military capabilities, be it at land or sea. This development was not taken lightly by the GOSL, which exacerbated the whole issue of the access to the sea and accused the SLMM of having warned the LTTE of an ongoing SLN patrol, hence violating the national security of Sri Lanka. In late 2004, a message was conveyed from the President's office to the Norwegian Facilitator that Her Excellency Madame Kumaratunga Bandaranaike deemed Mr. Tellefsen as untenable in his function. Tellefsen returned to Oslo for consultations as a *de facto persona non grata* in Sri Lanka. Following several weeks that appeared to observers to be a stand-off between the facilitator and GOSL on the function of the SLMM HOM, the Royal Norwegian Government declared that Tellefsen would take on a new command as the Head of Mission of the Temporary International Presence in Hebron (TIPH) and would be succeeded by his predecessor Mr. Furuhovde, who would take on a second term as SLMM HOM in early 2004. The tide would shift again on the issue of access to the sea. Later in the year, the SLMM would officially state that according to international law, the LTTE had no rights to operate in Sri Lankan sea waters. Non-state actors could not rule open sea waters or airspace, it was added.

The LTTE never accepted this ruling and said so openly. However, following the ruling, things calmed down somewhat, and there were fewer incidents of a level that could spark a full-blown crisis for the CFA. At the end of the year, a Tsunami struck the eastern and southern coast of Sri Lanka with such devastation that it destroyed most of the fishing vessels and equipment of already desperately poor fishing communities, both Tamil and Sinhalese. As international aid was pouring in for reconstruction of whole villages along the Sri Lankan shores, the Sea Tigers were forced to show more constraint in their operations and the Sri Lanka Navy would try to be on its best behaviour. There were hundreds of international aid workers present and the international community was watching the rebuilding efforts with a discerning eye. This was not the time to be observed as an aggressor in the waters of the traumatised sea bordering villages, where the dire need for the population was to be re-equipped with boats and fishing gear in order to sustain itself.

# 12

# The Tsunami—a Missed Opportunity for Reconciliation

Arugam Bay, with its cozy and quaint guesthouses along the coast in a remote south-eastern corner of Sri Lanka, had long been considered a well hidden gem for alternative tourists in Sri Lanka. The settlements had originated from humble huts of fishing communities that had gradually been replaced with lodges and modest two-storey hotels. Located in Ampara district about forty kilometres south of the sometimes troubled Muslim town of Akkaraipattu, Arugam Bay was just far enough away from the ethnic conflict to be considered relatively safe for foreign visitors. They consisted mostly of crowds of hip and cool youngsters who came from various parts of the world for the excellent surfing conditions, affluent Sri Lankans who sought retreat from the hustle and bustle in Colombo and middle class Muslims from further up north. There was a relaxed atmosphere in the air, and if the Muslim hotels did adhere somewhat conservatively to the rules of not serving any alcohol, some of the other beach lodges offered its young and carefree customers a quite distinct sense of freedom. In the evenings the surfers would gather for refreshing drinks in the seaside bar lounges, listening to classic hippie music by the Doors and the Beach Boys and sometimes there would be a faint but unmistakable scent of marijuana in the air. One could hardly enjoy a more relaxing afternoon than lying on a beach chair facing the seaside observing the powerful waves of the Indian Ocean roaring onto the shores.

On the morning of 26 December 2004 most of the seaside resorts in Arugam Bay were wiped out completely by a giant Tsunami wave that brought unprecedented death and destruction to the whole of the eastern and southern coast of Sri Lanka.

The natural catastrophe had originated from a massive earthquake in the seabed of the Indian Ocean off the northern tip of the island of Sumatra. The earthquake had sparked giant Tsunami ocean waves, which gathered momentum as they raced towards the shores of the adjacent countries hitting seaside communities in the whole region with devastating effect. The Aceh region in northern Sumatra was hit the worst reporting a staggering 100,000 deaths due to the catastrophe. Although Sri Lanka was more than thousand kilometres away from the epicenter of the earthquake, its eastern and southern coastline was hit with such an impact that 35,000 lives were lost. Various estimates indicate that around 100,000 houses were destroyed in the Tsunami rendering more than half a million Sri Lankans homeless. Furthermore, around two-thirds of the island's fishing fleet or 24.000 boats were wrecked resulting in a complete lack of income for the thousands of fishing communities from Jaffna in the north to Galle in the south. Tamil and Muslim communities suffered disproportionally as they traditionally lived along the whole of the eastern seaboard. Nevertheless, Sinhalese dominated communities were also ravaged in the south and in one particularly harrowing tale of grief almost the total population of the village of Peraliya, just north of the popular Hikkaduwa resort town, was extinguished in the giant wave. To add to the unspeakable misery, the coastal train *The Queen of the Sea, engine 59*, was swept off its tracks at Peraliya with around twelve hundred passengers losing their lives in arguably the worst train catastrophe in history.

The Tsunami seriously affected around two-thirds of the coastline of Sri Lanka, leaving a destroyed infrastructure sometimes several hundred metres inland and tens of thousands of survivors either badly maimed or suffering intractable psychological scars. Ampara district suffered the most bemoaning over ten thousand dead with Hambantota to its south recording almost five thousand fatal casualties. In Sri Lanka's magnificent Yala National Park, which was shared between Ampara and Hambantota, a mysterious phenomenon was noted, there were almost no dead animals to be found in the affected coastal area. It appeared that somehow sensing the danger the elephants, the monkeys and the leopards had moved further inland ahead of the frightful impact of the ocean waves.

In the aftermath of the Tsunami, the Government of Sri Lanka faced an enormous challenge to come to the aid and rescue of the survivors along the coastline, with hundreds of thousands homeless having lost all their earthly belongings. Apart from all the destroyed houses, coastal infrastructure including refurbishing roads, bridges, railways, power and telecommunication grids, water supply points and fishing ports would also have to be rebuilt. As terrible as the impact of the Tsunami had been in a one thousand kilometre stretch of the Sri Lankan coastline, fortunately the most sophisticated infrastructure in the western part of the island including the all important modern port of Colombo had been spared. This meant that foreign aid that immediately started to pour into Sri Lanka could be processed through due logistic channels without too much difficulty. Or that is what representatives of major foreign donors thought, as they had not reckoned with the intricate and absurdly intransigent bureaucracy of the administration in Sri Lanka.

Sri Lanka was showered with goodwill and donations from all over the world flowed abundantly to the warehouses in the port of Colombo. The newly appointed special envoys of the UN on Tsunami relief, ex-Presidents of the USA, George H.W. Bush and Bill Clinton, visited Sri Lanka in February and met with villagers in the south and the east who had lost both their dearest relatives and their meagre belongings. These grand elderly statesmen, once the most powerful men in the world, made a great impression on the people of Sri Lanka as they exuded optimism and defiance in face of the terrible tragedy that had happened. The ever charismatic Bill Clinton suggested that the longstanding ethnic grievances should be put aside to focus squarely on a joint effort of rapidly rebuilding the destroyed coastal areas.

Nevertheless, it soon became evident that the humanitarian aid was not flowing as efficiently to the north and the east as should have been expected. Countless international non-governmental organisations were operating in the coastal areas, to a large extent in the LTTE-controlled areas where the GOSL found it hard to have any control of the aid implementation and the rebuilding of infrastructure. As had become an inherent quirk within the administration in Colombo, the international aid workers were eyed with considerable suspicion by GOSL. Many were thought to be too eager to assist in LTTE-controlled areas. It seemed difficult for Cabinet Ministers in the south to understand the western notion of turning towards those that seemed to be in the worst position first, that is, those in areas devastated not only by the natural catastrophe of the Tsunami, but also those who had suffered the military clashes of the ethnic conflict. Some of the INGOs complained about random and malicious taxation of aid goods. In other cases, operational assets such as four-wheel drive vehicles would be stuck in the customs area of the port in Colombo for weeks and months before being put to good use in the catastrophe areas. Some of them had been released only after import duties that amounted to significant ransoms had been paid. To be sure, the ethnic conflict complicated the flow of aid from abroad through Colombo to the areas affected the worst.

After the shock of the Tsunami had subsided somewhat the LTTE, which had taken on an enormous task as the prime protector of civilians in Vanni and in the southern Trincomalee area, started to put forward distinct demands on GOSL. The Tiger leadership was angered by the slow disbursement of funds, goods and especially building material towards Vanni due to excessive red tape and corruption in Colombo and complained bitterly to the Norwegian facilitator. The international community subsequently was informed that the LTTE were considering the fate of the CFA if the GOSL would not agree to a joint mechanism in the post-Tsunami effort. The LTTE soon openly demanded to have a significant say in the organisation of how the aid was delivered and in the rebuilding process. This activity would become known as the Post-Tsunami Operational Management Structure or P-TOMS.

As the pressure from the international community, that was bankrolling the bulk of the aid and rebuilding efforts in Sri Lanka, mounted on the President, she was warned specifically by the Marxist-nationalist JVP not to agree to any arrangements such as the P-TOMS with the LTTE. President Mrs. Kumaratunga was in a tight spot politically. Although it was obvious that the aid efforts had to be stepped up in the north and the east, the SLFP lead coalition government was dependent on the JVP for its majority in Parliament. It seemed like a dreadful prospect for Mrs. Kumaratunga, who was scheduled to step down at the end of the year, to have to accept the fall of her government in one of the direst years in the history of Sri Lanka and one which would be her last in power. A decisive nudge at the end of May seemed to help shape her decision. Bill Clinton, on his second visit to Sri Lanka as the UN special envoy for co-coordinating the tsunami rebuilding process, decisively stated in public that he urged the political parties in the south to give their support for the P-TOMS including the LTTE and a Muslim component as well. Leaning quite substantially out of his core mandate he further stated that the experience of an inclusive joint mechanism could also lead to peace and reconciliation. Mrs. Kumaratunga finally gave in as the Norwegians and other influential representatives of the international community appeared to have received assurances from the leader of the main opposition UNP, Mr. Wickremasinghe, that his party would not exploit the mayhem to bring down the government. As the intention of the

President to enter into a formal arrangement with the LTTE on the P-TOMS became known, the JVP withdrew from the ruling coalition and its Cabinet Ministers resigned.

The P-TOMS agreement was signed on purpose by a GOSL official rather than a high-ranking politician from the ruling SLFP. In that way Mrs. Kumaratunga sought to downplay the significance of the agreement. The LTTE in accommodating that intention co-signed the agreement through a low-ranking official within their organisation. Nevertheless, it was an important event in the peace process in Sri Lanka, which the international community hoped would be expedited by the tsunami catastrophe rather than be undermined by it. Following on to the all-important CFA, the GOSL had entered into an agreement that went far in acknowledging the *de facto* responsibility of the LTTE for the well-being and security of Tamils living in LTTE-controlled areas. The P-TOMS agreement was welcomed both by the US administration and Kofi Annan, the Secretary-General of the UN. On a visit to Sri Lanka that same year, it became evident that GOSL had barred the UN leader to visit Kilinochchi and meet with the representatives of the LTTE. It was a measure that angered the Tamil Tigers immensely and would later have consequences for the Foreign Minister of Sri Lanka, who the LTTE thought had been pivotal in hindering the UN Secretary-General from visiting Vanni despite his apparent wish to do so.

The P-TOMS appeared promising for donors who hoped it would speed up the distribution of aid and goods through newly opened channels as stipulated in the agreement. But the most radical elements in Sri Lanka made sure that it would become a virtual non-starter.

First, the LTTE, choosing a moment in time that was extremely sensitive for the south, assassinated a high-ranking SLA military intelligence officer in a traffic jam at the busy Baseline road entering Colombo. Major Muthaliff was the highest ranking military officer killed by the LTTE since the commencement of the CFA three years earlier. His murder came as a shock to the military and GOSL at a time when it was grappling with the notion whether to accept the LTTE as a responsible partner in the P-TOMS or not. It was an extremely negative act on the part of LTTE which made the peace facilitation of Norway even more difficult than it had already been at that junction in time.

Second, the JVP which had stormed out of the GOSL in fury over the decision of the President to reach out a reluctant hand to the LTTE, contested that the P-TOMS agreement was in breach of the Constitution of Sri Lanka and took its petition to the Supreme Court. The magistrates of the court suspended several important articles of the P-TOMS agreement until September when there would be a new session on the issue. At that next meeting the Supreme Court postponed a decisive decision until November. Finally in November the court postponed further proceedings indefinitely with several suspensions of articles in place.

Following the Presidential elections in November 2005, Bill Clinton arrived in Sri Lanka on his third visit to the island. He met with several representatives of aid organisations to get a picture of the ground situation. The Tamil Relief Organisation accused Colombo of having centralized most of the flow of aid, funds and goods, despite the nominal P-TOMS. Furthermore, the newly elected Mr. Rajapakse, in his first policy speech to Parliament simply and without much ado told the representatives that he had nullified the P-TOMS agreement. A seemingly rattled and disappointed Bill Clinton met with the new President of Sri Lanka a few days later.

Bill Clinton had on several occasions highlighted the development following the tsunami in the Aceh region of Indonesia. It had also suffered a lingering ethnic conflict for years as Aceh-based insurgents fought for increased autonomy from Djakarta. In the wake of the catastrophe in Aceh, both the government and the leaders of the Aceh militants had come to the conclusion that in the face of the human tragedy they would have to set aside their differences and join hands in rebuilding the devastated region. A small EU mission oversaw the negotiations between the parties and the Aceh insurgents eventually surrendered their arms against a comprehensive package of devolution that could have served as a sort of precedent for Sri Lanka.

Instead of following the example of Aceh, the post-tsunami year of 2005 in Sri Lanka was a year of suffering and grief, a year of squandered opportunities for reconciliation and a lost year for peace.

13

# The Monopoly of Tamil Representation

One of the core elements of the LTTE strategy, under the leadership of Velupillai Pirapaharan, was to demand sole representation of the Tamil people in Sri Lanka. This had to a large extent been achieved in a sustained campaign in the late eighties when Pirapaharan's LTTE, ruthlessly crushed other Tamil paramilitary forces and political parties in an epoch of fratricidal terror. Young Tamil activists had conducted assassinations against their political competitors, scores of community leaders disappeared and political offices of competing Tamil splinter parties were blown up.

Pirapaharan had been right to some extent in his callous analysis of the situation. Tamils were divided into supporters of several regional splinter groups, with most of its leaders still preferring a political struggle with the Sinhalese majority in the south rather than a morally questionable and extremely dangerous armed uprising in the north and the east. Factions such as PLOTE, TELO, EROS and others crumbled under the domination of the LTTE. During the deployment of the Indian Peace Keeping Force in Sri Lanka from

1987-90, which counted tens of thousands of soldiers, the LTTE changed its stance from first welcoming it as a stabilising force into engaging in a direct combat with the Indian soldiers all over the jungle in the Vanni and particularly in Jaffna proper. Following difficult years for the IPKF, in the deeply troubled north of Sri Lanka, where it suffered over a thousand casualties, the force was withdrawn from the island. Delhi had been immensely frustrated by the tactics of the LTTE and saw little point in staying on as both the GOSL and the Tigers could barely contain their glee as the forces of the giant neighbour returned to their home.

In the wake of the withdrawal, a certain vacuum of power emerged temporarily in the Tamil-dominated areas and LTTE moved quickly to tighten its grip on the population, as good as extinguishing any internal opposition for all practical purposes. A number of brave Tamil politicians resented the way LTTE had grabbed all effectual power within the Tamil community, but there was little they could do other than live in fear for retribution by the LTTE for any misgivings voiced regarding their reign of terror. Only one other substantial Tamil organisation remained truly operational, the Eelam People's Democratic Party (EPDP). However, its offices could only be maintained and kept open due to a heavy presence of SLA at their premises, thus it came to the SLA to protect the only remaining opposition to the LTTE.

There were many attempts, some heroic, by influential Tamils to try to break up this political deadlock imposed on them by the LTTE, but most failed. The more prominent the individual Tamil voice became against the actions and methods of the LTTE, the more likely it was that it would be silenced by its cadres. Furthermore, within the LTTE itself, copious amounts of blood would be shed as Pirapaharan moved to eliminate his competitors for power in a thoroughly ruthless Stalinist manner. Some of these inner struggles have been described in media and research. However, little is factually known other than that many of the original battle-fatigued companions of Pirapaharan who had fought with him in the initial years of the LTTE movement, disappeared mysteriously. Even legendary cadres that had been believed by outsiders to enjoy the unconditioned trust of the leader were not spared.

After almost twenty years of fighting, when the emissaries of the Royal Norwegian Government travelled deep into the Vanni jungle to discuss terms of the Ceasefire Agreement with Pirapaharan and his commanders, the former was very much in command. After impressive military victories over the SLA, the general impression was that this branch of the Sri Lankan armed forces had been humiliated and that the morale of its troops had hit rock bottom. Thousands of army deserters who fled the war lived a miserably life of subsistence, fugitives from the State, scarred by alcoholism and drug abuse. Under these circumstances, Pirapaharan was in a strong position to negotiate terms and one of his most important points would be that the LTTE be acknowledged as the sole representative of the Tamils in any peace process, which the CFA would presumably trigger. EPDP and what little remained of opposition to the LTTE within the Tamil community was effectively silenced and the GOSL even accepted the LTTE demand for the disarming of Tamil "paramilitary groups" within 30 days. That mostly pertained to the EPDP, which had to some extent been fighting a weak proxy war in some pockets of the north and to a lesser extent in the east against the LTTE, with the tacit approval of the SLA. For others, the disarming of the remaining few voices that dared speak on behalf of the Tamils opposed to the LTTE, would also lead to the silence of these same voices as they would not be able to protect themselves any more. In the end, Pirapaharan got what he wanted. He was now the sole representative of the Tamils in the north and the east with other splinter group marginalised just as the Muslims, who had tried in vain to be accepted as a third signatory to the CFA. The lonely EPDP offices scattered here and there, primarily in the north with its greatest support in Jaffna Town and on the islets of the coast, were turned into small fortresses, covered by barbed wire and sandbags, protected by heavily armed SLA sentries.

14

# The Reign of Chandrika and Political Infighting in the South

Sri Lankan politics, since before independence from the United Kingdom in 1948, had been somewhat clan driven and dominated by family dynasties. The most prominent of the political dynasties was that of the Bandaranaike family. In 1994, Chandrika Bandaranaike Kumaratunga had been elected President of Sri Lanka after a flash career in politics following a lengthy exile in the UK. She had stepped into the giant footsteps of her father and her mother, who remarkably had both served as Prime Minister in the then relatively newly independent Ceylon. The family had reached the highest offices in the island and had been extremely successful politically, but had also paid bitterly for their prominence at the centrestage of power. Chandrika's grandfather had held one of the highest posts domestically during colonial rule as advisor to the British Governor. Her father had been the charismatic S.W.R.D. Bandaranaike who was a co-founder of the United National Party (UNP). He later broke away from the party, which was the then dominant force in Ceylon, to form its main rival in the island's future political battles, the Sri Lanka Freedom Party (SLFP). The SLFP went on to win the 1956 parliament elections where the main Sinhalese parties campaigned on a strong nationalistic ticket to the detriment of the Tamil and Muslim electorates and other minorities. The Prime Minister was a vocal supporter of cementing the power of the Sinhalese majority and elevating Buddhism to a state religion. However, his most controversial political issue was the "Sinhalese only" agenda, which relegated Tamil and English to secondary languages in the island. Even so, his political goals were not radical enough for the extreme hardliners in Ceylon and S.W.R.D. Bandaranaike was somewhat cynically assassinated by a Buddhist monk in 1959. He was succeeded as Prime Minister by his widow, Sirimavo Bandaranaike who became the first female holding such a high office in the world. Sirimavo Bandaranaike would hold this office three times on the last occasion being appointed by her own daughter. She served in the office as Prime Minister almost up to her death in 2000. Her daughter Chandrika had been one of the privileged few, studying abroad when the economy of Ceylon was faltering, mostly due to disastrous economic schemes of nationalisation by her mother's government, which led to an almost complete drying up of foreign investment in the island.

The young Chandrika studied in Paris at the time of the student revolution and would adhere to her socialist views whilst later in office. She returned to her native island in the early seventies when its name was changed to Sri Lanka and married a highly popular actor-turned politician, Mr. Vijaya Kumaratunga. She was active in politics during the seventies at the end of which her mother completely fell from grace politically. This period coincided with Chandrika Kumaratunga Bandaranaike switching her support to her husband's SLMP. Mr. Kumaratunga was assassinated in 1988 by Sinhalese insurgents associated with the militant JVP. It was repeating its militant past again attempting a disastrous Marxist revolution which would be crushed by the authorities just as the previous one in 1971, believed to have cost 20.000 lives. Having become a widow in these tumultuous and dangerous times in Sri Lanka, she went to the UK where she stayed in self-imposed exile for years. She returned in triumph to Sri Lanka, becoming elected Prime Minister in August 1994 and winning the presidential election in November that same year, crushing her opponent from the UNP, the party which had held the Presidency for seventeen years. The Sri Lankan constitution had been amended several times in the course of its young independence and Her Excellency Kumaratunga Bandaranaike became its fourth Executive President. This political system afforded the President most meaningful executive powers including the post of Commander-in-Chief of the armed forces. Nevertheless, even as the President is the dominating political figure in Sri Lanka, the Parliament elects the government and the post of Prime Minister. During the times when the President has the support of the Parliament, the post of Prime Minister becomes largely symbolical, as seemed to be the case after the elections in 1994 and 2004. However, when an opposing coalition holds the majority in Parliament, the uneasy cohabitation between a President and a Prime Minister can become cumbersome. This would seem to be the case at the beginning of the CFA in 2002.

Chandrika Kumaratunga Bandaranaike, as a young, glamorous President, educated at the prestigious Sorbonne in Paris, sought a dialogue with the LTTE at the outset of her Presidency. The feelers to the LTTE bore no fruit. On the contrary, a new Eelam war erupted, resulting in the Tamil Tigers managing to take the major towns of Kilinochchi and Mullativu in the north-east and hold on to them. As Chandrika faced growing pressure domestically and the security forces were unable to subdue the LTTE, she called for early presidential elections in 1999, five years into her six-year legislation period. She narrowly escaped an assassination attempt by the LTTE at an election rally. The attempt on her life was widely believed to have boosted her prospects in the election that took place only days after, in which she regained her grip on the Presidency by beating the UNP candidate Mr. Ranil Wickremasinghe with 51 per cent of the votes against 43 per cent. Mr. Wickremasinghe supported the

Norwegian attempts at creating a direct dialogue between the GOSL and the LTTE, which Chandrika rejected. In the parliamentary elections in late 2001, however, the UNP won a somewhat sweeping surprise victory and Mr. Ranil Wickremasinghe became Prime Minister. He swiftly pushed on with the Norwegian-facilitated negotiations with the LTTE for a permanent ceasefire agreement. It was duly signed in early 2002, despite the reservations of the President, and took effect on 22nd February. However, it was signed by Mr. Pirapaharan, the supreme leader of the LTTE, and the Prime Minister of Sri Lanka, Mr. Wickremasinghe, but not the President of Sri Lanka and thus the Commander-in-Chief of the armed forces. This would become a bone of contention within the political system in Sri Lanka for years to come and would lead to the extreme nationalist Buddhist and Marxist parties of the JHU and JVP respectively contesting the validity and legality of the government signed CFA, irritating the LTTE and the proponents of a negotiated peace within the Sinhalese south. Nevertheless, the CFA did take hold and remained very successful in its first two years, despite the sporadic lamentation of the President.

The President was never at ease in her relationship with the governing coalition of Mr. Wickremasinghe's UNP, the party she and her parents had fought bitterly for decades. Moreover, her own SLFP and its junior partners in the People's Alliance had only been able to forge coalitions through the support of the JHU and the JVP, who both advocated a military solution to the ethnic conflict. At the end of 2003, HE Chandrika made a surprise move: she suspended Parliament, sacked the government and nominally took over key ministries. This toppling of the democratically elected government occurred at a time when Prime Minister Wickremasinghe was conveniently travelling abroad. In a Machiavellian move, she formed the United People's Freedom Alliance (UPFA) with the Marxist JVP. The UPFA won the ensuing election in April 2004 at the same time as the LTTE was starting to suffer from the unexpected split of the Karuna faction in the east. After some infighting within her SLFP, her own brother Aruna had to settle for a lesser ministry as well as her long-time advisor Kadirgamar who became Foreign Minister, whilst the maverick southern politician from Hambantota, Mr. Mahinda Rajapakse, was sworn in as Prime Minister.

The LTTE was confronted with a totally new situation in the east where cadres loyal to the Vanni leadership were battling for power with the Karuna faction and the Tigers now saw their claim of being the sole representative of the Tamil cause greatly diminished. As the security forces sat on the sidelines, they could observe a bitter and bloody fight escalating in the Batticaloa region. Here, targeted assassinations of LTTE and Karuna cadres increased dramatically shifting the focus from the stalled peace negotiations between the LTTE and GOSL to a battle for predominance of the Tamil communities in the east. The Tigers were infuriated by this unexpected course of events in their struggle for the elusive Eelam and claimed that the security forces of Sri Lanka were covertly assisting and protecting Karuna's fledgling movement against the wrath of the battle hardened LTTE. There was circumstantial evidence for this, but it was extremely difficult to prove. The security forces could only gloat over this remarkable turn of tides in the volatile east, where the LTTE seemed to have lost its grip due to the somewhat surprising resilience of Karuna and his supporters. As it became evident that the LTTE could not suppress the Karuna faction anytime soon, the LTTE leadership became restless on the larger issue of devolution of powers towards the north and the east. The LTTE angrily demanded some tangible progress on their core political issue, which was the establishing of an Interim Self Governing Administration (ISGA), for the merged northern and eastern provinces with the LTTE squarely in control. This was the fundamental principle for which the LTTE had fought for over twenty years. Furthermore, it was a political notion that was understood and partly accepted by moderate politicians in the south, with the UNP and Mr. Wickremasinghe appearing to be the most genuine sympathisers. There were, however, many caveats to the ISGA.

The LTTE had been called upon by a number of observers and stakeholders, both from the southern polity and the international community, to clarify how they wanted to proceed with the modalities of a proposed ISGA. The LTTE would only come up with stringent proposals which suggested that it basically wanted administrative powers for the whole of north and the east to be handed over to them by the GOSL on a silver plate and without significant limitations. Furthermore, in a remarkably clumsy and undiplomatic proposal that resembled an ultimatum, they demanded control over more than half of Sri Lanka's coastline and the corresponding waters. This was too rudimentary to be acceptable politically in the south and would be in clear breach of the Constitution of Sri Lanka. Moreover, the insistence of the LTTE being the sole voice of the Tamil population and a ruler by decree was not helpful. There had been considerable progress achieved on this issue at peace negotiations in Thailand the year before but the modalities had never been worked out. Furthermore, when asked how and when the LTTE would be willing to concede to a process of democratic legitimacy by agreeing to allow the Tamils in the north and the east to choose its political representatives through elections, the Tigers would retract on the issue and try to sidestep it.

As the peace talks had broken down and the LTTE was now faced both with an inner Tamil struggle with Karuna for domination in the east and a more hostile and hawkish government in the south, the chances for establishing an LTTE-controlled ISGA appeared remote. It was very difficult to see how the JVP would support the establishing of an ISGA at all, and even more so if it meant handing it over more or less unconditionally to the detested LTTE. Mr. Tamilshelvan, the political wing leader of the LTTE, who interpreted his status as at parity with the Prime Minister of the GOSL, did not appear helpful in this core issue of the legitimate representation of the Tamil people. He would tell the Norwegian facilitator that elections were neither convenient nor feasible in the north and east for the foreseeable future.

15

# The Presidential Election in 2005 and the LTTE Decree of Abstention

President Chandrika Kumaratunga Bandaranaike had ruled Sri Lanka for over ten years seemingly unable to come up with successful initiatives of her own on the ethnic conflict. Her years in power had seen her initially reaching out to the LTTE. However, in reality there had been very little tangible on offer for the Tigers. The military hostilities had resumed into an open war during the late nineties and the LTTE, convinced that it could not reach a negotiated agreement with Mrs. Kumaratunga in power, had tried to assassinate her days before the 1999 elections. It was understandable that the attack not only left her physically scarred but also deeply wary of the LTTE's intentions and credibility as a negotiation partner. Her UPFA government had to rely on the JVP, which hampered it considerably in its pursuit for a peace and socio-economic dividend from the CFA.

Furthermore, the era of Mrs. Kumaratunga as President of Sri Lanka was slowly coming to an end. She had called early elections in 1999 and her six years in office should thus come to an end in 2005. She was obviously not cherishing the prospect of leaving office and came up with an initiative to extend her tenure as President, at least by one year, as she claimed she had been forced by the state of affairs in Sri Lanka to call elections one year early in her first election period. Her efforts on this issue appeared to undermine her popularity. Critical articles on the President started to appear in the privately owned press and her alleged eccentricities were highlighted. She was accused of being too prone to superstition and believing in the mystical, a humane notion actually quite common in the region and attributed to some other prominent politicians. However, she was also accused of living too grandly, spending too much time on lavish travels abroad and appearing nonchalantly tardy at public functions, sometimes leaving a large crowd of people waiting for hours for an inauguration of a monument or official facility.

In the year 2005, her last year as President, her government had to come to terms with the absolutely devastating aftermath of the tsunami catastrophe. This was a tall order for a third-world country, crippled by a protracted civil war, desperately relying on international aid and coming to terms with the inevitable political infighting in the run-up to the Presidential election. Moreover, much energy and public sympathy were spent on the futile pursuit of one more year in office, which was in the end categorically turned down by the Supreme Court. For the LTTE, Mrs. Kumaratunga was a lame duck at the end of her tenure. The Tigers would have to wait and see who would succeed her and take it from there. Furthermore, the conflict had also to be put on a back burner as the LTTE, which was first and foremost a military organisation, now had to find ways to alleviate the plights of the Tamil communities living in LTTE-controlled areas, who had arguably been hit the worst of all by the tsunami.

It was evident from the outset that the 2005 Presidential election would be a close call between the candidates of the SLFP and the UNP. Much would depend on how these two towers of Sri Lanka politics would be able to rally the support of smaller but decisive parties who would not realistically stand a chance by putting forward their own candidates.

There were some anticipations of a power struggle within the SLFP, where Prime Minister Mahinda Rajapakse seemed to be the front-runner, but nevertheless did not appear to be to the liking of the incumbent Mrs. Kumaratunga. She was believed to be contemplating backing the much respected Foreign Minister Mr. Lakshman Kadirgamar, a rare Tamil statesman in such a senior position. However he was gunned down by the LTTE. Chandrika's brother, Aruna Bandaranaike, who succeeded Kadirgamar for a short period as Foreign Minister after the assassination, was also believed to be a possible contender for an extension of the family legacy. It was clear that the sometimes flamboyant Mr. Rajapakse, who had in his early career appeared in a few films as a handsome young man, had been underestimated. He had initially performed largely a symbolic function as a subservient Prime Minister under President Kumaratunga, best known for donning a traditional white mantle with a burgundy red shawl. This attire was chosen as a tribute to his uncle who had taken the family into high level politics from a strong rural base in the southern-most part of Sri Lanka. Rajapakse had built his own political network in the south and had been elected to Parliament at the tender age of twenty-four, but disappeared somewhat from the centrestage under the predominance of the UNP during the early eighties and into the nineties, bursting back with the SLFP political triumph in both Parliament and presidential elections in 1994.

Since being catapulted to the office of Prime Minister he had very shrewdly and skillfully consolidated his political network and grew steadily into a role as a strong man in the SLFP. He could, however, not keep the erratic JVP within the government fold in 2005, that crucial year of the reconstruction of the communities in the eastern and southern seaboard. The JVP had walked out protesting to the important role of the Tamil Tigers administering and organising the inflow of international humanitarian aid in LTTE-controlled areas. Nevertheless, Mr. Rajapakse managed to steer his minority government through the turbulence leading up to the elections.

Mr. Rajapakse would contest the elections against the UNP's Mr. Wickremasinghe, who had managed to put in place the longest lasting ceasefire with the LTTE since the beginning of the ethnic conflict. He could count on the vast traditional electorate of the UNP, which had held the Presidency for seventeen years before the ascent to the office by Mrs. Kumaratunga. Mr. Wickremasinghe was perceived of as a soft-spoken intellectual and an advocate of a more market-based economy in Sri Lanka. He wished to end to the conflict, which had drained the state budget for such a long time. He would need the support, however, of parties representing the ethnic minorities of Sri Lanka in order to clinch the election. This became ever more evident as Mr. Rajapakse managed to bring both the JHU and more importantly the JVP on his side. The endorsement by these two parties came at a substantial political cost, however. Mr. Rajapakse would continue to claim publicly that he would pursue a negotiated settlement with the LTTE, just as his opponent. Nevertheless, it was widely understood that he would have to concede on key issues in order to appease the JVP leadership. These issues were believed to entail limiting or terminating the role of Norway as a facilitator in the peace process and revising the CFA. Furthermore, he would have to denounce the notion of a federally based Sri Lanka with substantial powers given to a LTTE-controlled administration of the north and the east and at least nominally pursue an economic policy of centralisation and strong state-owned enterprises.

As Sri Lanka and the international community were preparing themselves for a close outcome of the Presidential election, the LTTE took a surprising stand in the contest. It was understood that the leader of the Tamil Tigers, Mr. Pirapaharan, had issued a decree ordering the Tamils living within LTTE-controlled areas to boycott the polls. It was a stunning act of defiance of the candidate Mr. Wickremasinghe, who had co-signed the CFA with Mr. Pirapaharan in 2002. Findings of various pollsters and analysts had indicated that Tamil voters were widely in favour of Mr. Wickremasinghe. He had already secured the endorsement of the Ceylon Workers' Congress, representing the Hill Country Tamils, who had managed to stay out of the ethnic conflict despite their close ethnic relations with the Tamils in the east and the north. More importantly, the main Muslim party, the Sri Lanka Muslim Congress, advised its members to vote for him. The Muslims in Sri Lanka had often been caught between a rock and a hard place in the ethnic conflict and had sometimes suffered terrible grievances at the hands of the LTTE. A vote for Mr. Wickremasinghe could potentially lead to an ISGA of sorts where the LTTE would be in command but apparently the leadership of the Sri Lanka Muslim Congress saw this as a lesser evil given the other option of a likely shift to a more implicit Sinhalese hegemony under a JVP-backed Rajapakse presidency.

The main enigma, however, was the position of Tamils in LTTE-controlled areas. Surely, it was wiser for them and the LTTE to cast their votes in favour of the UNP candidate, an outspoken proponent for a negotiated peace with the Tigers. Remarkably, the LTTE would not budge from its position. The voters were told to boycott the election. They knew it would be best for their own security to heed that decree as the LTTE did not take insubordination lightly.

In Kilinochchi the LTTE put on an apparent display of democratic decision-making as the political leadership met with their parliamentary proxies in the Tamil National Alliance to discuss the stance on the Tamil franchise and the upcoming elections. After the meeting the media were told that Tamils had suffered under the leadership of both the SLFP and the UNP, and, thus, there was no reason to put their faith in either candidate. There was bountiful speculation on the issue leading up to the elections. In the end, there was almost no turnout by voters either in LTTE-controlled areas or in GOSL-controlled Jaffna. If a handful of brave Tamil voters ventured to the local voting station, they would have to take into account roadblocks and other hindrances reportedly set up by youths and thugs supporting the LTTE decree. There were reports of minor clashes in Jaffna during election day but the security forces seemed to have managed to keep the situation relatively under control as the vast majority of voters quite simply abstained from using their franchise.

The LTTE decree of abstention from the presidential election in Sri Lanka appeared to be a decision from the top, and as such non-negotiable. The logic of the LTTE could sometimes be strange and its erratic tactics frequently reflected that, much to the puzzlement of the representatives of the international community based in Colombo. However, as diplomatic meetings with the LTTE at a top decision-making level were few and far between, and as there was no transparent decision-making process, representatives of the international community sympathetic to the Tamil cause and proponents of the peace process could only shake their heads in disbelief.

Quiet discussions behind the scenes in Kilinochchi rendered no other information than that made public after the joint LTTE and TNA meeting underscoring that for the inhabitants of "the north" it made no iota of difference who was the President of the Sinhalese in "the south". This, of course, amounted to declaration of total detachment from the political process in Sri Lanka and as such could only be interpreted as a major snub for the more moderate forces in the Sri Lanka polity, most notably the UNP. Furthermore, it exposed some of the least appealing facets of the LTTE, being a fundamentalist organisation lacking the will of problem-solving through compromise, led by a deeply reclusive autocratic leader, who was sitting in a hidden HQ somewhere in Mullativu district.

The presidential elections went down to the wire, with Mr. Mahinda Rajapakse winning with a narrow margin claiming 50.3 per cent of the electoral vote as Mr. Ranil Wickremasinghe had mustered 49.4 per cent.

16

# The New Era of Mahinda Rajapakse

Following the inauguration of HE Mahinda Rajapakse in November of 2005 as the fifth Executive President of Sri Lanka, he sought to clarify his stance on a number of key issues. This was to be a balancing act as he was addressing different audiences, first the general electorate at his inauguration, shortly thereafter the political elite in Parliament and finally the representatives of the international community in Colombo. He would make important nuances in his stance on key issues relating to the peace process, hence his real policy seemed to be somewhat a matter of interpretation. At the inauguration and at his first policy statement at the opening of the new session of Parliament, he seemed to be determined to go head on with the LTTE, rejecting both a federal solution and the notion of a homeland for a specific ethnic group in Sri Lanka, constituting a clear policy against LTTE's main demands. The newly elect President went on to propose an inclusive peace process inviting opposition parties to participate in the procedure in order to reach a broad consensus on the issue. In this conjunction, he criticised the United Front Government's peace efforts for having been confined only to the government and the LTTE.

The new approach would have a noble tone to it, but in reality it would be extremely cumbersome and probably impossible to arrive at a consensus in the southern polity, given its nationalistic element's fierce opposition towards any concessions for the LTTE that would come remotely close to any proposal acceptable to Kilinochchi. Furthermore, President Rajapakse demanded a re-examination of the CFA calling for an introduction of an open and transparent ceasefire-monitoring machinery. Presumably, he was not satisfied with the way the SLMM had conducted its operations in Sri Lanka and how SLMM had interpreted the CFA. In addition, the new President appeared to be snubbing the Norwegian facilitator deliberately as he told his audience that the meditation extended by the United Nations, other such organisations, friendly countries and India would be organised and utilised, opting not to mention the arduous efforts towards peace undertaken by Norway for so many years. It was tempting to read into this a simple and clear message, the SLMM and Norway were not wanted in Sri Lanka anymore. However, it had to be noted that here was a charismatic, impressive and shrewd political leader playing for his home gallery in the embryonic days of his presidency.

The key policy statement made by President Rajapakse coincided with the time of year of the annual Heroes' Day speech given by the LTTE leader. In Colombo, there were different camps regarding the significance of the message from the supreme Tamil Tiger. In the media, some opinion-shapers dismissed his message as ranting of a criminal and bloodthirsty madman hiding in a jungles. Others, tried to analyse and interpret some core messages planted in the rather lengthy rhetoric. There was a strong element of surprise in the way Mr. Pirapaharan greeted the new President of Sri Lanka. Notwithstanding the fact that the distance between President Rajapakse and the LTTE was vast in terms of policy, according to the LTTE leader, the Tamil Tigers would wait to observe his political manoeuvres and actions for the time being, as President Rajapakse was considered by the LTTE to be a realist committed to pragmatic politics. This was a surprisingly positive stance towards the new President as he was widely viewed as taking a more hardline approach towards the LTTE and the CFA than his opponent. As usual, there was room for much speculation on the position of Mr. Pirapaharan and the policy of the LTTE. The remarks made in the Heroes' Day speech could arguably be interpreted as an explanation for the LTTE boycott of the election. Maybe, the Tigers thought it would be easier to conduct business with a strong President Rajapakse, who had managed to appease and secure the votes of the ultra-nationalists in the south.

President Rajapakse responded the following day by welcoming the remarks of Mr. Pirapaharan and reiterating an invitation for fresh peace talks. Addressing the representatives of the international community in Colombo, a distinctively different audience from that of the Parliament, Mr. Rajapakse now started that Norway was to be consulted on further peace efforts along with its co-chairs of the Tokyo conference, Japan, the USA and the EU. Furthermore, President Rajapakse reaffirmed his government's commitment to continue the ceasefire. All in all, the much-awaited first exchange of firm words between the new President of Sri Lanka and the head of the LTTE appeared to have gone remarkably well.

It was a poor and short-lived indicator, however, of what would unfold in the coming year.

Despite the official remarks made by Mr. Pirapaharan in his Heroes' Day speech, hinting at a grace period for the new Rajapakse administration, the LTTE would soon set out to test the new President with a whole range of operations and incidents that at times appeared to be clear provocations. In many of the incidents igniting the conflict in early 2006, the LTTE actions seemed unwise in political and propaganda terms, not the least towards the international community, which was slowly losing its patience with the increasingly erratic Tamil Tigers. Some of their actions, however, were clearly of retaliatory nature. Nevertheless, this was hard for them to explain to the outside world, as they had limited access to both the diplomatic community in Colombo and the international press, who was suffering somewhat from a post-Tsunami fatigue syndrome with Sri Lanka and was also busy reporting on the much more high-profile conflicts in Iraq, Afghanistan and Darfur.

President Mahinda Rajapakse's first full year in office would be a testing one, scarred with countless atrocities conducted and suffered by both parties. Sadly, there would be thousands of civilian casualties in the coming years.

# 17

## The Black Tigers and the Terror of the Suicide Attacks

The Liberation Tigers of Tamil Eelam were arguably the first guerrilla movement in the world to concentrate resolutely on the dreaded use of suicide bombers. This was a major weapon in their arsenal to sustain their asymmetric warfare with the armed forces of Sri Lanka. The LTTE were extremely proud of their Black Tigers as the suicide cadres were called. They were trained very specifically for their chilling task and the level of discipline exercised and callous efficiency achieved by the hundreds of Black Tigers that blew themselves up in the conflict drew attention globally and a grudging recognition from the adversaries in the south. The infamous conduct of child recruitment into the LTTE fighting machine could to some extent explain the sheer determination and discipline of the Black Tigers as most of them would have been formed, trained and brainwashed for their horrific destiny from quite an early age. The inevitable concomitants of total war would also play a key role in their determination to lay down their lives for a cause that they obviously believed vehemently in. Many of the Black Tiger recruits would have lost a parent or a sibling in the conflict.

Some would have spent their childhood years in a damp hut in a jungle clearance or in a makeshift shelter of plastic on the outskirts of an older settlement. Others would have experienced the sheer terror of being on the receiving end of artillery bombardments. There would remain many a tough childhood memory from the seemingly endless bloodshed in the northern and eastern battlefields of the island. The war in Sri Lanka was one where prisoners were seldom taken and the Geneva conventions were sometimes ignored by both parties. The LTTE cadres made a point of not letting themselves be taken alive by the enemy as they invariably wore a cyanide capsule around their neck, as a last resort. Furthermore, the ruthlessness of the jungle fighting resulted in the grim fact that death was a likely outcome for any fighter in the course of time. However, none was as assured of that as the Tamil youngsters, many of them females, training in grayish fatigues in the secret camps of the Vanni jungle.

The Black Tigers were at times displayed by the LTTE in photos disseminated to the friendly local Tamil press and to international media. Moreover, with the advent of the Internet, the TamilNet website, a LTTE media proxy, would regularly publish slightly blurred pictures of the Black Tigers posing with Mr. Pirapaharan a few days earlier as a prelude to their operations. The meetings with the leader of the LTTE would signal to the youngsters that their days were numbered, yet some appeared to be cheerful. These pictures were published after they had completed their lethal missions, often causing massive carnage in the south. They stirred a strange and morbid sensation with the observer. It was quite disturbing to watch the images of young people with their friendly and polite smiles to the camera, fully aware they would sacrifice their lives in a few days time. Furthermore, given the fierce determination so obviously put on display, these human bombs were a frightening prospect for the security forces of Sri Lanka and almost impossible to intercept.

Mr. Pirapaharan had instilled in his LTTE a fable for mystique and remembrance in conjunction with the gruesome activities of the Black Tigers. Each year, the LTTE would commemorate Black Tiger's day on 5 July as a veneration of the hundreds of suicide bombers who had blown themselves up for the LTTE struggle. LTTE supporters would gather round on that day in various towns in the north and the east, hoisting the LTTE flag and giving speeches of their battle for the liberation of the Tamils in Sri Lanka. Relatives of the Black Tigers were shown sombre dignity and adoration and improvised floats with pictures of youngsters who had sacrificed their lives for the LTTE cause were taken through the streets. This particular day of veneration had been chosen to commemorate the first spectacular LTTE suicide act, which had occurred in 1987 in Jaffna. The first Black Tiger, sporting the *nom de guerre* of Captain Miller, had infamously driven a truck packed with explosives into a SLA garrison at the Nelliyadi School in the northern part of the peninsula killing as many as two hundred soldiers. Although the exact number of casualties was not fully known, this horrific incident had been a defining moment of terror in the early stages of the Eelam wars.

One of the tangible signs of how remarkably effective and comprehensive the ceasefire agreement, CFA, was in its first years was very visually displayed in the form of a statue of Captain Miller close to the Nelliyadi College. The site and the statue were openly revered by the LTTE at public gatherings where the bronze painted sculpture was garlanded by relatives and LTTE officials. It was amazing that the SLA would show such restraint during the CFA to allow this statue to remain intact and the site open for LTTE supporters to visit and acclaim. The same could be said of the momentous LTTE cemeteries so meticulously kept nearby. The statue of Captain Miller had been hidden in 1996 as the SLA regained full control of Jaffna. It had been put back on its pedestal in 2002 as a result of CFA presence. In itself, this taunting symbol of LTTE defiance was probably a good indicator of the state of the CFA at any time, as in late August 2006 it was destroyed by unknown armed men.

The daunting plague of suicide attacks in the south, especially in

Colombo, had not only a demoralising effect on the Sinhalese majority but also instilled a deep hatred for the LTTE and the means it resorted to in its epic struggle with the security forces of Sri Lanka. In the last few years leading up to the negotiations which resulted in the CFA, the LTTE had scored spectacular, if also horrifying, successes in and around Colombo. In one particularly bloody attack, the LTTE had in an astonishing way been able to drive a lorry through all checkpoints into the heavily guarded financial and administrative district of Fort, just by Colombo's busy harbour, and had blown up enormous quantities of explosives resulting in widespread carnage and collateral damage. The black clouds of smoke from the fire raging afterwards in several adjacent business towers could be seen from all over the city. The impressive international airport at Katunayaka, a forty-five minute drive up from Colombo, had not been spared either. A year into the new millennium a group of Black Tigers and LTTE commandos had broken through the security perimeters killing and blowing up what they could manage including half of Sri Lanka's commercial air fleet. This was both a great setback militarily and also a terrible blow for the tourism industry, not only an extremely important source of foreign currency for the Treasury of Sri Lanka, but also a particularly sensitive one. High-level politicians had been assassinated in the past, including President Ranasinghe Premasada in 1991, with the incumbent Mrs. Kumaratunga only escaping narrowly, losing one eye, in a 1999 explosion. It was understandable that the politicians in the south would be divided into different camps, some calling for a halt to the senseless slaughter by any political means, others calling for revenge and the annihilation of the LTTE.

With the CFA, the scourge of the dreaded LTTE suicide attacks seemed extinguished. For more than two years, no attack was carried out in Colombo and check-points and sentry points were dismantled and vacated in many parts of the city. The metropolis eased up to concentrate on its merry mercantile hustle and bustle and wondrously erratic flow of traffic and people. This pleasant atmosphere of hope and optimism was widely enjoyed in the city. There seemed to be a marked increase of people wandering around in the colonial parks and down the pleasant promenade of Galle Face Green, from where one could observe the sun setting gently into the Indian Ocean. The security level in Colombo was, however, to change sharply again as the sinister plague of suicide attacks reappeared out of nowhere in July 2004.

The SLMM and most other stakeholders were taken completely by surprise as a young woman blew herself up in a police station a few minutes walk up the Galle Road from where the SLMM HQ was located. The woman had been intercepted by police officers as she had sought to meet with the well-known Tamil politician, Mr. Douglas Devananda, a Cabinet Minister in the Government of Sri Lanka. He was a prominent leader of the Eelams People's Democratic Party, the only major remaining rival Tamil organisation that had not been crushed by the LTTE, and as such ranked close to the top of the Tiger's hit list of political opponents. The incident exposed the difficulties for the security forces in preventing such acts to be undertaken by the LTTE in Colombo proper. Due to strict cultural codes, it was very difficult for servicemen to simply rip off the clothes of a female, however strongly she was suspected of carrying an explosives belt under her attire. And as such it was relatively much easier for female cadres to slip through checkpoints and other forms of security inspections. In this particular case, the woman had been barred from getting into the office of Mr. Devananda. However, she had been afforded the time and means to blow herself up even after having been brought out of the building to the nearest police station for further investigation. One would have assumed that this young woman would have appeared shy and avoided direct eye contact with males as such was the custom. She had probably been pretty, as most young women in Sri Lanka, and was slender and delicately built. That did not change the fact that she detonated her explosives devise with an uncanny determination and ruthlessness, the bomb tearing her apart and ripping with her four police officers and injuring many others.

The first suicide attack in Colombo, since the commencement of the CFA more than two years earlier, was an extremely negative and damaging act that destroyed a lot of hope and undermined the little goodwill there was for the LTTE in the south. Although the LTTE would categorically deny any involvement in this particularly calculated violation of the CFA, the *modus operandi*, the means and the motive and the target, all rendered the LTTE's proclamation of innocence ridiculous.

The suicide attack had taken place off Colombo's most busy downtown street and although the target had been sitting in an office building a bit further away, the female bomber had in the end blown herself up in a Police Station quite close to the highly guarded Prime Minister's residence at Temple Trees. It was important to examine why such a high profile attack had taken place at this time. Could this mean a watershed for the CFA and the general security situation in Colombo?

Quite often, the international community and the foreign-based media concentrated too extensively on the shocking impact of LTTE's lethal and cold-blooded attacks instead of putting the killings into a more rational and coherent context of asymmetric warfare. And as such, the LTTE was not too helpful in explaining their logic, preferring to keep their tactical rationale shrouded in a cloud of deadly defiance and mystery. It also has to be kept in mind that the LTTE was also quite isolated from the international media and foreign representatives, sometimes complaining bitterly that its acts were primarily performed in self-defence or as a response to atrocities committed by the Army. The LTTE certainly felt itself completely misrepresented by international media which it claimed almost totally disregarded offensive actions by the security forces of Sri Lanka. There was some truth in that, as a conventional military assault on a target in the north would simply not attract attention of the international media in the same manner as a suicide attack, even though the casualty figures in the former incident could be much higher. That indeed appeared to be a worldwide phenomenon, an air strike on civilians, intended or not, would not draw the same media attention as a suicide explosion in a city.

The suicide attack in Colombo on 7 July was to mark a return to the days of uncertainty for high-level opponents of the LTTE. It was also to mark a creeping return to ever expanding inspection measures by the security forces and soon parts of the city would be dotted with checkposts as a reminder of an actual war going on, despite the CFA.

What was not markedly noted in the media was the fact that only two days earlier, the LTTE had held grand Black Tiger day celebrations in GOSL-controlled Jaffna and Trincomalee. The stipulations of the CFA allowed the LTTE political cadres to arrange such celebrations and they could operate relatively freely without too much harassment by the SLA. There was, however, a rather sinister tone in some of the speeches that day. Mr. Elilan, the head of the LTTE's political wing in the important Trincomalee area, was usually a relatively calm and reasonable man, if fiendishly stubborn sometimes. Yet he was not mincing his words this time as his speech was laden with threats of the use of force. Trincomalee was always a tricky area for the LTTE, with a mixed population in Trinco town and the large Muslim segment in Mutur on the southern shores of Trinco bay. However, the LTTE had been in relatively strong position before in Tamil dominated Batticaloa further to the south-east. This was no longer the case though after the Karuna split. As a matter of fact, it was allegedly their newly established opponents that chose one of the symbolically most important days for the LTTE to strike at the Tigers.

Batticaloa had become tense after the Karuna split and was plagued by tit for tat killings of LTTE and Karuna cadres. This was GOSL controlled area, so the LTTE was not allowed to carry arms. The LTTE had both manpower and access to weapons stored away in the area, but the Tigers could not operate freely. The same was assumed for the Karuna faction. However, the LTTE had complained bitterly that the security forces were now extending co-operation to armed Karuna cadres and protection. It was not only a paranoid LTTE ranting about the Karuna faction. The SLMM and other international agencies now frequently came across Karuna cadres in the area and they were very visibly carrying arms. This constituted a fundamental violation of the CFA which stipulated that all Tamil paramilitary groups should be disarmed according to its article 1.8.

On the morning of 5 July 2004, Black Tiger Day for the LTTE, Mr. Senathi, the head of the LTTE political wing and his assistant were shot at a junction in Batticaloa. On the same morning another two LTTE cadres where shot just north of Batticaloa with one of them killed on the spot. Mr. Senathi would succumb to his injuries later, being posthumously declared Lieutenant-Colonel, one of the highest ranks given within the LTTE, and buried with full military honours. He was the highest ranking LTTE figure assassinated in the east to date. These shootings could very well be interpreted as an indication of the LTTE being beaten on a retreat in the region. The LTTE was furious as it held the Sri Lanka Army and police responsible for security in Batticaloa in accordance with the CFA. A dangerous fratricidal battle appeared to have erupted in the Batticaloa region with the GOSL observing with some covert gloating as the political activists of the LTTE were being picked out and ambushed one after another. The LTTE, in an angry public statement, warned that if the political killings in the east, controlled by the SLA, were not stopped immediately, it would respond to the war thrust upon it. This was a common phrase used by the LTTE and history had shown that it was usually not wise to interpret this as an empty threat. An evidence of that could be witnessed in Colombo two days later.

The killings that had been going on for a few months did not recede in the east. On the contrary, scores of mostly Tamil males of either side would continue to be assassinated with the LTTE blaming the SLA for assisting and protecting the Karuna cadres.

In Colombo, the highest political officials had been extremely wary of the designs of the LTTE until the year of 2002 with the commencement of the Ceasefire Agreement. There had been a few remarkable years of security in Colombo, but now things seemed to have changed to the worse. In the year of 2005, dominated by the repercussions of the tsunami which had laid waist to most of the eastern coast, the LTTE could only sit back in Kilinochchi and watch from afar as some of the highest political dignitaries of the world stopped by to offer their condolences and help to this troubled island. As Sri Lanka was recovering from the natural catastrophe it was also receiving the most international attention it had ever experienced in its history. In Colombo, up in the charming old colonial mansion in the Fort district, the Foreign Ministry was busy accommodating these high-ranking emissaries and explaining the situation in the country.

The eloquent and elegant, long serving elderly statesman from Jaffna, Mr. Lakshman Kadirgamar, had become Foreign Minister for the third time in 2004. He was considered to be both a possible contender for the upcoming Presidential elections and a close advisor to the out-going President Mrs. Kumaratunga. However, as one of the most notable Tamils in the country, who had risen through the mainstream political system of Sri Lanka to the highest of offices in government, he was a menace to the LTTE. The person of Mr. Kadirgamar and his brilliant career were both an antithesis for Mr. Pirapaharan's LTTE which based its struggle on the presumption that Tamils could not expect a fair treatment in a Sri Lanka dominated by Sinhalese chauvinism. The Foreign Minister in turn appeared keen on delivering the message to the outside world that for him Mr. Pirapaharan was a cold-blooded thug and tyrant. Mr. Kardigamar strongly advocated to all of his interlocutors that the LTTE should be condemned and banned internationally as a terrorist organisation. On August 12, 2005, Foreign Minister Lakshman Kadirgamar was assassinated by a sniper, at his heavily guarded residence in Colombo.

Following the inauguration of President Rajapakse in late 2005, the SLA Chief of Staff Lieutenant-General Sarath Fonseka was appointed Commander of the Army. He had not gone the smooth way of the military management ladder through desk jobs, on the contrary, here was one of the most battle hardened officers of the SLA put in the commanding position. He was considered a through and through Sinhala nationalist and a hardliner as such, favouring a military solution for ending the conflict. He was quite outspoken and prone to uttering politically incorrect remarks to the press sometimes causing embarrassment for the political chiefs of Sri Lanka, not the least in relation with the representatives of the international community. Lt. General Fonseka had fought epic battles against the LTTE and was credited with having master-minded the retaking of Jaffna in 1996. He was certainly not believed to be as fond of his memories from the Elephant Pass debacle some years later, when his SLA suffered a crushing defeat at the hands of the Tamil Tigers.

Under the command of Lt. General Fonseka, the army was blamed by the LTTE and the Tamil media to respond very heavy handedly to minor incidents and alleged LTTE violations of the CFA. Thus, the tension increased considerably in the first months of 2006, which should have been the honeymoon days for the two new incumbents of Sri Lanka's highest and most important offices, those of the President and the Army Commander. Scores of fighters on both sides were killed as the death toll rose dramatically from the previously low levels for which the CFA was justly credited. The toll of civilian casualties from SLA bombardment also rose sharply. The days of restraint seemed to have gone by in an arrested conflict that lacked further steps forward in the peace process.

In April 2006, Lt. General Fonseka was on his way with his escorts within the SLA HQ in the heavily guarded compound across the street from the peaceful Galle Face Green pleasure ground. The northern and the southern entrances to the compound were guarded thoroughly and along the western side ran a long brick wall dotted with foxholes and sentry posts. The eastern flank was completely guarded by the tranquil waters streaming into the idyllic Beira Lake close to the Temple Trees compound. This was indeed a formidable High Security Zone. However, there was a maternity ward open to civilians at the Military Hospital, deep within the compound, and access to it was given to pregnant women with valid and vetted papers. It was reported that the suicide bomber had feigned pregnancy which would have given her an added advantage, as good as completely ruling out a potential body search by the soldiers standing guard, and quite some space for explosives. A young woman had charmed her way through the soldiers at the southern entrance and was now approaching her target. The young woman detonated her lethal package as the convoy of the Army Commander passed her by. Seven of the Commander's entourage were reported killed and others badly wounded among them the Lt.-General himself who survived miraculously and apparently against all medical odds. It had been an extremely close call and the carnage had been massive. It was a classic case of a LTTE suicide attack.

However, the blast at the SLA HQ so clearly aimed at its Commander was never ruled against the LTTE as a violation of the CFA as the embarrassed and enraged SLA refused SLMM monitors access to the scene. To be sure, the Tiger's up in Vanni were cheering and celebrating the successful infiltration of the SLA HQ. It had exposed the weaknesses in the defenses of the security forces and indicated, despite heavy security measures in the south, that the LTTE would be able to strike at almost anyone in the military or political hierarchy of Colombo.

# 18

## Mannar Island—the Remote Gateway to India

The situation in Mannar had been very strained for years and it was the most vulnerable area controlled by the GOSL, both at land and sea. In essence, the security forces only controlled the A14 highway from Anuradhapura towards Mannar and the A30 road from Vavuniya, which merged with the A14 halfway towards Mannar. After the merging point at Paraiyanalankulam, there was a stretch of almost 40 kilometres surrounded by jungle on both sides where the LTTE was capable of conducting operations with relative ease. This was accordingly one of the most dangerous roads in the world and would serve the LTTE as a venue for increasing Claymore mine attacks on the Sri Lankan security forces. To the north was LTTE held Vanni and to the south was the mostly abandoned jungle merged with the giant Wilpattu National Park. Its northern part had been claimed by LTTE for almost twenty years, but as the Norwegian facilitator and the SLMM had tried to establish demarcation, GOSL would refute the LTTE claims. However, the realities on the ground spoke for themselves. The GOSL security forces did not dare to patrol freely in the park, with the northern part apparently completely and the western section mostly out of bounds. Nevertheless, the southern part of the Park had been opened to some limited safari tourism, following the commencement of the CFA in 2002. Before the CFA, the Wilpattu National Park, Sri Lanka's largest, had been completely closed for over a decade due to the conflict. Its main ruler had been the majestic Sri Lankan Leopard, which was considered to be one of the very few to actually benefit from the conflict, as the Leopard population had stabilised and some observers even believed it had increased, in the absence of human intrusion.

Mannar itself was a largely homogeneous Tamil town on the Mannar Island stretching out from mainland Sri Lanka through the Palk Bay towards the southern-most shores of Sri Lanka's giant neighbour, India. On the way towards Mannar Island, just before reaching the coastline, one would pass the breathtaking natural wonder of the Giant's tank, one of the most important landmarks on this north-western coast of Sri Lanka. It was as its name indicates a vast storage of water after the rainy season, which would sustain the local farmers for the remainder of the year. The tank was a natural wonder in itself which seemed to have been created by a higher being for its purpose only to be perfectly completed with some ingenious engineering skills by long gone generations. The spiritual saying had it that it was left as a footprint from a giant that had roamed this part of the island thousands of years ago.

En route the A14, past the Giant's tank, military camps and sentry posts dotted the landscape towards the coast. A large bridge served as a crossing point towards Mannar Island proper at which eastern shores, closest to land, lay Mannar town, with its tightly clustered low-rise buildings, apparently peaceful and quiet for the visiting eye. Further south from the bridge, there was another bridge ruined by the conflict, upon which had once been a perfectly built railroad stretching all the way towards the western-most point of the island, Talamannar. At Talamannar, there had been great commercial activity in the distant past at the ferry jetty, which had served as a redistribution centre for all sorts of goods being ferried over the shallow Adam Strait towards India. Where people had gathered to embark on the ferry to India, there were now no civilians to be seen, as this was a High Security Zone and the main harbour in the north-western part of Sri Lanka and seat of the Western command of the SLN. The important railway system left behind by the British colonial administration had faded in memory as in most parts of northern Sri Lanka. Indeed, Mannar was one of the remotest areas of Sri Lanka, and with the breakdown of the railway infrastructure and the militarisation of the Talamannar ferry point, legal commercial activities had ceased. The island itself was, as so many other places affected by the conflict in Sri Lanka, very beautiful. It was relatively flat with abundant sub-tropical vegetation and coconut trees surrounding small farm houses and occasional villages. The southern coastline was mostly pristine, with magnificent sand dunes and a clear and unspoilt view towards the dark blue seas in the Gulf of Mannar. On the northern shores there were countless colourful fishing boats awaiting the predawn sailing in the following morning and foreign visitors were greeted with shy smiles from the locals.

The police would be the key component of the security forces in Mannar town assisted by the SLA on bigger incidents. In the past, the most frequent and difficult incidents had been flag hoisting and hartals. On specific commemorative days, determined young men would hoist the LTTE flag by the main square downtown or at the wide sporting ground close to the SLMM office. The SLA would arrive and disperse the crowd, sometimes demanding the flag being taken down by the organisers, on other occasions simply pulling it down themselves at the risk of riots in the town afterwards. However, compared to other theatres of the conflict Mannar Island had been relatively peaceful during the first four years of the CFA. This was about to change dramatically.

Further to the west of Mannar Island, the oversight of security was conducted by the SLN through its naval infantry. The navy would engage with fishermen from Pesalai, a pretty fishing town on the northern shores of the island roughly midway between Mannar town to the east and Talamannar to the west. At times the interaction between the SLN and the fishermen would be tolerable, at other times this relationship would be very strained. This depended also on the commanders of the SLN at each given time, some were very professional and commanded their men in a disciplined and orderly way, others were wary of the Tamils and suspected them of collaborating with the LTTE. Moreover, as in other areas of the conflict, the patience with the CFA would inevitably wear thin as the situation on the ground and at sea was escalating in a trend that seemed to forebode a full resumption of hostilities. The fishermen frequently complained bitterly about being harassed by the navy. They had to adhere to strict regulations on when to fish and how far they were allowed to sail from shore. This was indeed a complex situation, as the further out they would sail for fishing, the more abundant the catch, but also the closer they would get to Tamil Nadu, and the further from the prying eyes of the SLN. Mannar Island was a well known transition point for contraband being smuggled on small boats from India to Sri Lanka. This could be ammunition, dissembled military hardware, radio equipment, fuel, cement and other useful items. There was also a fairly steady stream of narcotics arriving in Sri Lanka from the main land most of it to be channelled to Colombo where there was a great demand for illegal drugs as in any metropolis. Of course, the police had very limited means to intercept drug running, but occasionally astonishing quantities of heroin were intercepted.

It was believed that some of the smuggling was organised directly by the LTTE, namely, the transport of tactical equipment and goods. Moreover, even though the LTTE was very strict on alcohol policies, let alone drugs, the drug trading was so lucrative that it had to be exploited as a means to a nobler end. It was impossible to fully know how much of the heroin smuggling was directly organised by the LTTE but there were strong indications that a substantial part of it was outsourced in a way to commercial drug dealers. The LTTE was, however, keeping a close eye on this criminal activity as it was levying the illegal trade as well as it could. To be sure, it was given that the proximity to India and the abundant availability of small vessels in the area was driving clandestine activity, which benefitted the LTTE enormously both in material and financial terms. It was the tactical task of the Sri Lankan Navy to try to curtail this activity at sea with all reasonable means.

There were occasional outburst of violence in Mannar Island and numerous incidents over the years, but the situation would take a turn for much worse in 2006 with terrible occurrences about to happen.

There were some stories being brought to the attention of the SLMM of SLN harassment of the local fishermen getting out of control. Most of the lower rank Sea Tigers did not wear a combat uniform and could not be distinguished from the local fishermen. Most of them would wear very similar garments, consisting of a traditional male cut sarong, a sort of colourful skirt, or some inexpensive trousers, and chequered shirts or faded T-shirts. When the SLN intercepted boats that had ventured further out than the usually regulated three miles zone, they were not sure if they had encountered a fishing boat commanded by simple fishermen trying out their luck in disobeying fishing regulations, or Sea Tigers or their smuggling proxies. This frustrated the SLN enormously and sometimes their lower ranked personnel forgot about their supposed discipline and took matters into their own hands. There were frequent incidents when fishing gear was confiscated, which was a big setback financially for the crew, or the boats were confiscated or even destroyed. It is hard for outsiders to understand how poor these fishing communities are and how vulnerable they were economically to such treatment. But there would sometimes be even more sinister outcomes of the encounters at sea. Some fishermen would be detained and interrogated on land; others would remain in custody for lengthened periods of time if they were suspected of having strong links with the LTTE. On a number of occasions the SLN was reported by the locals as having thrown Tamils overboard, some of whom could not swim and thus drowned. It was, of course, difficult to verify such accusations, but some would appear credible following a thorough enquiry into reported incidents.

This was the backdrop to some of the Sea Tiger activities from their bases on the western coastline north of Mannar Island, with the closest being at Vidattaltivu less than ten nautical miles away from Mannar town as the crow flies. It was also widely understood that the Sea Tigers possessed vessels operating from small bases on the coast south of Mannar Island. These were believed to be hidden away in the jungle when not in the water. As the infrastructure had not been rebuilt in this area since the cessation of hostilities in 2002, roads were littered with giant potholes and in some areas had been reduced to jungle dirt tracks and many bridges had been demolished. Hence, these bases were almost completely inaccessible for any outsiders, other than the SLMM with its robust four-wheel drive vehicles. Even so, the SLMM was clearly not a welcome visitor in these parts of the woods, notwithstanding guarantees of full freedom of movement and rights of enquiry by the CFA, co-signed by the leader of the LTTE.

Trying to understand and verify what had happened after incidents in the Mannar area would have been a cumbersome and difficult task for professionals with knowledge of the local population, its language and its social structures. This proved to be an almost impossible task for the security forces who were seen as a foreign intruder mostly not in command of the local language. There were a few Tamil-speaking police officers, but in the navy this was extremely rare. For the SLMM, it was, of course, difficult to establish facts, and its mandate was not to undertake criminal investigations. However, given the enormous trust vested in the SLMM by most of the local population, its access to a pool of extremely talented and dedicated national staff and operational resources, not the least in communication technology, it stood perhaps the greatest chance of reporting what was really going on in Mannar. But this also depended on a good working relationship with both the security forces, local community leaders and representatives of the LTTE political wing.

There would be occasional killings in Mannar, even in times when the general situation was assessed to be relatively calm and quiet. There could be a plethora of motives behind such killings and in the Mannar area there would be a pool of possible perpetrators. In some instances it could be a plain result of gangster infighting. It could also be an act of the LTTE punishing people who did not pay their levies. Furthermore, it could be an act of drunken soldiers getting out of hand. It could also be the summons of justice handed out to perceived informers, either by the security forces or the LTTE. These matters would become even more complex as extortion of middle class Tamils and small business owners, by unknown gunmen in GOSL controlled areas, increased dramatically following the Karuna split. For the SLMM, business went on as usual, enquiries were made and although these were not criminal investigations, enough information could usually be gathered to make a very educated guess. This result resulting in ruling incidents against either the LTTE or the security forces, or in some cases drawing the conclusions that incidents were non-CFA-related. Mannar would remain a remote and tricky outpost for the SLMM and the security forces, but an area with its own intrinsic challenges to the rule of law and the security of its local community.

19

# The EU Proscription and Increased Isolation of the LTTE

The LTTE felt increasingly misunderstood and isolated after President Rajapakse came into power. There was a common perception developing in Kilinochchi that were it not for the international Tamil diaspora, the LTTE would find itself almost completely isolated outside of Sri Lanka. The one place where there was substantial support for their cause was on the other side of the Palk Strait in Tamil Nadu. The political leaders of Tamil Nadu, however, were also wary of the violent past of the LTTE, which was believed to have conducted the infamous assassination of former Indian Prime Minister Mr. Rajiv Gandhi on an election campaign in this southern-most federal state of India, in 1991. Much speculation on the assassination had been documented in volumes of books, but the LTTE, or rather the mastermind behind the murder, Mr. Pirapaharan, had never officially taken responsibility for it. However, statements from the main political counsel of the LTTE, Mr. Balasingham, a Tamil resident of the UK, who was extremely influential in setting the political agenda for the organisation, as good as amounted to a full confession in early 2006.

Above: President Chandrika Kumaratunga (right) and Prime Minister Ranil Wickremesinghe, long-time political rivals, chat during a ceremony to mark Sri Lanka's independence celebration in Colombo, Sri Lanka, 2002. *(AP Photo/Gemunu Amarasinghe)*.

Below: Sri Lankan President Mahinda Rajapakse greets supporters after laying a wreath to fallen soldiers on National War Hero's Day in Colombo in June, 2009. The celebrations came as Rajapakse's government troops ended the over three decade old armed rebellion of the Tamil Tigers. *(AFP Photo/Ishara S. Kodikara)*

Above: Norwegian special envoy Erik Solheim greeted by LTTE leader Pirapaharan in Vanni. *(Stein J. Bjørge / Aftenposten / Scanpix)*

Below: The recluse: Pirapaharan surrounded by his trusted bodyguards. *(Stein J. Bjørge / Aftenposten / Scanpix)*

Right: Female Tiger Cadres at sea. *(n.n.)*

Below: Youngsters operating Sea Tiger attack craft. *(n.n.)*

மில்லர்
வல்லிபுரம் வசந்தன்

Left: The statue of LTTE´s first suicide bomber, Captain Miller, in northern Jaffna. *(JOS)*

Above: The A9, Kilinochchi celebrating Black Tiger day. *(Thorfinnur Omarsson)*

Right: Front side of the deadly Claymore controlled mine used with devastating effect by both sides in Sri Lanka. *(Sverre-Andreas Waldal Iversen)*

Below: SLMM HOM and Puleedevan inspecting Pooneryn ferry jetty. *(LTTE )*

Above: Ambulance in Vanni after SLA Claymore attack. *(Sverre-Andreas Waldal Iversen )*

Left: An LTTE Commando. *(Stein J. Bjørge / Aftenposten / Scanpix)*

Below: Body count after the SLA debacle in Muhamalai. *(L. B.)*

Above: LTTE allowed to fly its flag over its cemetery in government controlled Jaffna. *(JOS)*
Below: Vintage SLA tank destroyed when Elephant Pass fell to LTTE. *(JOS)*

Above: The central train station in Jaffna ruined by the war. *(JOS)*

Below: SLA Forward Defence Location at Nagarkovil in the north. *(JOS)*

Above: LTTE Political Wing leader Mr. Tamilshelvan and family shortly before he was killed in an SLAF airstrike. *(L.B.)*

Right: LTTE Black Tiger memorial in Kilinochchi. *(JOS)*

Below: The LTTE office in Kalmunai, one of many where the LTTE was allowed to conduct 'political work' inside government-controlled areas. *(JOS)*

Above: SLMM inspecting the frontline in the north. *(JOS)*

Right: LTTE propaganda poster at the outskirts of Kilinochchi. *(L. B.)*

Right below: Aftermath of assassination of SLA Brigadier General Kulatunga in Colombo. *(L. B.)*

Below: Mineclearers in Vanni: Large swaths of land remain contaminated by mines. *(L. B.)*

Above: Pesalai Burning: Sri Lanka Navy personnel's revenge for a devastating Sea Tiger attack. *(Sverre-Andreas Waldal Iversen)*

Left: A Sri Lanka Navy Dvora at full speed in Trincomalee´s magnificent harbour. *(Kristjan Guðmundsson)*

Below: Discussing future: SLMM monitors with local fishermen in Pesalai. *(JOS)*

Above: The LTTE police officers in their distinct blue uniforms. *(JOS)*

Right: At the beginning of the six year-ceasefire: Jaffna-Kandy highway A-9 refurbished and opened for traffic. *(Iresha Kariyawasam)*

Below: Batticaloa seen from an SLAF helicopter. *(JOS)*

Above: LTTE suicide attack on SLN buses in Habarana leaves over a hundred dead. *(Constantin Karamé)*

Left: A Claymore attack by the LTTE in the streets of Colombo´s diplomatic quarter. *(L. B.)*

Below: Sri Lankan Naval presence in Bay of Bengal to intercept LTTE smuggling vessels. *(Kristjan Guðmundsson)*

Right: Tiger fighters in the jungle west of Batticaloa. *(Thorfinnur Omarsson)*

Right centre : Inspecting a shanty town outside of Vavuniya, one of LTTE´s child recruitment centres. *(JOS)*

Right below: Sri Lanka Army soldier keeps watch on no-mans land, Omanthai. *(JOS)*

Below: Local boys enjoy a quiet swim far away from the main fighting, Ampara. *(JOS)*

Above: Kilnochchi in ruins after the decisive push by the Army to clear out the LTTE from its main stronghold. *(Kristoffer Rönneberg)*

Left: A T55 tank destroyed by the LTTE in Muhamalai. *(LTTE)*

Below: The endgame. Sri Lanka Army soldiers clearing out the last pockets of resistance of LTTE. *(Kristoffer Rönneberg)*

Mr. Balasingham was by then terminally ill and appeared as wanting to appease the Indian authorities. Despite the avowal by such a high-ranking individual, who was one of the few who was reported to be able to speak his free mind with Mr. Pirapaharan, the government in Delhi appeared reluctant to break the international isolation of the LTTE and to engage in the conflict again.

To this backdrop, there had also been some major changes in world affairs, changes that would affect the conflict in Sri Lanka as well, if only by association. Most importantly, the US President Mr. George W. Bush had officially declared a war on terrorism. This had been the response to 9/11 which took place half a year before the commencement of the CFA. It must be considered rather likely that the attack on the Twin Towers and the wrath of the US that followed, particularly against terrorism in general, and against Muslim jihadists in particular, had an impact on the LTTE. In such circumstances, it could be wiser to enter into a ceasefire agreement than to continue the bloodshed.

In the years that had followed, the US, vowing to fight terrorists globally, had already conquered Saddam's Iraq and was fighting an increasingly protracted war with its coalition partners in NATO against the Taliban in Afghanistan. Furthermore, the US having relied mainly on the UK and Spain and a coalition of smaller willing nations for its fighting in Iraq, was increasingly pressuring its more sceptic allies in Europe to join in the global war against terrorism. There was increasing pressure on the EU to align its list of proscribed terrorist organisations in the world, with that of Washington.

The proposal of the EU proscribing the LTTE as a terrorist organisation was a disturbing prospect for the LTTE and the Tamil diaspora, but it could also have a very negative impact on the whole peace process in Sri Lanka.

The clandestine international funding of the LTTE, through the Tamil diaspora had obviously been a matter of great concern to GOSL, which had appealed to western governments to try to put a stop to it. But that was easier said than done. Credible evidence had been obtained both in the UK and Canada on such funding activities. It seemed to follow a two-fold pattern of levies imposed on Tamils by the LTTE contact groups in the west and to some extent extortion of small to medium Tamil-owned businesses. Formal complaints against extortion were reported to be relatively rare occurrences as in Sri Lanka proper. The LTTE was feared by many Tamils living abroad, as its network was believed to be well informed on Tamil immigrants. However, the LTTE and the Tamil liberation cause also enjoyed widespread support in the Tamil diaspora, manifested by large demonstrations being organized every now and then in the UK, Canada, France, Switzerland and Norway. If the international community would align itself in proscribing the LTTE as a terrorist organisation, the authorities in some of these countries would be given a much wider mandate to try to quench the LTTEs funding activities internationally.

Both the Norwegian facilitator and the SLMM, however, believed that proscribing the LTTE as a terrorist outfit, four years into the CFA, could derail the whole peace process, fragile as it was already. Taking away the legitimacy of the LTTE as a negotiation partner on behalf of the Tamil people could surely complicate all efforts, however feeble, to try to return to a peace dialogue.

The SLMM was composed of contingents from the five Nordic countries, three of which were members of the EU, which was now seriously contemplating proscribing the LTTE on its list of terrorist groups. The LTTE warned the international community in general and the EU in particular that such a move could bring about the end of the SLMM and thus the end of the CFA.

The then SLMM Head of Mission Major-General Ulf Henricson communicated his dire view on the outcome of an EU ban on the LTTE both in writing and in meetings with high-ranking diplomats in Colombo. It could spell the end of the ceasefire and a return to full scale war in Sri Lanka. These warnings were duly noted, but it is not clear at which decision-making level they were discussed within the EU. Mr. Henricson himself a Swedish national was in a key position to communicate his misgivings to Stockholm, where the issue of a possible proscription of the LTTE was discussed as in other EU capitals.

In May 2006, there was a flurry of diplomatic activities regarding the imminent proscription of the LTTE by the EU. The LTTE strongly objected against any such move and came close to declaring that it would retract its commitment to the CFA would the ban take effect. Mr. Solheim, the Norwegian minister for International Development, and former Special Envoy to Sri Lanka, met with President Rajapakse and seniour GOSL officials on 26 May, among other issues discussing the impact of an EU ban on the peace process. He was accompanied by Mr. Jon Hanssen-Bauer, Norway's Special Envoy, who would meet with the LTTE in Kilinochchi the day after. The proscription of the LTTE by the EU had its clear advantages for the GOSL, as it would mean that authorities in most of Europe could curb LTTE funding activities and freeze assets of Tamil organisations believed to be operating as subsidiaries for the LTTE within the EU. To be sure this would be a welcome move to GOSL as it should severely hamper the LTTE in funding its clandestine arms procurement programme which was believed to be fairly sophisticated. However, this tangible gain in the fight against the LTTE could come at a political cost, as it could jeopardize the brittle CFA and lead to a full retraction of the LTTE from the peace process. Years of strenuous dialogue with the leadership of the LTTE could end in vain.

Mr. Hanssen-Bauer discussed the alternatives with the LTTE at the meeting in Kilinochchi and Mr. Tamilshelvan spoke harshly about the international community's commitment to the peace process. He stopped just short of declaring an end to the CFA in the case of an EU ban. Time was running out, however, for diplomatic efforts of Norway.

Up to this point, there had appeared to be a balance of sorts within the *ad hoc* group of international players that had assumed a degree of ownership of the conflict in Sri Lanka, the co-chairs. The co-chairs had been formed at the Tokyo donor conference in 2002, where international donors had pledged funds in excess of 4 billion USD for rebuilding of infrastructure in Sri Lanka if the Parties adhered to the CFA. The funds would be released in accordance with incremental steps in the peace progress following the commencement of the CFA. The co-chairs consisted of Norway and the EU, which were seen as relatively understanding of the Tamil cause, and the USA and Japan, the latter sometimes perceived as reluctantly supporting the former in a more hardline approach against the LTTE. The co-chairs were scheduled to meet in Tokyo on 30 May to review the alarming development in the ground situation in Sri Lanka, where increasing violence and military attacks appeared to be undermining the credibility of the CFA to such an extent that a return to war seemed likely.

The view of the facilitator on the proscription issue was clear, Norway believed it could seriously jeopardise the whole peace process and could lead to a swift end of the CFA. Results gained by the CFA could evaporate and the situation on the ground could be rolled back by years. The SLMM HOM had warned that it could mean the end of the SLMM, effectively abrogating the CFA and its achievements. Discussions with high-ranking EU officials in Colombo revealed the pattern of logic behind the EU deliberations on its future stance on the LTTE. It seemed that the EU through the diplomatic services of their member-states with Embassies in Colombo had come to the conclusion that the LTTE was dragging its feet in the peace process. A school of thought had emerged somewhat in unison with the US policy, that only by weakening the LTTE could the Tigers be brought to the negotiation table. This chain of thought seemed to overlook the fact that the LTTE had only agreed to the CFA in the first place as it perceived itself holding a very strong hand.

The warning messages were not heeded by the EU which at a council meeting of its Foreign Ministers in Brussels on May 29, 2006, officially proscribed the LTTE as a terrorist organisation. This made a dramatic impact on the political balance of power within the co-

Chairs, which met the day after in Tokyo. The Norwegian facilitator appeared increasingly isolated in its peacemaking efforts and its standing vis-à-vis the GOSL had been diminished. Surely this was unintentional, however, there were indications that as the Norwegian role appeared to be reduced, other interested parties might increase their stake in Sri Lanka. The US Assistant Secretary of State for South and Central Asian Affairs, Ambassador Richard A. Boucher, visited Sri Lanka in a buoyant mood the following day. This was his first visit to Sri Lanka in this capacity. For observers of the situation in Sri Lanka, it would appear that there had been a shift in the position of the international community to a more hawkish US-led stance. It remained to be seen what impact this would have on the frail CFA and the peace process. Moreover, how would GOSL and LTTE react?

20

# War Resumes in Mannar as Pesalai Burns

As the CFA started to falter in 2006, tension increased markedly in Mannar. Despite the smuggling activities, the drug running, assassinations and the general friction between the security forces and the local population, Mannar had been considered a relatively quiet and isolated outpost. However, the difficult relationship between the Sri Lanka Navy and fishermen was turning from bad to worse. Furthermore, given the SLMM stance on the sea, that it should be exclusively GOSL controlled, the Sea Tigers saw it necessary to oppose this ruling by overtly asserting themselves as a *de facto* lethal sea fighting force, provocating the SLN when it could and even engaging in outright naval battles.

The SLN was extremely wary of the Sea Tigers who operated with outlandish ruthlessness, not hesitating to conduct suicide attacks on navy vessels when given the opportunity. It was not easy to defend a larger vessel from a one-man fiberglass boat laden with explosives capable of homing in on its target at extreme speed. The mutual hostility was profound and prisoners were rarely taken.

On 17 June 2006, war resumed in Mannar Island and sparked

sustained violence in faraway corners of Sri Lanka. At dawn, the SLN was reported to have sent out three small plastic boats with a total crew of eleven to inspect the fisheries off the shores of Pesalai in a routine operation. As out of nowhere numerous Sea Tiger vessels appeared on the spot, according to the fishermen interviewed they could have been as many as fifteen. The SLN sailors were completely outgunned and the Sea Tigers did not hesitate but went on a full-fledged attack destroying the three navy boats and massacring all of the SLN seamen. Having ruthlessly extinguished the life of the young sailors, the Sea Tigers moved their vessels closer to shore firing against the police station in Pesalai and hurtling bombs and heavy weapons fire at the navy camp close by. Both the navy and the police returned the fire but after half an hour or so the Sea Tigers retreated and disappeared to the north-east. As was to be expected, the brothers in arms at the navy camp were completely enraged when they learned about the slaughter. This bode not well for the local Tamil community.

A few hours later, disturbing reports reached Colombo, indicating that the navy had gone berserk in wild spree of retaliation and revenge in the village of Vankalaipadu close to Pesalai. As tension had been on the rise in most conflict areas in recent weeks, the local population started to gather at the church premises in the afternoon only leaving for their huts and daily activities in the morning. That Friday night a particularly large assemblage had stayed overnight in the church itself. Thus in the early hours of Saturday morning, hundreds of civilians were crammed within the church proper and in the courtyard of the parish perimeter. Eyewitnesses were consistent in drawing up a sinister picture of the events unfolding that morning after the fatal encounter of the SLN dinghies with the Sea Tiger squadron. One elderly woman was killed due to injuries sustained by an exploding grenade that had been thrown through a window into the crowded church. Unidentified men wearing blue clothes had also charged into the entrance area of the church and opened fire, wounding up to forty civilians seeking shelter. Moreover, fires had been set to dozens of huts and houses and boats and fishing gear were burning as well. Four fishermen had been shot at close range down by the shore and one body had been obtained from a drifting boat, which could have been caught up in the crossfire from the Sea Tiger attack earlier. The wounded civilians were rushed to hospital in ambulances and makeshift vehicles, some of them seriously injured. As the SLMM arrived on the scene, a large part of the village of Vankalaipadu was burning, the attackers were gone but the police and military personnel were enquiring with a terrified and traumatized gathering of the villagers. Their collective story was coherent and logical given the anger that would have been enkindled within the inhabitants of the close-by SLN camp as the sailors realised that eleven of their fellow seamen had been brutally wiped out by the Sea Tigers. Sadly, the inclination of the local population to seek refuge from the SLN in case of a major incident taking place had been justified.

It was fairly clear for all to see what had taken place at the church premises in Vankalaipadu. In the next few days the death toll would rise as some of the injured succumbed to their wounds. The respective authorities would promise to initiate a thorough investigation into these terrible events. However, as with most such cases, the judicial procedure would probably drag on for years and in the end it would be overtaken by other terrible criminal acts and wither away without anyone being brought to justice. The sheer wrath and violence inflicted upon this defenseless community of simple fishermen would certainly evoke a deep hatred for the Sri Lankan security forces within the Tamil population of Mannar, for years to come. The burning of Pesalai was yet another futile, sad and callous incident of civilian suffering due to the rampant ethnic conflict in Sri Lanka.

As the conflict would continue to escalate through most of 2006 and into 2007, Mannar would be the stepping stone for many Tamils to get away from Sri Lanka. The western-most tip of Mannar Island was only twenty kilometres away from the closest shores of India in Tamil Nadu. As the name would indicate, this southern state of giant neighbour India was populated by an estimate of forty to fifty million ethnic Tamils sharing a similar language and cultural background with the Tamils of northern Sri Lanka. There was a considerable sympathy for the Tamil cause on the other side of the Palk Strait, if limited economic means to accommodate those Tamils who chose to flee the conflict in their island. The seas directly west of Mannar were quite shallow and only barely managed to cut off a land link to the subcontinent. A string of small sandy islets, called Adams Bridge, dotted the strait separating Sri Lanka from India and between them there were short intervals of water. It would, indeed, probably be feasible for the athletic and able-bodied to swim and walk over this bridge if the security situation had allowed it. Many families, however, chose to try their luck with a passage on a trawler or a larger fishing vessel in the darkness of the night. Hundreds of fleeing Tamils from Mannar and other remote areas in Sri Lanka were intercepted by the Sri Lanka Navy in the months following the revenge attack on the Lady's Church in Pesalai, only to be returned to the police authorities in Tallaimannar. No one could tell how many Tamils had managed to get across the strait seeking refuge in the economically poor but relatively peaceful Tamil Nadu.

# 21

# Close Encounters with the Tigers

For the GOSL, the CFA had in a way been a desperate measure to arrest an internecine war which seemed beyond being brought to a halt through an outright military victory. The State of Sri Lanka was on the verge of bankruptcy at the beginning of the twenty-first century. Its infrastructure was ruined in the north and the east and hopelessly outdated and neglected in most parts of the south. Its military had suffered humiliating defeats by the LTTE and thousands of soldiers had deserted from the SLA in previous years. Nevertheless, the GOSL saw itself as the sole legitimate ruler over all of Sri Lanka and no politician in his right mind would indicate that he or she would accept the stringiest demands of the LTTE, which amounted to an independent Tamil state in the north and the east. Furthermore, even though the GOSL had entered into the CFA on premises of parity, the GOSL would constantly play down the legitimacy of the LTTE and seek to diminish its role as a sole Tamil interlocutor. Hence, the GOSL saw the conflict as very asymmetric, not only tactically in the fighting fields, but also politically.

The LTTE, of course, had a completely different view. They had been expanding and consolidating the territory controlled by them before the ceasefire agreement and had scored some spectacular military victories in Vanni. Moreover, they were holding strategically important land south of Trincomalee, and were a military force to reckon with on the ground level all the way down to Yala National Park in the south-east of Sri Lanka. The CFA also gave the LTTE a welcome chance of obtaining some legitimacy as a liberation movement for the presumably oppressed Tamil population, locked in poverty in the remote corners of the island, far away from the seat of government in Colombo. The LTTE had entered into the CFA full of confidence and saw itself, through the agreement, enjoying political and military parity with GOSL for the first time. The CFA could also be interpreted as a major stepping stone towards a political settlement of the conflict. Should there be distinct progress in the peace process, it was to be expected that this would further strengthen the role of the LTTE and cement its position as the principal representative of the Tamil population in Sri Lanka.

However, the LTTE sometimes seemed too eager to demonstrate its role not only as a military adversary, but also as an astute political counterpart legitimised by the CFA as a co-signatory. This was a strategic misinterpretation of how the GOSL regarded the same document and its consequences. These asymmetric views on the respective roles of the parties to the CFA, from both sides, would often lead to a stalemate in the peace process, as trivial matters as protocol could lead to a breakdown in otherwise promising diplomatic engagements.

The LTTE was sometimes viewed by the international community with curiosity and interest as it had developed into a formidable fighting organisation that had managed to hold its own against an increasingly sophisticated SLA for decades, and had even kicked out the massive Indian Peace Keeping Force (IPKF). However, there were also large segments of the international community that perceived of the LTTE as a strangely knit band of jungle terrorists dominated by a bloodthirsty and reclusive leader exercising his power via Stalinist terror and Maoist subjection of his underlings. This external interpretation of its movement, the LTTE found very hard both to digest and accept.

In essence, the LTTE was not very well understood by the outside world. There were only a handful of high-ranking representatives from the international community who had made the arduous journey up north to Kilinochchi through the frontlines to meet with high level LTTE leaders. And the supreme leader of the LTTE, Mr. Pirapaharan, was mostly hiding in his fortified commando post believed to be somewhere off the A35 road between Kilinochchi and Mullativu. He had met with the representatives of the Royal Norwegian Government at the beginning of the CFA and had shortly thereafter granted a brief encounter with representatives from the international press. His press conference in April 2002 was the first in more than a decade. It was a memorable event, where over three hundred local and international journalists were cramped together in a meeting hall in Kilinochchi. The Tigers pointed guns at the media during the press brief and explained to the puzzled reporters that the life of the LTTE leader was so important that if there were any quick and surprising movement by the press, they would shoot just to be on the safe side. For a hectic press meeting, the hands of the journalists went quite slowly into the air for questions following these warning words. It was to be the last time that Mr. Pirapaharan was to meet with the Press.

He did, however, quietly meet with the Head of Mission of SLMM, Mr. Trond Furuhovde, a few times at the beginning of the CFA. Mr. Pirapaharan was always escorted by heavily armed guards and his staring dark brown eyes seemed to have a commanding effect on his collaborators. Mr. Pirapaharan had meticulously built up a strong cult regarding his persona and large posters and pictures of the supreme LTTE commander were prominently displayed in all LTTE offices and facilities. Nevertheless, he surprised the SLMM delegation over lunch, when he appeared to relax somewhat, joking that he was not a tyrant, that title he attributed to his wife who he said held full command of his household. After the last meeting in the spring of 2003 where Mr. Pirapaharan in a surprise move released two SLA soldiers in LTTE custody to the SLMM delegation, he was rarely seen by the outside world. He would only be visible on a few occasions each year through photographs of him commemorating fallen LTTE combatants such as the Black Tigers. These photographs were posted on the main media outlet used by the LTTE, the TamilNet news site. So rare were his comments on the conflict that they were mostly confined to his annual speech given on the so-called Heroes' Day on 27 November every year, incidentally the day after his birthday which was believed to be 26 November, although never fully confirmed by authoritative records. The deep reclusiveness chosen by the LTTE leader was interpreted to signal various elements of his character, his acute sense for security, extreme distrust of the outside world and to some commentators a complete lack of interest in any sort of political discourse. In the south, opinion-makers would ridicule the LTTE boss for paranoidly hiding out in the jungle fortress and there was bountiful speculation circulated claiming that he was living in luxury while his Tamil subjects were eking out a life of miserly subsistence. However, there were many observations made in Tamil-dominated areas indicating that large segments of the population supported Mr. Pirapaharan whole-heartedly and even admired its leader whose daily life was shrouded in a cloud of mystery. For the deeply superstitious and religious people in backward areas, it apparently made perfect sense that the head of the LTTE only appeared in public on a handful of occasions every year. It added strongly to the aura of mystery surrounding Mr. P.

The main voice of the LTTE and the key interlocutor with the outside world was Mr. Tamilshelvan, head of the political wing of the LTTE. He resided on the outskirts of Kilinochchi town with his wife and two young children. Mr. Tamilshelvan would be the interface with the international community on all important issues regarding the LTTE, the CFA and the peace process. The LTTE also commented on military matters through its military spokesman

Mr. Irasaiah Ilanthiayan, nicknamed Marshall, who would mostly give his statements exclusively through the TamilNet website. A third key figure for the outside world was Mr. Puleedevan, the director of the LTTE Peace Secretariat, an office that had been established mostly due to the CFA and the facilitator, as a counterpart to the Secretariat for the Co-ordination of the Peace Process (SCOPP), in Colombo.

Mr. Tamilshelvan was a youngish looking man approaching forty who had been injured in combat and hence limped somewhat and thus invariably supported himself on a cane. He personified the image in which the LTTE wanted to represent itself politically and culturally, always neatly clad and groomed, smiling deceptively even as he was giving firm and authoritative statements. He would be extremely tough on both broader strategic issues and smaller practical and technical matters and very difficult to negotiate with. He was, however, always very polite to the high-ranking visitors granted audience but would not allow himself to get on personal terms with the more frequent visitors, be they either the representatives of the facilitator or the SLMM. He was a man feared and hated in the south, whose only weakness seemed to be his profound appetite for devilled cashew nuts, a small culinary delight, invariably served with the excellent Ceylon tea prepared for visitors to the meetings held at the modern and elegant premises of the Peace Secretariat in Kilinochchi. Marshall was a bit older and more seasoned military commander who usually managed to hide a considerable sense of humour behind his outward expression of seriousness and sadness. He was soft-spoken and as he chose his words carefully they were very much worth listening to. His manner of communicating on military matters was sometimes so subtle that his messages on future or past incidents involving the LTTE seemed to constitute more of a riddle or a puzzle than a statement. The most frequently met counterpart of the LTTE on the SLMM side was Mr. Puleedevan, head of the Peace Secretariat. He was a very lively and outgoing young man, apparently in his mid-thirties, who would burst into laughter at the most surprising and improbable moments. This could be perceived of also as a subtle defense mechanism against getting to cosy with the SLMM representatives permanently stationed in Kilinochchi. In the early years of the CFA, Mr. Puleedevan had visited Colombo regularly and had dropped by the SLMM HQ at Galle Road for a chat every now and then in a cheerful mood. As the conflict regained momentum in 2006 and the parties seemed to be returning towards full hostilities, a visit by any high-ranking member of the LTTE to Colombo seemed to be a very improbable and ludicrous notion of the past.

The Norwegian facilitator, mostly through its resident Ambassador to Colombo, visited Kilinochchi every now and then to discuss issues regarding the CFA and the peace process. The leadership of the SLMM would also engage with Mr. Tamilshelvan in important meetings in Kilinochchi, mostly to discuss modalities of the CFA, serious incidents caused by either party and later on, the military situation on the ground and the intentions of the parties to adhere to the CFA which was being weakened substantially and continuously from the end of 2005. These meetings would be cordial and mostly held in a sober but amicable atmosphere. It was hard to fit these counterparts into the image moulded of them in Colombo, where both the polity and the press would depict them as bloodthirsty, nihilistic madmen imposing an insane war of extortion and terror upon the peaceful people of Sri Lanka.

Strategic issues such as the refusal of the SLMM to accept LTTE claims to the waters of Sri Lanka would of course lead to a rather forceful objection by the former, but there was no shouting or screaming or threatening gestures. On the contrary, the SLMM was mostly met with great courtesy. The LTTE would not argue much against the rulings that the SLMM HOM had made against them, even regarding incidents of extremely serious and fatal nature. The SLMM HOM would sometimes publish his findings on severe violations of the CFA and post them as rulings to the parties. In fact, it seemed that the LTTE was not all too interested in the SLMM system of rulings at all. Maybe, they should have made a stronger effort in portraying themselves more favourably to the international media, but that was tough as GOSL controlled the access of reporters up to Vanni. The LTTE was bitterly disappointed with the lack of goodwill from the international press and the international community. The LTTE felt that its agenda and actions had never been represented fairly and the leading Tigers frequently expressed their deep disappointment with international actors and the lack of diplomatic intervention into the conflict from the outside world.

The SLMM had two liaison officers stationed permanently in Kilinochchi and they met with their counterparts at the LTTE Peace Secretariat on a daily basis. This was very useful to defuse difficult situations in the early years of the CFA. Later on, the SLMM would deliver urgent messages and proposals from GOSL, but the spirit of trying to develop the peace process further, avoid misunderstanding and refrain from military action, had evaporated by the beginning of 2006. The SLMM would increasingly declare serious violations of the CFA and rule such violations against either party, which in most cases did not win the mission any accolade. In the early days of the CFA, by far the most rulings were made against the LTTE, a fact that SCOPP made a big issue of in the press, both local and international. However, what was not so clear to the media was that most of the rulings against the LTTE were of fairly minor nature, given what was at stake in keeping the weapons silent on the battle field. Flag hoistings were typical for the LTTE in most of the conflict areas and the SLA and police would intervene and meticulously make formal complaints to the SLMM. Child abduction and forced enlisting into the fighting formations of the LTTE were, of course, a much more serious issue, but it was a difficult topic to discuss with the LTTE. They argued that a mandatory enlisting of soldiers into an army was a global phenomenon, and as they were fighting a war of liberation against Sinhala oppression, they had every right to enlist young men and women into the LTTE ranks. Previously, even children as young as twelve to thirteen years had been taken by force from their families, but in the course of time the LTTE would be more careful of taking teenagers of the ages of, say, fifteen to seventeen into their ranks. The presence of the SLMM had a markedly chastising effect on the LTTE in this regard and the SLMM intervened in hundreds of cases of child recruitment. Moreover, Tamil parents were encouraged to visit the SLMM offices to file complaints against the LTTE on the grounds of child recruitment which proved to be a quite successful deterrent against the LTTE snatching the very young into their forced ranks. Nevertheless, forced abduction of teenagers into the LTTE military wing continued and weakened the reputation of the LTTE immensely internationally. UNICEF and other international agencies were present in Sri Lanka in the north and the east and issued regular reports on this controversial issue. These reports had the effect of chastising the LTTE somewhat, and they were read, noted and digested by the upper echelons in Kilinochchi. Nevertheless, the LTTE continued to complain bitterly about the negative presentation of this *modus operandi* internationally and maintained that most of their recruits were in fact volunteers which, according to them, could not be claimed in the case of the SLA which suffered thousands of deserters.

The LTTE, of course, also had numerous deserters. However, to survive they would have to flee LTTE-controlled areas or they would be tracked down. In some instances the SLMM observed teenage boys who were able to make an escape out of Vanni to join their families and the LTTE left it at that if the SLMM was formally aware of the circumstances. In other instances, Tamil parents would be brave enough to report forced recruitments to the SLMM, which would then make enquiries. Some resulted in youngsters being released by the LTTE, whereas in a number of cases the teenagers stated that they wanted to stay on in the LTTE camps rather than returning home. In several cases, this decision was made by young females that indicated that they had fled domestic violence by their fathers.

There was always a danger of SLMM liaison officers staying too long in Kilinochchi, and to be sure, some of them probably got overly fascinated with the fighting spirit and the resolve of the LTTE. It was difficult to pinpoint exactly when such feelings had reached the point where it could be perceived that a SLMM liaison officer had lost his or her neutrality. The common rule was to rotate SLMM members out of Kilinochchi after a maximum of six months, but some stayed longer, in hindsight, maybe, too long.

The SLMM would be the main channel for the LTTE to communicate with GOSL in Colombo and also to engage with the international community, although the Norwegian facilitator also had an important role in this. The LTTE appreciated the fairly frank interface with the outside world that the SLMM provided. And the SLMM could also explain to the LTTE that some of their actions were considered completely barbaric, especially the use of suicide bombers and detonating explosives where civilians were at risk.

# 22

## Frosty Meetings and a Golden Opportunity Lost

Following the EU proscription, a big question mark was hanging over the ceasefire in Sri Lanka. The Norwegian Government, however, acted quickly and invited both parties to discussions in Oslo later in June. The LTTE accepted the invitation, but made it clear that these were not formal peace talks with the GOSL and that the representatives of the LTTE would only meet with Norwegian officials and the SLMM.

The coordination of travelling arrangements for LTTE delegations out of Sri Lanka, for meetings either in Norway or Switzerland, was usually a nightmare. Officially, the Norwegian Embassy would take the responsibility for the protocol issues. However, practical issues were a task for the SLMM. There was usually significant brainstorming to find adequate logistical and security solutions. Both the GOSL and the LTTE made the transit of the LTTE delegation even more difficult with their inflexibility. This was in sharp contrast to what had been offered by GOSL in the early years of the CFA, when it had been relatively easy to arrange the transit of the LTTE. In those days, the LTTE delegation was simply picked up by helicopter at the big central sports ground in Kilinochchi and via Vavuniya would be flown to the international airport at Katunayaka where there would be a VIP holding room made available for the group. The LTTE travellers would be escorted by SLMM members and a representative of the Norwegian Embassy at all times.

In June 2006, there were a number of problems related to the Norway trip that summed up the level of distrust between the parties at this stage. First, the LTTE made very difficult demands and would not consider travelling otherwise than in what they called VIP arrangements with diplomatic privileges. Secondly, the LTTE was, as it appeared, taking this opportunity to settle some other travel arrangements of very important nature to them.

The whole issue of co-coordinating travelling for the LTTE also included making sure that they would not feel snubbed by GOSL and its guidelines. There were numerous side issues such as that of pride, standing and diplomatic parity demanded by the LTTE. That was of course an illusion. A delegation of the renowned fighting outfit of the Tamil Tigers would not be regarded as a normal group of diplomats, say in the VIP part of Dubai airport on a stop-over. However, trying to accommodate both parties, the SLMM did everything in its power to facilitate the trips. There had been previous episodes proving how difficult this could be. The meticulously planned sea transfer of eastern based LTTE commanders to the Vanni in April, which had failed completely, was a case in point.

Two months earlier, the LTTE had agreed to a second round of peace talks in Geneva. Following the election of the new President, there had been some ugly incidents in early 2006, but at peace talks in Geneva in late February, both parties seemed genuine in advocating a return to the complete cessation of hostilities. It appeared to be a tremendous positive shift at the time. The following weeks had been tense and incidents had piled up. However, there were no major incidents threatening further talks. Now most stakeholders felt that if the peace dialogue could be kept going the peace process could hopefully gather a new momentum. Hence, the facilitator and the SLMM thought a second round of talks at Geneva to be of invaluable importance.

The LTTE had agreed in principle to the renewed talks. However, the Tigers stated that they would have to hold a Central Committee meeting with all its main commanders in Kilinochchi prior to Geneva II, to define its current position. The eastern theatre was getting ever more volatile, so this was not an unreasonable demand in itself. However, there were, of course, caveats regarding this, as was usually the norm in the conflict. In order to hold this particular meeting, the LTTE explained that the SLMM would have to arrange for a number of high-ranking LTTE commanders in the eastern theatre to be transported from the LTTE-controlled pocket south of Trinco bay to Mullativu, the naval stronghold of the Sea Tigers on the eastern shores up in Vanni. The LTTE fighters had been effectively cut off from Vanni as the practice of troop transport at sea had broken down earlier.

Now, the LTTE fighters could only take the land route from the eastern region in order to reach Vanni in the north. There was evidence of such movements emerging every now and then, but the Tigers would have to cross GOSL controlled territory and pass numerous SLA camps on their way. Furthermore, the LTTE cadres would have to cross the much travelled A6 highway, which was tightly guarded by the SLA, especially on its busy Habarana – Trincomalee section. So making the trip from the Sampoor area up to Kilinochchi was an extremely risky business, a risk that the LTTE was not willing to expose their commanders of the highest ranks to.

Now the LTTE demanded that the SLMM should arrange for a ferry to pick up a number of LTTE cadres in Mullativu and set sails for their stronghold in Ilakkantai south of Trincomalee, where a number of the regional commanders would be picked up and taken via the eastern seaboard back up to Mullativu. The SLMM was to have a Naval Monitor placed on the ferry and further Naval Monitors on any escorting SLN vessels. Moreover, the SLN vessels were not to approach closely to the ferry, which would be escorted by Sea Tiger vessels.

On the actual day of the execution of this plan, numerous SLMM representatives including the Chief of Staff, were present, in the early hours of 15 April 2006 on the beach at Mullativu. It was a nice and sunny morning with only few scattered clouds faraway on the horizon dotting the clear blue sky. This would be a real test of what level of cooperation could be facilitated between the parties through the SLMM at a time where the CFA had suffered seriously in the last few months, not the least concerning activities at sea. It was to be a fairly complicated exercise, but the experienced Naval Monitors thought it should be able to work out well, if both the parties conducted themselves according to the guidelines drawn up by the SLMM.

In short the operation failed completely, mostly because of common distrust between the SLN and the Sea Tigers. As the ferry nervously navigated towards a predetermined holding point close to the shore, the SLN escort vessels stayed a few nautical miles away. However, the Sea Tigers were in breach of the agreed procedure as they were moving heavily armed vessels up and down the coast. The SLN complained to the SLMM naval monitors, who sought clarification from the shore and there was also a dispute on how the LTTE commanders should be transported to the ferry and by which vessels. The LTTE was told to take them to the ferry on unarmed fishing boats and the first batch sailed out to the ferry. Then the Sea Tiger boats started moving out from the beach and the SLN got very nervous and demanded that they return, which was communicated through the Naval Monitors. As the LTTE had complied, their leaders on the beach started getting nervous as well about the notion of sending high-ranking commanders on a ferry to be escorted solely by the SLN. They claimed that this was not a part of the agreement. However, the SLMM would never have arranged such a transport on their own without the escort of the SLN and that position was explained to the LTTE. In the end the LTTE aborted the sea transport.

The failed sea transport of the LTTE commanders would have dramatic consequences for the evolution of the conflict. In a rare glimpse of emotional anger, Mr. Tamilshelvan, the head of the LTTE's political wing, wrote an angry letter to the Norwegian Ambassador Mr. Hans Brattskar, in which Mr. Tamilshelvan condemned the actions of GOSL in disturbing the travels of the LTTE commanders. He further stated that since the commanders from the east had not been able to travel via sea to Kilinochchi to attend preparatory meetings before the all-important upcoming peace talks in Geneva, the LTTE would not be in a position to attend.

At this critical juncture in the conflict, with the CFA on the verge of total collapse, the cancellation of the Geneva II talks was a devastating blow to the whole peace process. The positive declarations of both parties at Geneva in February had indicated that peace could be negotiated between the two strongmen as had been prophesised by the LTTE leader following the inauguration of President Rajapakse. Now a golden opportunity at the negotiation table had been carelessly squandered.

The June meeting in Oslo did, however, materialise in the end but rendered very limited results. The LTTE delegation refused to meet with the GOSL delegation as it claimed that a delegation headed by Mr. Tamilshelvan, could only be matched by a GOSL delegation headed by a high-ranking cabinet minister, most appropriately by the Prime minister of Sri Lanka. The GOSL had no intention to accommodate such an insistent demand and most likely did not feel that much would be gained from a high-level encounter in the current phase of the conflict. The Norwegian facilitator, however, managed to extract from both delegations a continued commitment to the CFA, at least nominally.

# 23

## A New Situation on the Ground—Mawil Aaru

Following the suicide attack on Army Commander Fonseka at the end of April 2006, the security forces had evidently shifted their posture from that of general restraint to taking the war to the LTTE whenever they were provoked and given an opportunity to strike back, claiming retaliatory operations. After the incident at the SLA HQ in Colombo, the SLAF had flown bombing raids in the Trincomalee area and the SLA had delivered sustained multi-barrel artillery attacks on the LTTE-controlled areas east of Mutur. These massive attacks caused widespread damage to infrastructure and houses, which resulted in thousands of civilians fleeing the area to the more secure Sampoor area further east. There were full-fledged military battles fought sporadically on the ground with the SLA finding it tough to gain ground in the difficult jungle terrain. Some of the area was also heavily mined and the LTTE had had years to consolidate their defence localities. Nevertheless, the SLA now completely outnumbered the LTTE in the area and also had firepower at its disposal dwarfing that of the Tiger's, who had few other options but to stay loyal to their asymmetric warfare tactics trying to avoid large-scale infantry clashes in a concentrated area.

Nominally, there was still a ceasefire agreement in effect, and as the international community was keeping a watchful eye on the events in the east, an all-out offensive by the SLA was not expected yet. However, as the security situation in the whole area had deteriorated massively, it was difficult for the SLMM, the main provider of credible information to the diplomats in Colombo, to venture in to assess the scale and scope of the reoccurring military clashes. The LTTE claimed that the SLA was softening up the area with continuous artillery bombardment and frequently flying the much-feared air sorties that spread panic among the Tamil residents in the area from Mutur east to Sampoor. Many of them had originally arrived there years ago as Internally Displaced Persons, fleeing fighting further north. They had been living in a state of insecurity and desperate poverty ever since.

There had been a clear and disturbing trend of escalation in the violence in other parts of the north and the east. Even as discussions had taken place in Oslo with both parties attending, the bloodshed continued unabated in Sri Lanka. The LTTE was particularly angered by the increased attacks of the SLA's deep penetration units (DPU), often well within LTTE-held territory. The DPUs consisted of small groups of soldiers who infiltrated LTTE territory and set up ambushes, sometimes deep behind the demarcation lines. In such ambushes the favoured weapon of both the SLA and the LTTE was the Claymore mine, an extremely lethal device indeed. Claymore mines were controlled in the sense that they could be triggered by wires or detonated on command, spraying a hailstorm of deadly steal pellets into a certain direction away from the controller. The operation of the deep penetration units in the Vanni area was in essence the Sri Lanka Army applying guerilla tactics usually solely attributed to the LTTE. Ambulances had been destroyed in Claymore mine attacks on a number of occasions and in early June the LTTE blamed the SLA for an incident in the Batticaloa region in which a tractor carrying around twenty civilians was blown to pieces. It could have been a large landmine, controlled or not. That did not matter much for the victims and the LTTE which listed the dead as ten civilians, three of them children and five women. Moreover, a few days later, a particularly horrid massacre of a family of four close to Mannar caught widespread attention. The extremely brutal pictures from the scene of the massacre were published in the Tamil media, clearly showing two children hanged after their father and mother had been murdered and the latter raped. All initial findings pointed towards rogue elements of the Army being the perpetrators. The Tamil community was shocked and the LTTE went on to produce a particularly disturbing collage propaganda poster put on display by the A9 entrance to Kilinochchi depicting Sri Lanka President Rajapakse as holding the strings of the hanged children.

The LTTE was enraged and claimed that the security forces were openly and with impunity killing Tamil civilians in heinous targeted attacks. In talks with the SLMM, the Tamil Tigers had often prided themselves on taking the responsibility for the security of Tamils in LTTE-controlled areas. Now Tamils were being killed, apparently by security forces in GOSL controlled areas where the LTTE could not protect them. Knowing the logic of the LTTE, the SLMM had an unpleasant feeling that a strong LTTE response on the ground would be imminent.

On June 15, 2006, one of the most shocking incidents of that year occurred when a passenger bus packed with civilians was blown up in a Claymore blast close to Vavuniya. Over sixty Sinhalese passengers were killed and almost one hundred injured. This tragic massacre of civilians underscored the fact that the situation in Sri Lanka was spinning completely out of control. The LTTE denied any responsibility, few believed them. It constituted an inexcusable act of sheer terror against innocent civilians. The carnage on the A29, close to the village of Kepitigollewa, triggered a marked increase in the air campaign of the Sri Lanka Air Force which flew bombing attacks in Mullativu in retaliation at the same time as the Army stepped up its bombardment in the east.

Within the GOSL-controlled part of the southern Trinco bay area there had long been a lack of security due to tensions between ethnic groups mired in the intricate mix of the region. Hostilities and hatred among the different ethnicities went back for decades and violence could erupt at short notice with random assassinations and disappearances being common. Nevertheless, the government of Sri Lanka was trying to address the needs of most of the people in the area through several aid programmes. There was also considerable activity by INGOs, some of whom had arrived with their aid projects in the aftermath of the tsunami that had hit some of the townships in the Trinco area particularly hard. Foreign aid was important for both GOSL and the LTTE although both parties continued to view the foreign aid workers with some suspicion. The parties wanted considerable control over what was being achieved with the foreign aid and the LTTE as in the post-Tsunami year demanded to have a strong say in GOSL financed projects within LTTE-controlled areas. This audacious stance of the LTTE would now lead to a massive misjudgment on their part in trying clumsily to force the government's hand in a highly sensitive matter in Sri Lanka—water.

The system of parallel administrative structures meant that the LTTE expected and demanded aid for civilians from Colombo in areas which they controlled. The GOSL was well aware of the dire needs of settlements both within their controlled areas and of those under LTTE control. However, it was, of course, much more complicated to distribute aid and conduct reconstruction in areas where the LTTE effectively was in full control. The GOSL had proceeded on a number of projects in the area south of Mutur in order to facilitate irrigation and to construct and refurbish facilities enabling poor villagers better access to drinking water.

In late July, when the heat was scorching in the southern-most Trincomalee region and wells were starting to dry up, the water supply was crucial for the indigent local farmers. Later in the year the monsoon rains would replenish tanks and wells and with increased water supply, this particular issue would subside in importance. However, the SLMM in Trinco now learned that local Tamil villagers had blocked the sluice gates of the water reservoir at Mawil Aaru situated in the Verugal area south of Mutur. This was within LTTE-controlled area, but the water stream from the reservoir was needed by Sinhalese settlements on the other side of the demarcation line in GOSL-controlled area, where it normally flowed through an intricate system of canals. The LTTE claimed they had nothing to do with the action, that it was sparked by the Tamil villagers themselves, demanding that GOSL conduct projects for the improvement of drinking water in their villages. They claimed that the needs of Tamil settlements had been neglected as opposed to the multitude of projects carried out to increase access to drinking water in the Sinhalese settlements.

It seemed like a typical local case of friction between the two ethnicities, a case which in the past would have been addressed by the SLMM and most likely solved at a district level through the SLMM Trincomalee Local Monitoring Commission (LMC), constituted of leading citizens and a SLMM chairperson. Regrettably, the mechanism of the LMCs had broken down for all practical purposes at this stage of the CFA. Nevertheless, this at first glance seemed like a trivial low-level problem that could surely be solved by the intervention of the SLMM and the facilitator exerting some pressure on the LTTE to resolve it. But the LTTE was not forthcoming at first. The Tigers were still fuming about the decision of the EU to proscribe them as terrorists and had already demanded that the bulk of the SLMM monitors, those from the EU countries, Denmark, Finland and Sweden, should leave by the end of August. Hence, the usually constructive dialogue with the SLMM was at a low at this junction in time. Furthermore, the LTTE leader in Trincomalee, Mr. Elilan, and his superiors in Kilinochchi, probably completely miscalculated the outcome of this apparent blackmail through the withholding of water at Mawil Aaru. Few realised that the name of Mawil Aaru would soon become well known to most Sri Lankans and to the diplomatic corps in Colombo. Indeed, Mawil Aaru would be the name associated with, maybe, the most important turn of the tide in the protracted ethnic conflict in Sri Lanka.

The SLA under the command of the recuperating Lt.-General Fonseka jumped on this unexpected opportunity and so did the GOSL. The whole issue was immediately blown completely out of proportion in Colombo and the media there was screaming about a major humanitarian catastrophe in the making, due to the cynical LTTE move to deprive desperate Sinhalese settlements of water. As if on cue, the SLA military machine sprang into action and a full-blown war erupted in the Mutur area. The SLMM Head of Mission was deeply involved in finding a way to settle the dispute through peaceful means, but Army Commander Fonseka, who had so narrowly escaped with his life intact from the LTTE suicide attack earlier in the year, grabbed the initiative and held on to it. Here was the perfect excuse for teaching the Tigers a lesson, even if it would demand enormous sacrifices of the SLA's front soldiers.

In the following days all hell broke loose in the region. It was impossible for anyone to verify fully what was happening during the next two weeks. There was much guess work and collection of bits and pieces of information from various sources trapped inside the fighting zone. As the dust settled somewhat, the SLMM sought to draw up what had taken place in fairly broad terms. Initially, the armed forces of Sri Lanka bombarded the LTTE positions east of Mutur with all they could muster from land, from air and from sea and followed it up with launching a full infantry attack backed by tanks. Following early successes, the SLA was, however, as some had expected, beaten back. The LTTE had then launched a counter-attack which saw the Tigers successfully advancing over the old front-line positions and temporarily taking Mutur town. The Muslim population had already fled the fighting in panic. The Sri Lankan Navy infantry was also engaged in the battles at Mutur at some stages, but principally the Army bore the brunt of it. LTTE artillery made use of its strategically located positions on the southern shores of the entrance to Trinco bay north of Sampoor, from where their shells could just about reach the SLN Trincomalee naval base itself. The danger for the LTTE of using its artillery towards the naval base was that this would increase the risk of the heavy guns being spotted by new radar-based weapons system which could guide the SLA and the SLAF towards the artillery positions in order to destroy the hardware. This would seriously limit the LTTE firepower in the case of SLA trying to push into the Sampoor area. For the time being, the fighting was concentrated on the Mutur area and further south. After some days of fierce fighting the LTTE claimed they had voluntarily withdrawn from Mutur town to settle at their original positions or those that had been specified in the CFA more than four years earlier. Both sides had obviously taken horrendous casualties, but the figures presented by either side were routinely skewed completely so it was very difficult to estimate the total and actual death toll. Even though the LTTE was claiming that it had stood its ground firmly and resolutely, the LTTE leadership in Kilinochchi seemed a bit rattled by the determination of the SLA to resolve the Mawil Aaru affair by military means.

Even though the SLMM HOM had secured an arrangement for the opening of the sluice gates at Mawil Aaru as soon as the security situation allowed for him to go and monitor the event himself personally, the GOSL and SLA would not settle for such closure of this episode. The official line in Colombo now was that the government would not give in to blackmail by terrorists and that the Army would liberate the area within twenty-four hours. The intervention of the Special Envoy of Norway, Mr. Hanssen-Bauer, who had arrived in Sri Lanka, was to no avail. Army Commander Fonseka had been given the opportunity to unleash a war on the LTTE, which he must have hated immensely after the brutal and cold-blooded attempt on his life. He was obviously a very determined and gifted military man and now he ordered his troops to go on the offensive again, after the LTTE had retreated from Mutur. It was a deadly campaign through a dense jungle territory not lending itself well to conventional warfare. Nevertheless, what emerged in the fighting to take control of the sluice gates of Mawil Aaru was a Sri Lankan Army fighting with more determination against their battle-proven adversaries than had been expected. The LTTE was probably quite surprised by the ferocity of the SLA onslaught. The latest epic battles between the SLA and the LTTE had been fought before the CFA took effect and had seen the LTTE come out victorious as their fire power seemed to equal that of the SLA, but the determination of the Tamil Tiger fighters had appeared to tip the balance decisively in their favour. The SLA, in those years, had sometimes made the impression of a reluctant and demoralised force. Now it cast this image with venom.

During a lull in the fighting, Mr. Hanssen-Bauer met with Mr. Tamishelvan in Kilinochchi. At the meeting Mr. Tamilshelvan, promised that the sluice gates be opened for humanitarian reasons and as a goodwill gesture. This was obviously too little too late for the SLA. The SLMM sent a delegation headed by its HOM and reached Mawil Aaru after a cumbersome and extremely dangerous voyage through an area which had just witnessed the most substantial military battle in Sri Lanka for five years. Even though GOSL had been informed about the SLMM HOM's intent to reach Mawil Aaru and see that the LTTE kept its promise, artillery shells started to land in the vicinity of the delegation, with the SLMM party, the LTTE and locals running for cover. The LTTE would later state that the SLA had deliberately tried to wipe out the HOM of SLMM at Mawil Aaru, but GOSL would claim it had been an unfortunate result of a string of miscommunication at their end. The international community in Colombo was shocked by how close the SLA had come to killing the SLMM members, hapless guardians of a clearly defined ceasefire that both parties claimed they still respected, lying through their teeth.

The SLA Commander had stated boldly that his troops would take Mawil Aaru when the furious fighting had started and that he was clearly not going to renege on that commitment at any cost. So the SLA marched on and a few days after the SLMM shelling episode the SLA had indeed secured its control, not only over Mawil Aaru but also the whole of the Mutur east area. This was the most successful land campaign of the SLA in almost a decade, although a clear and gross violation of the CFA and one that was likely to put its entire existence in doubt. The success of the SLA was, as could be expected, wildly celebrated in the south. Lt.-General Sarath Fonseka had shown that he was now commanding a formidable army, prepared to suffer enormous losses of men in order to fulfil its strategic objectives. The LTTE, on the other hand, was stunned by its momentous defeat. It would soon lead to further disasters for the Tigers, both in the north and the east.

One of the most appalling occurrences in the lead up to a full resumption of war in Sri Lanka was uncovered shortly after the fighting in Mutur had stopped. Seventeen aid workers of the French INGO "Action Contre la Faim" (ACF) had been found dead within the aid agency's compound in Mutur. Most of them, who were Tamils apart from one Muslim, had been shot execution style in the head at close range. They were wearing ACF t-shirts which further should have identified them apart from their presence at the ACF office. It was a ghastly and horrible act that had taken place in Mutur, and for once it was widely reported in international media.

The execution of the ACF aid workers was a difficult matter for the SLMM, both parties blamed each other for the murders and both parties had been in control of the town periodically in the last days. After the SLA took full control of Mutur, the SLMM was barred from entering the town to inspect the ACF compound and enquire into the massacre, citing "security reasons". The Head of the SLMM pointed out that the SLMM was held back, even as news reporters were given guided tours of the much more dangerous Mutur east area, which the GOSL proudly put on display for the media, having grabbed it by force from the LTTE a few days before. The Swedish Major-General Ulf Henricsson had arrived in Sri Lanka in the spring to head the SLMM. He had taken over from Head of Mission Hagrup Haukland of Norway who had served the SLMM for years and had been its Chief of Staff in the initial years and its embodiment. In those days the SLMM HOM had enjoyed a commanding authority in Sri Lanka as the guardian of the CFA. However, in the short spell of the new SLMM HOM Mr. Henricsson's time in Sri Lanka, the CFA had unravelled almost completely and there was little he or the rest of the SLMM could do to urge the parties down from the brink of all-out war.

Mr. Henricsson had not shied away from criticising both parties repeatedly for their lack of commitment to the CFA. He had been the most public of all SLMM HOM's, and had just narrowly escaped alive at Mawil Aaru having to scramble for safety away from SLA shells. Mr. Henricsson would have to leave Sri Lanka at the end of the month as he was from Sweden and LTTE had reiterated that all SLMM personnel from EU countries must leave the mission before 1 September, as the Tigers would withdraw their security guarantees at that time. So, in a sense, diplomatically speaking, Mr. Henricsson had little to lose as he went public on the execution of the ACF workers just before his departure from the island. The outgoing SLMM HOM, after thorough findings and interviews with stakeholders in the area, representatives of other organisations and well-informed locals ruled that the Sri Lankan military was responsible for the massacre. SLMM was convinced, following its inquiries, that there could not have been any other armed group than those of the security forces behind this evil deed, which was also termed to be one of the most serious recent crimes against humanitarian aid workers worldwide. This was a harsh and blunt statement which did not go well down with GOSL. Colombo would establish several investigative committees and groups, including foreign rule of law dignitaries, to try to rebuke the SLMM verdict. The dignitaries would later complain that their work had been systematically hampered and these findings would not render any final judicial verdict on the case. The SLMM sting towards GOSL on the ACF murders was somewhat levelled off by including in the ruling the explicit blame on the LTTE for the devastating attack on the passenger bus near Kepitigollewa, which had caused horrendous civilian casualties.

Although the relationship between the SLMM and the GOSL became somewhat strained following the dramatic events in Mutur, the mood in Colombo was optimistic and buoyant. The GOSL took extreme dislike in being criticised internationally for its dismal record on human rights issues, but the military victory sparked by the Mawil Aaru affair was far more important than worrying about what was being written in the international media on the human rights situation in Sri Lanka. Fonseka's SLA would march onto the east and south of Trinco bay and eradicate pockets of LTTE resistance until it had taken complete control of Sampoor. This led to massive movements of tens of thousands of Tamils fleeing the incoming security forces and joining the LTTE in a retreat along the coast to the south in the direction of Vakarai. In the next few months, the priority for the SLA would be to consolidate its hold on the region south of Trinco Bay and to evaluate when a push to the south would be viable. For the first time in a decade or so, the security forces of Sri Lanka held a firm grip on all of the Trinco Bay area. The LTTE now only controlled a stretch of land and a short coastline wedged between Trincomalee and Batticaloa. The whole campaign had been a triumph for those who opposed a negotiated settlement with the Tamil Tigers.

# 24

# A Desperate Grab for Jaffna

Jaffna was very densely populated and it was difficult to determine where Jaffna town ended and where the small adjoining villages started. The western part of the peninsula, where most of the Tamils lived, looked practically the same, very flat with thick vegetation and few proper landmarks. It was in essence a perfect place for staging ambushes and slipping away into the darkness of the bush. Therefore this was a very difficult area to control for the security forces, especially for soldiers who came from the south of Sri Lanka and were unfamiliar with road signs in Tamil. For many years, there were regular occurrences of low-level incidents, abductions, assassinations and harassment of politicians who favoured a political dialogue with the Sinhalese establishment in the south rather than an armed conflict. In such an environment, it was difficult to command soldiers who had to fear for their lives on patrols at random points and junctions within the town proper and in remote corners of the peninsula. Jaffna's famed university was packed with youngsters, who might or might not be partaking in armed assaults on the police and the SLA. The security forces were fighting an enemy that did not wear uniform and melted into the environment with the ease of a chameleon. It was logical, if regrettable, that sometimes elements of the security forces would lose their nerve following attacks on themselves. This was also an evident sign of their lack of professionalism and discipline. To the grief of the inhabitants of Jaffna, deplorable incidents of revenge were a regular feature of the intrinsic distrust between the security forces and the whole community. In 1981, the famed Jaffna library, a beautiful colonial building, was burnt down, allegedly by soldiers and police officers gone berserk with anger after attacks by local paramilitaries which had cost a number of lives. In 1983, the cold-blooded killing of thirteen service men in an ambush by the LTTE sparked a full-fledged armed conflict that would last for a quarter of a century.

At times, the LTTE had claimed almost full control of Jaffna, which the Tamil Tigers considered the ancient Tamil heartland. During the first half of the nineties the LTTE had gone from strength to strength tightening its semi-official grip on Jaffna. In 1987, GOSL had signed an infamous and in Sri Lanka widely detested accord with India, which resulted in the stationing of the massive Indian Peace-Keeping Force (IPKF) in Jaffna and Vanni. The Indians, who had ironically trained the LTTE in the first place, were soon seen as arrogant and insensitive intruders by both the LTTE and GOSL. In the following years, Mr. Pirapaharan, the LTTE leader, ever nurturing his paranoia and overt megalomania, decided that the presence of the IPKF was no longer helpful. This view was apparently shared by GOSL in Colombo as both adversaries in the ethnic conflict felt their status undermined by the IPKF presence. Years later, the fantastic stories still circulated in Jaffna, describing how the GOSL had secretly provided the LTTE with arms which the Tigers used to attack the bewildered IPKF. The huge Indian contingent had thought one of its core missions was to protect the Tamils from the Sri Lankan security forces. In 1990, the IPKF had had enough and withdrew from Sri Lanka after having suffered over a thousand casualties in ambushes and combat with the LTTE. It was indeed remarkable how determined the leader of the LTTE was in keeping India out of the conflict in Sri Lanka for good. In 1991, in a surprise attack that shocked the whole world, India's young and dynamic Rajiv Gandhi, who had taken over at the helm of the political family dynasty and had already served as Prime Minister, was brutally murdered at a campaign rally in Tamil Nadu. He had been killed by a young female suicide-bomber in a fashion that bore all the hallmarks of the LTTE. The IPKF debacle in Jaffna and Vanni and the murder of Mr. Gandhi resulted in India's hands-off stance towards the ethnic conflict in Sri Lanka, even though local politicians in Tamil Nadu would continue to support the LTTE struggle.

After the ascent of Mrs. Chandrika Kumaratunga to the Sri Lanka Presidency in 1994, the GOSL had tried to engage in a dialogue with the LTTE in order to find some means to negotiate an end to the armed conflict. However, the LTTE was far from being a simple organisation to negotiate with and in the end Colombo lost its patience. In 1996, a massive military campaign was launched by the SLA in order to bring Jaffna under government control. Troops were redeployed towards the combat zones in the north in order to crush the LTTE. The SLA had increased its firepower considerably by acquiring brutally efficient heavy artillery which was used to pound the LTTE defenses into Jaffna. The Tigers stood no chance in such an encounter of conventional warfare and made a very adept strategic decision in shifting out of Jaffna under the onslaught and migrating some of its most hardened fighting formations instead to the east. Later in the year, as the SLA had brought Jaffna under full government control, the LTTE in turn had wrested control over large areas of land in the Trincomalee and Batticaloa regions in eastern Sri Lanka.

Although the LTTE smarted from the loss of Jaffna, there was little they could do about it for the next few years. However, at the turn of the century, the LTTE seemed to have grown enormously in strength and launched a renewed war on the SLA, dubbed Eelam War III. In 2000, in a spectacular offensive, the LTTE managed to overrun the biggest military complex held by the SLA in the north at Elephant Pass, the narrow strategic entry point into Jaffna peninsula. The LTTE pushed further north and towards Jaffna town, but were eventually halted at Muhamalai on the main road and at Nagarkovil on the only alternative land road up the peninsula. Although both sides were dug deep in at the FDL on either side, there was a very real danger for the GOSL that the LTTE would be able to push into Jaffna, which could result in a horrendous blood bath for either side, as the SLA was not only controlling Jaffna but also, in a worst case scenario, trapped with thousands of soldiers who would not be able to retreat from an onslaught. This was the delicate stalemate that had now been in effect for six years.

The CFA calmed the extremely tense situation regarding both the Army defense line at Muhamalai and the overall situation in GOSL-controlled Jaffna. There were numerous complaints by the LTTE on modalities of the CFA, especially regarding the so-called High Security Zones (HSZ), which had been established at the perimeters of key military installations, mostly by establishing generous buffer zones for the armed forces. One of the main concerns of the CFA was to bring back normalcy to previous areas of high tension between the parties and this called for the SLA evacuating official installations such as schools and administrative buildings where they had set up Army camps. In the case of Jaffna, however, so densely populated and so prone to covert ambushes and attacks on the security forces, Colombo would not give in and insisted on the continued presence of HSZs. This meant that unlike in many other parts of Sri Lanka, the commencement of the CFA would not automatically allow Internally Displaced Persons to return to their houses close to military camps. This was a bone of contention for the LTTE for years to come. Nevertheless, there would remain significant HSZs surrounding the Air Force Base at Palali, the Navy's northern command at Kankesanturai harbour and south of Jaffna town at Jaffna Lagoon of which the SLA controlled the northern shores and the LTTE the opposite side.

The fact that the CFA cemented the SLA's control over Jaffna for years was considered a serious calamity by the LTTE. However, the

CFA also clearly stated that the LTTE could operate politically in Jaffna, which meant that they could exert their unofficial control over the Tamil population. The LTTE was accepted by large segments of the population in Jaffna as the *de facto* ruler of Jaffna politically and in many socio-economic affairs, however there were others that loathed their use of force and intimidation and questioned their right to a monopoly in representation of the Tamils. The LTTE's only surviving paramilitary rival, the EPDP, enjoyed considerable support in Jaffna town and especially on the islets of the coast. However, it had been forced to disarm completely under the stipulations of the CFA. The few EPDP offices were now turned into heavily fortified bunker-like installations guarded by SLA sentries. The LTTE would nevertheless sometimes stage attacks on its rival organisation and it was only for the brave and the determined to continue their work for the EPDP.

The CFA completely shifted the atmosphere in Jaffna for the better. Economic activity increased massively after the opening of the A9. INGOs flocked to Jaffna to set up aid projects and the security situation improved markedly. Worshippers flocked to Hindu temples, some of which had been evacuated by the SLA in accordance with the CFA. At the large and imposing temple at the end of one of the main roads in Jaffna, to which it had given its name, one could even see the odd tourist taking photographs, a sight evoking reminiscence of better times long gone. The magnificent library was rebuilt and opened to the delight of the intellectual leaders of the community and the faculty of Jaffna University. Its gardens of luxuriance were neatly kept and from the newly painted balcony one had splendid view of the clock tower, the old Dutch fort and the undulating waves of the peaceful waters in the shallow bay. Shops popped up at street corners and a new lucrative housing and catering business emerged. There were some excellent guesthouses and inns established at Temple Road where the expatriates gathered at night to exchange information and gossip. It was even considered fairly safe to walk the short distance home from the pub in the night if not recommended for those faint of heart who disliked being accompanied by hoards of homeless and hostile dogs in the mosquito-plagued darkness.

As the CFA wore thin over the years, in the absence of any meaningful developments in peace talks, large-scale hostilities resumed and life in Jaffna changed for worse. Jaffna was ripe with speculation on an imminent onslaught by the LTTE and the security forces were on high alert. Draconic curfews had been in place for over a year and many INGOs had left the area, among them demining teams that had been so positively symbolic for the gains initially brought about by the CFA. Assassinations were on the increase, there were constant reports of disappearances and the SLA was accused by the local media of conducting itself in a manner of a foreign tyrant occupant force. To be sure, there were many who had to fear for their lives, informants for either side, bagging tiny sums for the upkeep of their families, having to take into account terrible reprisal if found out. The immensely feared white van squads were busy operating at night, and many a male Tamil would be dragged out of his hut or house in front of a panic-stricken wife, never to be seen again dead or alive. Conditions at the Jaffna prison were appalling where hundreds had sought "preventive" incarceration, preferring to spend their days and nights in badly sanitised cells, stinking of urine and rot, rather than risking discreet but lethal visits to their dwellings after dark.

In the immediate aftermath of the SLA advance in the Mutur area, in 2006, where the LTTE had lost control of a sizeable area of land, the Tigers launched their attack on Jaffna. LTTE commandos attacked the SLA FDL in Muhamalai whilst small groups of LTTE fighters landed in various places on the shores of the peninsula. There were many but conflicting reports on the nature of the LTTE attack, which the propaganda machine in Kilinochchi claimed was a defensive battle against an onslaught by the SLA. The SLMM had always based its reporting on interviews with the military leaders of both parties and other local stakeholders who often proved to be remarkably accurate sources of information. Furthermore, it was sometimes surprising how candid the military commanders would be in assessing the overall situation. Even so, one had to analyse the information on the backdrop of the clear and conflicting overall objectives of the parties to the CFA.

The picture that could be drawn up in the aftermath of the intense but short-lived LTTE attack on Jaffna was that of a strangely bungled operation, probably sparked by a notion of desperation in Kilinochchi after the debacle in the Trincomalee area.

At the FDL at Muhamalai it was reported that the LTTE operation had started after a group of female cadres had managed to get through no-mans land in a decoy passenger bus after which they had unveiled firearms and started attacking the guardsmen at the checkpoint. At the same time a forward party of LTTE commandos had attacked from the LTTE FDL from the south. A wave of LTTE fighters soon advanced to follow on joining in on this surprise attack. There had been penetration through the SLA lines, but little was known about how substantial the initial advance had been. Mortars were reported incoming from the south and artillery barrages could be well heard in Jaffna town, where rumours of an LTTE breakthrough at the frontline were circulating. The fact of the matter, though, was that following some intense hours of fighting, the LTTE advance had been soundly beaten back by the SLA. It was also reported that helicopter gunships had been involved in the SLA defense of Muhamalai and that these had been extremely efficient and formidable in repulsing the LTTE commandos. On that same morning, SLMM was alerted to reports stating that small groups of LTTE fighters had landed in various places on the beaches of Jaffna and on Kayts Island. They were also trashed by the security forces.

The whole LTTE operation was wide in scope but there appeared to be a surprising lack of punch in the assaults. This seemed out of character for the LTTE's usually fierce fighting capabilities. In essence, the spectacle seemed to depict a truly failed operation, which the SLA had managed to crush even when taken by surprise initially.

The outcome of the battle saw the Sri Lankan Army going on a counter-attack and gaining a foothold in the former no-man's land, effectively kicking the LTTE southwards a few hundred metres. Hence the SLA had taken the FDL positions of the LTTE and the *de facto* demarcation line had been pushed slightly to the south. This also meant the "border crossing" facilities were now squarely in the hands of the SLA and the LTTE would have to start digging fast to consolidate new trenches and improvised bunkers in order not to be pushed even further down into Vanni.

In practical terms, the ill-fated LTTE grab for Jaffna would have very concrete logistical and tactical consequences. The LTTE had lost most of the infrastructure needed for inspecting vehicles and people and conducting "duty clearance" of goods brought by lorries. Moreover, following the attack, the SLA closed down the crossing point into Jaffna indefinitely. The A9 link from Vanni into Jaffna had been so important tactically and logistically for the LTTE as it was the only link to the Tamil heartland from which they were seeking their support and the credibility for their armed struggle. The opening of the A9 had been the very backbone of the CFA and its most important achievement, having been closed for the best part of a decade prior to the Norwegian facilitated peace efforts. Now it had been closed down, perhaps for good, and the LTTE seemed entirely to blame.

The LTTE would later on quietly deplore the fact that they had not committed more resources into the attack. They claimed that at one stage in the battle they had been very close to breaking decisively through the SLA defense formations. However, the disparity in fire-power had clinched the battle for the SLA and apparently the LTTE did no longer possess surface-to-air-missile capability to take down the helicopter gunships. This could have been the decisive factor for the defeat. The LTTE would at times talk frankly about military clashes, but this time they would stop short of admitting to what seemed there for all to conclude—that the desperate grab for Jaffna amounted to a military debacle.

A further conclusion could perhaps also be drawn from the battle for Jaffna. It might be inferred that the LTTE was simply running out of either men or firepower to launch ground offensives and engage into conventional battles with the SLA, even on such a narrow and limited fighting ground. The SLA would surely draw its own conclusions from the battle and, maybe, contemplate putting the LTTE further to the test.

# 25

## A Fine Diplomatic Effort—a Final Rendezvous in Geneva

After the dramatic events of August 2006, a lull of battle fatigue seemed to have set in and the fighting subsided temporarily during September. It was also a time for both parties to reflect upon the new situation that had emerged after the dust had settled somewhat. It was clear for all to see that there had been a dramatic shift in the situation on the ground, by far the biggest shift since the commencement of the CFA in February 2002. In broad and general terms, the CFA had functioned better than even the greatest optimists had dared to hope, for four and a half years. Maybe, even to such an extent that it had become a nuisance to the trigger happy on both sides of the conflict. The CFA would officially continue to be in force, but after the events of August 2006, it would pertain to a completely different situation. The preceding years of hope for a negotiated peace settlement and of relative calm, without major fighting on the ground, seemed to be a thing of the past. For many an observer in Sri Lanka, the CFA was in fact dead and buried.

The LTTE had made a colossal tactical blunder in the Mawil Aaru affair. At times the tactics of the Tigers would take the SLMM and other international observers with complete surprise, not to speak of the GOSL that sometimes appeared stunned by the strange logic of some of the LTTE's actions. Usually, after a thorough analysis of the motives and goals of the Tamil Tigers, be they short term or strategic, a certain logic would appear. Although sometimes such analysis was based on a lot of guess work, also depending on how candid the LTTE leadership would be towards the SLMM liaison officers in Kilinochchi. At times there would be preciously little coming from that end. Such was the case with Mawil Aaru.

In factual terms, the immensely strategic region south of Trinco bay had been overrun by the SLA with the security forces regaining full control of the whole access routes to Trinco harbour and eliminating the menacing artillery positions of the LTTE north of Sampoor at Foul Point. Furthermore, the SLA was now in a position to start chasing the LTTE down the coast line towards Batticaloa, hence potentially denying the LTTE access to the whole eastern seaboard, where the Sea Tigers had run rampant for years and been a serious threat to the SLN eastern command in Trinco.

In the North the A9 was squarely closed, with 600,000 Tamils in Jaffna having to depend on the sea corridor for essentials such as food staples and fuel. This would moreover present GOSL with a massive logistical problem in the face of international criticism of the humanitarian situation for the local population. The inhabitants of Jaffna were at times subjected to harsh curfews and lingering harassment by the 40.000-strong security forces which the LTTE labelled an occupation force in the Tamil heartland. Nobody knew when the A9 would be reopened. Recent history was not reassuring, the highway had been closed for over a decade before the CFA took effect.

The Norwegian facilitator had negotiated the CFA with both parties as joint owners of the ceasefire and the SLMM monitoring it, with the co-chairs exerting diplomatic pressure on both sides to find ways to reach a negotiated settlement. However, recently, on the apparent behest of the US, the EU had proscribed the LTTE as a terrorist organisation, cutting the Tigers almost completely out of the diplomatic loop. Judging by recent events on the ground this had obviously proved disastrous. Hence, in the wake of the EU decision, one party, the LTTE felt itself scorned in its quest as the champion for Tamil rights and became dangerously isolated from the outside world. Within the GOSL, the supporters of a "military solution" to the conflict were gaining confidence and more moderate tones were gradually being silenced.

A return to peace talks seemed remote.

However, the Norwegian facilitator had been busy behind the scenes. A flurry of diplomatic meetings had taken place in Colombo and even the US had apparently applied significant pressure on the President, with its classic carrot-and-stick approach. Japan and Norway, as usual, could wield some leverage with a hint towards even more generous funding of development projects which was tempting for an administration amassing an ever growing fiscal deficit in an environment of a falling Rupee and constantly increasing inflation. Furthermore, the EU would have to re-evaluate the whole situation from a diplomatic perspective. As the proscription issue had completely alienated the LTTE and appeared to have given GOSL an unconditional backing in the conflict, now was a time for the Europeans to make a reverse shift and join, however subtle, in putting some pressure on the GOSL.

As the diplomatic activities were just that, quiet and efficient meetings and talks with a plethora of GOSL dignitaries, the media and hence the public were not completely aware of how persistent this latest initiative of the international community was. However, there was notice made of the fact that the President agreed to a joint meeting with the four Ambassadors of the co-chairs early in October. Nevertheless, given the ferocity of the recent clashes on the ground many observers and not the least the public were taken with surprise as the facilitator announced that the parties had agreed to a round of fresh peace talks in Geneva on the 28-29 of October. The press release announcing the new round of peace talks was issued by the

Norwegian Government on 10 October 2006, with Erik Solheim thanking Switzerland for hosting the talks. A sigh of relief could almost be heard in the country, however, there were also powerful elements within Sri Lanka that would not be overly enthusiastic about this news. Their response would be extremely swift.

26

# A Dismal Battle in Muhamalai

Just before dawn on 11 October 2006, massive fighting started at the frontline in Muhamalai where the Sri Lanka Army and LTTE had been in a stalemate at the narrow gateway between Jaffna peninsula and Vanni. The SLA had started a major offensive to the south, just a few hours after the breaking news of an agreement for fresh peace talks in Geneva later in the month. Even for Sri Lankan standards, this was surely the most grotesque of all possible responses to the renewed diplomatic efforts of the international community. The highest military command seemed to be squarely conveying contempt for the latest peace making efforts.

The battle itself would result in a terrible bloodshed. The October tragedy on the Muhamalai killing fields would arguably become the single most deadly military clash globally in 2006. Astonishingly, it would only generate a ripple in the waters of the international media. Apparently, the outside world did not take much notice of hundreds of young soldiers being wiped out within a day's fighting in remote Sri Lanka.

In the preceding days of the Muhamalai offensive, the SLA had been busy moving troops and artillery and the LTTE had warned the SLMM that something of a major nature was in the making. A few days earlier, the LTTE claimed they had repulsed a SLA reconnaissance unit and killed five, well within no-mans' land, close to the LTTE side of the forward defense location. This was impossible to verify for the SLMM as the monitors had neither the protection equipment nor the means to venture into the frontline. When the shelling started on the morning of the battle, however, the massive impacts from the array of heavy artillery fire from the Multiple Barrel Rocket Launchers used by the SLA could be clearly heard at the SLMM office in Kilinochchi, with windows rattling madly before the break of dawn. The SLMM monitors in Kili were not equipped to monitor a combat situation at first hand and had been restricted in their movements by the SLMM HQ in Colombo, so the principal information of what was unfolding came from the LTTE. They claimed that the SLA had moved infantry ground troops across the frontline, pouring hundreds of soldiers into the battle zone, supported by tanks, and that heavy fighting was ongoing deep inside LTTE controlled territory. Apparently the SLA had opted for a two-pronged tactic proceeding with waves of soldiers at two entry points trying to gain ground and hold it well within the LTTE defence line. The LTTE often insisted that they resorted to a tactical withdrawal when they were hit especially hard by a concentrated effort of the SLA. These were the widely recognised tactics of asymmetric warfare with a fully trained conventional army on one side and a guerilla fighting formation on the other side. Thus, the LTTE would drop back initially. However, as the battle raged on, the SLA began suffering horrible casualties as the government soldiers got stuck in the difficult terrain, littered with landmines and barbed wire. As would be credibly verified later, the LTTE managed to push forward on one of the flanks, circumventing the bulk of the SLA intrusion and shut down one of the two gateways into the combat zone, virtually trapping hundreds of the SLA soldiers. As the battle raged on, the tanks were destroyed by the LTTE and the SLA offensive would first ground to a halt and then be beaten into a retreat towards the remaining gateway under a lethal barrage. LTTE snipers would pick out scores of the badly covered SLA soldiers desperately trying to make their way back to safety, resulting in a ghastly bloodbath before the fighting was over.

In the silence after this devastating and disastrous offensive by the SLA, a picture of horror became apparent. Fallen combatants were littered all over the ground riddled with bullets, most of them SLA soldiers. This was an incredibly futile sacrifice of life in Sri Lanka, the worst since the commencement of the CFA, which was left in tatters, apparently hardly worth the paper it was written on.

Both the SLA and the LTTE routinely overstated enemy casualties following combat and downplayed their own losses. However, this time there was no room for interpretation as the LTTE went on to stage a morbid display of dead enemy corpses in order to manifest to the outside world their fighting capability. The battle had indeed amounted to an apocalypse for the SLA.

The LTTE officially claimed they had killed over 200 SLA soldiers. This was hard to deny by the SLA, as the day after a staggering 74 dead SLA bodies were put on display in the sporting ground of Kilinochchi town. These soldiers had obviously been killed so deep within LTTE controlled territory that the Tigers had felt secure enough to collect their remains without being in range from the other side, which after the battle would have been in deep shock following the disastrous campaign. The horrid and unnerving sight of such a number of decomposing bodies being put on display for propaganda reasons underscored to which means the Tigers would resort to defend the territory they controlled. It was a stark reminder of the reality in which both parties had found themselves before the ceasefire agreement took hold.

It was impossible to tell how many other bodies were left to rot in the scorching heat of the tropical sun in the following days, but arguably, they would not conceivably be fewer, given the nature of the battle. Furthermore, the battleground would be left with scattered mines and a huge amount of unexploded ordnance, making it an impossible task to fully clear the terrain for months to come. Based on the circumstances and facts available, the LTTE claims on the casualty figures for the SLA seemed credible.

Questions would arise bountiful after this amazing military defeat of the SLA in the northern front. Why had the SLA engaged in a massive offensive, bearing resemblance to the futile military tactics of WWI in Flanders Field? Who had ordered the biggest and most ambitious SLA assault on the LTTE since the commencement of the CFA, only a night after the news had broken that GOSL and LTTE were scheduled to conduct peace talks in Geneva later in the month? Was it a completely bungled attempt to come to the peace talks with a strong hand following a massive show of force? Had the military high command properly explained the dimensions of this attack and coordinated it with the President, who was the Commander-in-Chief of the armed forces? Had the President given his consent or had the Army Chief Lieutenant-General Fonseka acted on his own initiative?

As could have been expected, no clear and concise answers to these imperative questions would ever emerge.

In the aftermath of the epic battle, a hefty discussion took place within the GOSL establishment in Colombo. There would be rumours that the doomed debacle would lead to Lt.-General Fonseka being relieved of his command, but it did not materialise. The fact that the international media never really covered this appalling and tragic event gave the GOSL and the SLA breathing space to lick its wounds and downplay the whole affair. Remarkably, the most insistent and condemning criticism of the apocalypse in the north was published in the Sri Lanka daily *The Island*, the most hardline nationalistic newspaper, famed for its close ties to, and admiration of, the armed forces. Weeks after this madness had been allowed to happen, the daily would not let go and it reported from a briefing given by Lt.-General Fonseka, on a courtesy visit with high military counterparts in Washington, that it was now unofficially acknowledged that the SLA had lost as many as three hundred soldiers in the hours of fighting on 11 October. Months later, in discreet talks in Jaffna, the local commanders would go even further and quietly, with distinct remorse, reveal that up to four hundred coffins had been transported to the south in the aftermath of the failed operation.

Tactically, the Muhamalai offensive had cost the SLA dearly. There would emerge an unofficial consensus within GOSL that the LTTE could not be broken, with conventional means at the northern front, under current circumstances. It appeared evident as well that the strangely weak and apparently uncoordinated attack of the LTTE on the SLA forward defence localities in August that led to the closure of A9, had not reflected its true fighting capability. That in return begged the question of the motives and tactics of the LTTE during that futile assault, so soundly crushed by the SLA. In short, the high command of the SLA had gotten the signals wrong.

To be sure, there would have to be some lessons learned even though there were no personal consequences apparently for the most seniour officers of the Army. The offensive had been commenced at the end of the dry season, when the ground would presumably be the most firm, hence most inviting for mechanised infantry, supported by tanks. Yet it had failed. The monsoon season was imminent, which would turn fields into marshes and was generally considered giving the LTTE an advantage in the asymmetric warfare. The most logical conclusion to this would probably be to concentrate SLA offensive efforts in a wider front, and further away from Kilinochchi, the main seat of the LTTE, as the LTTE would presumably be more vulnerable where it had to cover a broader frontline. In strategic terms, it would be tempting to simply deduct that a decisive push into the Vanni would have to come from the south at multiple theatres, say, from Vavuniay and Mannar, at the same time. But that remained to be seen.

27

# The A9 Stays Closed

The SLA offensive in Muhamalai had not come as any surprise to the LTTE. Hence they were relatively well prepared. In fact the LTTE had warned vehemently against a large-scale offensive by the SLA in the making in the days leading up to the battle. A few days earlier the LTTE had both addressed its concerns to the Norwegian facilitator and the SLMM. The LTTE had claimed that the SLA had moved hundreds of soldiers towards Muhamalai and that transports of military hardware had also been observed in the area. The LTTE further demanded that SLMM be given proper access to the SLA FDL to verify that a military build-up had taken place. Mr. Tamilshelvan took urgent contact with the SLMM HOM and even demanded that a message be drafted to be handed over directly to Sri Lankan President Mr. Rajapakse. The Tigers also threatened in no uncertain terms that they would take retaliatory action if the SLA would indeed launch their premeditated attack. Even though the LTTE had repulsed the SLA soundly in Muhamalai, they would soon own up to their threats on striking back at the security forces in the south.

On 16 October, the LTTE launched a horrendous attack on the security forces. Dozens of buses transporting Sri Lankan Navy troops were gathered at a parking ground at a busy traffic junction in Habarana. Suddenly a lorry was driven into the cluster detonating its lethal cargo of explosives with devastating impact. Over three hundred sailors were believed to be gathered at the ground taking lunch on a transport break. Around one hundred were killed, most of them on the spot, others succumbing to their injuries on the way to hospitals. Another one hundred were injured, some of them severely. The buses had been on their way from Colombo up the A6 towards Trincomalee to relieve Navy personnel that was travelling in the opposite direction for leave. The meeting point in Habarana was well known, so security precautions had failed miserably in this terrible attack.

The LTTE did neither claim nor deny responsibility directly. However, an interview with their military spokesman Mr. Ilanthirayan or "Marshall", on TamilNet, all but formally confirmed the LTTE being behind the atrocity. He stated that the SLA had engaged in several offensive actions against the LTTE and Tamil civilians in recent weeks, either through artillery assaults or air attacks. In a response to those attacks far away from the forward defence localities of the LTTE, retaliatory strikes against military installations were accordingly legitimate. The suicide attack in Habarana and its accompanying statement from Kilinochchi was a bold and unmistakable message to the south that the LTTE would not hesitate to resort to the most devastating actions if it felt itself provoked by the security forces. It was also a very unhelpful message to the outside world.

Instead of managing to restrain its armed formations before the upcoming peace talks in Geneva both parties had launched spectacular offensive assaults resulting in the death of hundreds of combatants. The timing for these clashes could not have been worse.

The peace negotiations, or general discussions on the situation on the ground, that were conducted in Geneva at the end of October 2006, rendered no results. The LTTE had pushed its major point relentlessly; the A9 would have to be reopened before any other steps towards defusing the military situation could be taken. The GOSL delegation had apparently neither the authority nor the intention to undertake anything of the sort. That was in many ways an understandable stance. First, the A9 had been closed, up at the FDL in Muhamalai, because of an apparent tactical blunder of the Tigers. LTTE fighters seemed to have tried to take command of the SLA FDL in a covert operation that went badly wrong. Second, the transit of goods via the A9 to and from Jaffna had become a strategic financial issue for the Tigers which GOSL would no longer tolerate.

The Tigers had routinely collected taxes on goods transported to Jaffna and reserved the right to withhold part of the supplies rolling through their territory, including essentials such as food and fuel. International aid organisations had also supplied important goods and materials for the consolidation of the infrastructure and the health services, but could not replace the steady supply stream through Vanni driven by basic commercial interests. The GOSL insisted that most of the financing of the LTTE fighting machine was generated through illegal levies on the commercial companies operating the steady stream of lorries up to Jaffna and back. The hawks within the GOSL saw the closure of the A9 due to the LTTE attack in August 2006 as a fundamental own goal by the Tigers and would advocate a policy of strangling the LTTE financially by keeping the A9 shut. The downside to this would be the grim fact that now the Tamils of Jaffna Peninsula had been shut off from the rest of the island and other means would have to be found to expedite goods to the local population and the massive contingent of troops stationed there.

Perhaps this latest point could explain the feebleness of the Tiger attack in Muhamalai. It was almost as if they had ventured into this whole operation with great reluctance. The manpower for such an operation was simply not applied, raising numerous question marks for military strategists. What had been the real intention of the LTTE with the attack on the SLA in Jaffna? Could it be that it had been a decoy attack? It was not always easy to decipher the actions of the

LTTE in the battlefield and convert them into logic. However, the ineffectiveness of the assault gave food for thought and speculation. One likely explanation was that the LTTE had merely been testing the fighting power of the SLA and its response to a head on military attack on their FDL. Tactically that might make sense, but only barely, as the element of surprise, so priceless in warfare, had been eliminated. Another possible explanation might be of a more strategic and political nature. Following a surge in violence in Jaffna in the period from April to June, tough restrictions by the security forces, such as thoroughly monitored curfews, had brought the situation under control and the violence had subsided. Life in Jaffna had generally resumed some sort of normalcy over the years in which the CFA brought back economic activity and an open lifeline to the south both for the transport of commercial goods and people. Maybe, life had been getting to close to normal for the liking of the LTTE.

Thus, the LTTE might have felt an erosion of support within the Jaffna population and had determined that temporary isolation of the Tamils being controlled by the Sinhalese-dominated SLA would turn the tides. The most likely reason for the poorly executed grab for Jaffna was the desperation felt by the LTTE and the anger, having lost their immensely strategic stronghold in the whole southern Trincomalee region. That was a heavy blow and also begged the question of the real current strength of the LTTE, two years after having lost its recruitment base in the east due to the Karuna split. Even though the LTTE tried to keep its cool in front of the SLMM liaison officers, they could be very erratic and rash in their decision-making. The prospects of losing their Trinco base, in an outright military battle, after having lost most control in the east could well conceivably have driven them to the conclusion that only a lucky punch towards seizing control of Jaffna could bring them back to a position where they would still command respect from GOSL in further negotiations for a peaceful settlement of the conflict.

At the end of 2006 the situation was such that the A9 would probably not be opened unless the SLA would score an outright military victory in the area and push the LTTE deep into the jungle. To be sure, the permanent closure of the A9 crossing point to Jaffna indicated to many observers that the CFA had become meaningless. One of the most outspoken officials of the GOSL, acting Defence Secretary Gothobaya Rajapakse and younger brother of the President, told foreign correspondents as much at a closed meeting in Colombo in the beginning of 2007. The President and his closest circle of advisors seemed ever more tempted to abrogate the CFA. GOSL, however, still apparently hesitated due to the impact such a move would have on Sri Lanka's standing in the international community.

28

# The Poonaryn Incident

As A9 had been closed for several months, the general situation for the population in Jaffna had deteriorated considerably. Essential supplies such as rice and fuel had to be taken by ship instead of lorries. However, frequent skirmishes between the SLN and the Sea Tigers in the waters off Mullativu would complicate the transport of goods and people at sea. Mullativu was an enormously important strategic point for the LTTE, home to the principal striking force of the Sea Tigers and conveniently located on Sri Lanka's north-eastern coast, ideally placed to expedite boats to intercept vessels sailing from the only major port in Jaffna, Kankesanturai (KKS), controlled by the Navy, and to Trincomalee and back.

Following the closure of A9, basic staples had become scarce, the price level had shot up for food and other goods and the general atmosphere in Jaffna had deteriorated substantially as the Jaffna Tamils now perceived themselves as trapped in their peninsula with an Sinhalese occupation force in their midst. The Tamil press and the political machine of the LTTE were portraying the situation in Jaffna as critical with the supply crisis leading to a sharp deterioration in living standards among the Tamil population in Jaffna peninsula.

GOSL was trying to alleviate fears of Jaffna sinking into a state of poverty and hunger and was determined to ship fundamental supplies through its government agencies.

The LTTE was successful in a paradoxical campaign, severely hampering the flow of goods at sea through frequent attacks on patrols in the waters of Mullativu. At the same time, the LTTE would point out the plight of the trapped population in Jaffna, where certain foodstuffs and fundamental goods such as fuel were getting scarce and the price level was rising dramatically. The LTTE's political unit with their Political Wing leader Mr. Tamilshelvan at the front would blame this deteriorating situation on the alleged total lack of flexibility of the GOSL on the A9 question. With the GOSL in a defensive stance towards the international community, SCOPP proposed to the SLMM HM in a meeting in November to convey a proposal to the LTTE leadership on opening an alternative road for goods and personnel transportation through Vanni, without opening the A9 crossing at the Muhamalai FDL.

The proposal was issued verbally at a routine meeting between the officials of SCOPP and the SLMM HM, which took place every week. As most minutes from the SCOPP meetings were now routinely leaked to the state-owned press organs, the proposal would be displayed prominently in the next morning's papers. However, there was some confusion on the proposal. The SLMM had apparently understood the proposal to entail the continued flow of lorries through the Omanthai crossing point following A9 up to Kilinochchi, taking a sharp turn to the left north of Kili with a new crossover into government-controlled Jaffna peninsula via the ferry point at Poonaryn. This proposal appeared as a graphic map in at least one leading newspaper the day after the meeting at SCOPP. Other news sources, however, mentioned a proposed opening of a land route further to the west. As the SLMM HQ tried to get a clarification from SCOPP, it was understood at their end that they were proposing the reopening of the immensely strategic A32 road that followed the coastline north of Mannar Island all the way up to Jaffna lagoon.

This seemed to be a peculiar proposal for several tactical and practical reasons. A glance at the map would lead one to be inclined thinking that the LTTE would never allow commercial traffic up this road. It would practically go through the most strategically important military positions they held in the area. Travellers on the A32 would pass directly by some of the most covert Sea Tiger bases in all of the northern theatre as the roadside was practically on the coast in the most sensitive area closest to the zone of separation between the SLA and the LTTE. Moreover, increased traffic along this road could also have a negative impact on the clandestine flow of contraband between Tamil Nadu in India and the Vanni. Furthermore, given the fact that long stretches of the road had been destroyed years ago in bitter fighting, it was indeed difficult to see the GOSL proposal as a viable alternative to the opening of the A9.

The incident that followed shortly at an inspection of Poonaryn would forcefully, in the literal sense, underscore the point that breaking the isolation of Jaffna via that ferry point would probably not be realistic in the current situation.

The SLMM had quite considerable obligations towards the parties to the CFA. Some were clearly formulated, others had been established informally during the years in which the CFA had functioned successfully. Conveying a message from SCOPP to LTTE or vice-versa was one of these obligations and usually carried out by the SLMM HOM if it was of high importance. Following fruitless and frankly disappointing peace talks in Geneva at the end of October, the CFA had never looked weaker and the SLMM was willing to act immediately if there be any chance of positive or at least defusing steps in the conflict. Hence the SLMM HOM, his Aide de Camp and a Kilinochchi-based SLMM liaison officer met with the LTTE leadership at the Peace Secretariat in Kili two days after the SCOPP meeting where they presented the GOSL proposal on the opening of the Mannar-Jaffna road.

In short, the LTTE was not impressed. It regarded the GOSL proposal as window-dressing for the co-chairs and the international community. The Tigers asked how it was to be expected that a ferry service could be established at Jaffna lagoon, which northern side was held by the SLA and proclaimed a High Security Zone, where no civilians were allowed to trespass. The Tigers also questioned how a ferry on the very shallow lagoon could accommodate large trucks filled with goods. There were no ferries around, and had not been there for ten years or so. The jetty was badly damaged and the former infrastructure had all but vanished at the ferry point. At later meetings with officials of SCOPP, it was evident that they had not realized that there were such fundamental problems with the proposal and some of their officials participating in meetings with SLMM did not fully understand what a High Security Zone was and its implied limitations to the transport of goods and people.

The LTTE were usually very polite but firm in their meetings with the SLMM at a seniour level. However, this time they did voice some angry dissent with the proposal and how SLMM had taken on its role in displaying it both to the LTTE and also responding to media enquiries on the feasibility of an alternative route to Jaffna. They obviously perceived the proposal to be a blunt attempt to shift focus from their demands for the reopening of the A9 crossing point at Muhamalai, and as such took it as a serious affront.

However, in order to convince the SLMM that the LTTE was not simply dismissing the proposal out of hand, but rather cited military technical reasons and a complete lack of infrastructure in Poonaryn, they proposed that they take the SLMM HOM to the jetty to see for himself straight after the meeting. It was a tempting offer on a beautiful day with partly clouded blue skies, an offer hard to refuse at the spur of the moment, but a very risky one that should probably have been turned down. But that was easy to say in hindsight.

Communications to Colombo from Kilinochchi were in many ways adequate if not perfect. At the SLMM office in Kili you could usually reach the SLMM HQ in Colombo via fixed line telephones, faxes could be sent as hard copy most of the time, if not always, and the email system was functioning remarkably well. There was no GSM, which probably was operationally sound, as GSM is usually relatively easily monitored. Notwithstanding the SLMM principle to engage with as great transparency towards both parties as possible, it was probably not operationally viable for the SLMM liaison officers in Kilinochchi to discuss their insight on such an open source. And then there were satellite phones for the special occasions where a message simply had to get through. The tricky thing with satellite phones that SLMM used were that the caller and the receiver have to be relatively static in their movements; you could neither reach someone driving in a car nor call from a moving vehicle.

The SLMM HQ was severely understaffed in the first two weeks of November in 2006, with actually only a handful of monitors around. During the transition from a 70-plus mission manned by Norway, Sweden, Finland, Denmark and Iceland to half that size with monitors only staffed by Norway and Iceland, the staff from those latter two countries had not been allowed to take proper leave during September and October. Now new faces had arrived and were deployed in the field offices, but many of the HQ Ops were away for a few days.

The SLMM Operations centre was a large open room with about ten work stations, nicely equipped with most recent IT and COMs capabilities and very accurate maps of the conflict areas courtesy of the SLA in the positive early days of the CFA. It was widely agreed within the SLMM top hierarchy that such maps would never have to be made available to it at the current time, so they were considered the treasure they justly were. Due to the severe personnel shortage, there were only two staffers present in the Ops Centre. Around half past eleven the Ops officer received a fax from the SLMM office in Kilinochchi. It was a message from the ADC, a following text should be forwarded to SCOPP in Colombo, giving notice that the SLMM HOM would go with his party and escorted by LTTE to inspect the jetty at Poonaryn. Expected time of arrival at Poonaryn was 1400 hours. It was a startling message, given the recent volatility at the northern front, but it was duly forwarded to SCOPP and also followed on via phone as the SLMM HQ tried to reach the SLMM travelling party in Kili for further details.

Two hours of trying to reach the SLMM HMs travelling party had not rendered any results, but suddenly there was a phone ringing in the SLMM HQ. It was the ADC on a satellite phone, in a squarely immobile situation, to say the least, speaking remarkably calmly in explaining his predicament. The SLMM HM with a group of officials from the LTTE Peace Secretariat were trapped at the Poonaryn Jetty by incoming SLA mortars fired from the other side of the lagoon. The explosions could be clearly heard in the background and the officer was scribbling the position of HM and his party down on a sheet of paper; *HOM at Poonaryn ferry, ADC—very close mortar attacks!* The SLMM monitors started phoning frantically. Although lists of GSM numbers of key military brass were at hand, it was difficult to find someone high enough in the chain of command to be able to authorise something swiftly. At SCOPP nobody seemed to have acted on the fax yet, and as contact was established with Dr. Kohona, the Secretary-General of SCOPP, he was obviously totally unaware of the travel notification and became very agitated and perplexed at the same time.

During this, up in Poonaryn, the SLA soldiers having the advantage of a clear sight over the lagoon towards the jetty were adjusting their mortars while shells were homing in on the SLMM group. There was only one viable option and that was to make a desperate run from the exposed position at the shore of the Lagoon. The reconnaissance group consisting of SLMM and LTTE officials was extremely lucky, managing to run to the cars and drive away, with the last shells landing so close that one vehicle left behind was blown off the road by air pressure. The SLMM HOM and Puleedevan, the head of the LTTE Peace Secretariat, got away with minor cut wounds. However, the incident was not over, as the SLA had the capability of calling in SLAF for air support in hot pursuit of the party. A minute later, the Chief Ops of SLAF had reached his Ops Centre, and the situation was explained. He was very forthcoming and promised to make sure that no aircraft would put the lives of the SLMM Poonaryn visitors in danger.

The SLMM was not a military mission, it was on paper a civilian monitoring mission. However, from the commencement of the mission, the management had tried to have a composition of one-third military background retired or active, one-third police officers and one-third civilians, many with special skills tailored to their positions within the SLMM. Female monitors were particularly valuable in the field and often excellent monitors, as the female population in the conflict areas sometimes was very reluctant to talk to male monitors. Nevertheless, it was important to bear in mind that the mission monitors were neither expected to monitor a war and war-like incidents, nor were they equipped to do so in material and vehicles. There were a number of close calls during the almost six years' tenure of the SLMM and CFA, but no casualties in the end which amounted to a miracle.

Poonaryn would be remembered as one of the closest calls and its significance was dramatically elevated as it involved for a second time a SLMM Head of Mission on the receiving end of Sri Lankan Army shells. The LTTE representatives, seasoned by years of military conflict, stayed remarkably calm during the incident and their photographer had the day of his life, coming away from Poonaryn with a vast array of digital pictures of the SLMM HM under fire at the devastated jetty, under conditions of a clear view over the lagoon. The incident begged both the question of security arrangements prior to such visits and also the rules of engagement now established for the SLA front soldiers. Apparently and despite a still existing formal ceasefire agreement, the rules of engagement for the SLA had gone back to the pre-CFA; shoot first—ask questions later. The same rules were more or less applied by the LTTE as well by now.

# 29

## An Irreversible Rift with SCOPP

News of the Poonaryn incident travelled extremely fast. It was soon on the wires widely reported in international media but splashing front page news in only two countries, Norway and Sri Lanka. In Sri Lanka, the GOSL-dominated media tended to downplay the whole incident at the same time as TamilNet had a field day with the exclusive digital photos taken by the LTTE during the visit and the shelling. The LTTE managed to make these photos available very rapidly and some of them appeared shortly after in Norwegian media.

In Norway the story would primarily be presented as a deliberate attempt by the Sri Lankan Army on the life of the SLMM head. Erik Solheim, who had been a special envoy of the Norway to Sri Lanka, and had played the most important role in securing the CFA, was called upon to comment on the incident. He had since moved on take on the post of Minister for International Development in the Norwegian Government, but to many media in Norway he was still the most important political authority on matters concerning Sri Lanka. It was obvious that Solheim was very quick to grasp what had taken place as soon as he had been properly informed. He would move to distance himself from the notion that had been published initially, which was that the SLA had deliberately targeted the HOM of the SLMM. Having travelled extensively in Sri Lanka and fully grasping the operational capability and limits of the Army, Solheim would draw the conclusion that this had in fact been an unfortunate incident involving the HOM nothing more and nothing less.

The fact that the presence of a well-marked white SLMM vehicle flying the SLMM flag at Poonaryn did not deter the SLA front line unit from immediately starting to launch mortar shells on to the old jetty point was quite revealing of how little was left of a ceasefire spirit at the demarcation lines. That was the underlying message to take away from Poonaryn. However much the CFA had been appreciated in the beginning, at the northern front a state of outright warfare prevailed.

GOSL saw the incident in a similar way as Solheim and went ballistic over the coverage in the foreign press and particularly that in the Norwagian media, which quite openly indicated that the SLA had sought to wipe out the SLMM HOM. SCOPP, immediately demanded a crisis meeting with HOM to clarify the issue. At the following meeting the atmosphere was markedly strained. The SLMM represented by its Chief of Staff conveyed the message to SCOPP that during an inspection trip to Poonaryn, undertaken as a result of the initiative of SCOPP to try to seek an alternative land route to Jaffna with goods, without resorting to opening the A9, the SLMM HOM had almost been killed by the SLA. The senior representative of GOSL at the meeting was Dr. Palitha Kohona, the head of SCOPP, a seasoned diplomatic hand, previously holding a high-ranking post at the UN in New York and a very close associate and advisor of the President.

Dr. Kohona did not take this lightly and remarkably for such a seasoned diplomat, completely lost his bearings and temper, jumping out of his seat and pointing agitatedly to the incident spot on a map on the wall, screaming that this was a warzone. That assessment was, of course, extremely revealing given the still nominally existing CFA. To be fair though, Dr. Kohona was, of course, right. The SLA was not a modern western army and lacked communications equipment. Informing SCOPP on a proposed trip by the SLMM HOM to the frontline with a few hours' notice was essentially meaningless. For such information to reach a forward unit of frontline SLA foot soldiers would take a day or two.

The relationship between the SLMM and SCOPP had sunk to an all-time low and would in reality never reach the necessary level of mutual trust again, in order for the CFA to have any chance of surviving. It was a grim fact that bode no good for the future.

In the past, the high-level meetings between SCOPP and SLMM, held weekly in Colombo, had been immensely valuable and useful in finding common ground and solutions to keep the CFA intact. As Dr. Kohona drifted into the camp of the hawks within GOSL, the meetings were relegated to a nuisance to both the SLMM and SCOPP, with rude and derogatory remarks on the conflict and the SLMM being the standard line of communication of the head of SCOPP. It was a shame as this completely undermined both the SLMM and the CFA, and most importantly destroyed the information exchange between the SCOPP and the LTTE, which SLMM had facilitated so well in the past.

There was another disturbing aspect to the meetings after that, relating to the security of the SLMM monitors in the field. A pattern of dissemination of information to the press emerged in late-2006. If Dr. Kohona was present at the SCOPP meetings, details of the discussions would be splashed in the state newspapers the day after. Usually, the minutes of the meetings were completely distorted, mostly in a way to ridicule the SLMM or question its sincerity. This routine leaking and twisting of sensitive meeting minutes resulted in the SLMM becoming extremely unpopular with the Sinhalese population who read and accepted this "news" in the state media at face value. The SLMM would become known as the "White Tigers" in the GOSL-owned press, which would stir up very negative emotions with the Sinhalese public. This would translate into an obvious security threat for individual SLMM staff, not the least in the capital Colombo, where the security assessment had been the most favourable for SLMM staff in the past. The donning of clearly marked SLMM shirts was quietly faded out at the SLMM HQ in Ward Place, Colombo. The monitors stationed in Colombo were told to be aware of their unpopular status and to avoid conversations on their purpose and mission, especially in restaurants and other public places.

# 30

## The Special Envoy Visit and the Targetting of the Defense Secretary

It was an ominous, deep and dark sound of an explosion that could be heard widely in downtown Colombo. From the SLMM point of view, the timing could not have been more bizarre. The SLMM Head of Mission had gathered his most seniour staff for a conference to be addressed by Jon Hanssen-Bauer, Norway's Special Envoy for Sri Lanka. The latter had just rushed into the meeting room on the top of the exclusive Cinnamon Garden's hotel resort as the suicide bomber detonated his Claymore mine two blocks away. The SLMM Heads of District stared at Mr. Hanssen-Bauer's astonished face and then everybody rushed to the window muttering something in disbelief.

On 1 December 2006, the LTTE almost succeeded in assassinating one of their most hated foes within the Sri Lanka administration. The target was Defense Secretary Gothabaya Rajapakse, among the most powerful men in Sri Lanka and younger brother to the President. It was an ugly picture that SLMM monitors saw when they rushed to the adjacent Cinnamon Gardens quarter. At the busy junction in one of Colombo's most travelled downtown arteries on

Dharmapala Mawatha road, a suicide bomber driving a three-wheeler autorickshaw had tried to get as close to the Defense Secretary's car as possible before detonating a massive explosive device. Mr. Gothabaya Rajapakse was stated to have been on the way to meet the President at nearby Temple Trees when he was targeted. He had been escorted by elite commandos who apparently had been able to squeeze their large Land Rover between the attacker and the armoured vehicle of the Defense Secretary. It was a sleek if unassuming grey BMW, but the Bavarians who built it had obviously known their craft well as it had withstood the impact from hundreds of steel pellets remarkably well. Defense Secretary Rajapakse, almost miraculously, escaped unscathed from the incident, with a minor cut wound. However, two of the commandos died on the spot and seventeen others were severely wounded, some of them uniformed escorts, others hapless passers-by. The body of the suicide attacker lay on the trunk of one of the many totally destroyed vehicles. The head had been completely blown off in the explosion.

The Defense Secretary was rushed to Temple Trees where he was embraced by an unusually emotional President. The whole dramatic incident and meeting of the Rajapakse brothers were shown over and over again on TV. The younger brother was a controversial figure in Sri Lanka who had been installed as a caretaker for his elder brother the President who formally also held the important portfolio of Minister of Defense and that of Minister of Finance. The third Rajapakse brother had been appointed as special advisor to the President. Mr. Gothobaya Rajapakse had not been given a mandate by an electorate and was probably best known for his notorious outbursts towards critical media people. He had been a career officer in the Sri Lankan Army retiring at the rank of Lt. Colonel. The suicide attempt on his life would completely change his public status. Overnight he became wildly popular in the south and was seen as a tough and resourceful hero who pledged to destroy the LTTE.

Back at Cinnamon Gardens, Mr. Hanssen-Bauer was rattled by the explosion, which had occurred only about eight hundred metres away. It was not so much that the deep and thuggish sound had made such an impact on him, it was probably more the alarming news of what had just happened in broad daylight a few blocks away in Colombo and what effect it would have on the whole of the peace process in general.

Mr. Hanssen-Bauer had tried to fill the big footsteps of Mr. Erik Solheim as a Special Envoy at a very difficult time in early 2006, when serious violations of the CFA were increasing rapidly. He was a scholar who had previously been involved in Norway's peace efforts in the Middle East where he had earned a fine reputation for his work. He was a charming man, mostly polite and pleasant and soft-spoken with his interlocutors be they in Colombo or Kilinochchi. There had been an overt rift between him and the outspoken Mr. Henricsson who as SLMM HoM until the end of August 2006, had tried to restrain both GOSL and LTTE from tit-for-tat attacks by going to the media and condemning such acts. Mr. Hanssen-Bauer was not a believer in using the media much in the conflict and thought frequent and bold media statements to be extremely counterproductive for the overall peace process.

In recent months, however, the SLMM had come under increasing media attacks by high-ranking cabinet members of GOSL, most notably by the defense spokesman of the Cabinet, Minister Keheliya Rambukwella. He was a colourful character in Sri Lanka politics and had served as a Science and Technology minister in the UNP government in 2001-04, but had crossed over from the UNP to join the SLFP and was rewarded with a ministerial post. He would invent absurd stories about the SLMM and its monitoring efforts and feed them to the media on his daily press conferences, managing to keep a remarkably straight face most of the time despite the ludicrous content of his declarations. He also delighted in spreading misinformation on the noble work of several other INGOs such as the ICRC, Amnesty International and the UN. As many of his statements amounted to outright lies, the SLMM spokesperson was sometimes asked to refute them publicly, especially if the Minister's comments were likely to put members of the SLMM at risk in the districts, where many common SLA soldiers read such remarks in the papers and believed them. Although the most seniour officers of the SLA knew better, throughout 2006, the GOSL propaganda campaign against the SLMM in most state-owned media gathered momentum and most of the military became deeply suspicious of the SLMM. Mr. Rambukwella's tireless efforts to portray SLMM monitors as blatant and biased LTTE sympathisers who were covertly assisting the Tamil cause of carving up Sri Lanka in two pieces was increasingly successful to such an extent that occasional critical media voices begged the question of why the CFA was not simply abrogated and the SLMM told to leave the island. There were no answers to that question from GOSL, yet. It did not take a crystal ball to prophesy that that would change.

Traffic came to a complete standstill for two hours in downtown Colombo after the suicide attack on Defense Secretary Gothabaya so the delegation of Mr. Hanssen-Bauer, who had to postpone other meetings, had ample time to discuss the strategic state of affairs in the peace process. The SLMM was on occasions simply too involved in monitoring tactical issues and chasing horrible incidents in the districts, to be able to see and understand the big political and diplomatic picture. Norway's Special Envoy had access to a wealth of important information channels and protagonists and was expected to give some insight in what was going on behind the scenes diplomatically and politically.

Mr. Hanssen-Bauer had rushed to Sri Lanka following the yearly speech of LTTE leader Mr. Pirapaharan, who indicated that the LTTE was on the brink of walking away from the CFA. His last visit had been six weeks earlier when he had managed to facilitate the latest round of peace talks in Geneva. In his role as Special Envoy to Sri Lanka he had to schedule his visits carefully as too frequent appearances in meetings and media in Colombo and Kilinochchi would surely dilute the effect of his presence. His task was formidable, as the parties had reached a point in the conflict where there sometimes seemed preciously little. Mr. Hanssen-Bauer or any representative of the International community could do in the later half of 2006 other than to observe the unfolding of military clashes and hope that things would quiet down in the aftermath.

A few weeks earlier, the latest peace talks in Geneva had rendered nothing tangible. Norway as a facilitator seemed to have lost considerable clout in mediation in the conflict with the US Ambassador coming ever stronger on the side of GOSL in what now appeared to be an outright third-world low-intensity war. The delegations of GOSL and LTTE had been invited to Geneva by Norway and Switzerland, focusing on three distinct issues, namely, human suffering, military de-escalation and reduction of violence and political components leading up to a political settlement. On the first two subjects, the LTTE had simply demanded the opening of the A9 and the SLA to show restraint, both points were more or less categorically rejected by the GOSL delegation. Point three was more subtle.

On the GOSL side, President Rajapakse was trying to attract backers for his coalition which did not command a majority in Parliament and was at times held politically hostage by two very tricky political movements, the dogmatic-Marxist JVP and the nationalistic-Buddhist JHU or the Monks. The President had claimed that he was sincere in seeking a negotiated settlement to the war with the LTTE, but his tacit support from the JVP and the JHU would surely crumble if any concrete proposals were laid on the table. Hence, the stance of GOSL was that of a waiting game, projecting a fair offer to Tamils somewhere over the horizon. The LTTE was deeply angered and frustrated by the lack of progress on the all-important issue of a final negotiated settlement. But they also had themselves to blame for this, as Mr. Pirapaharan had not been inclined to back down from an extremely uncompromising demand of a Tamil Eelam homeland, virtually independent from Sri Lanka. Surely a more realistic solution lay somewhere in the middle.

In order for President Rajapakse to find some way of securing political backing for a potential settlement with the LTTE he would have to reach out to the UNP, as his coalition was simply too vulnerable to the whims of JVP and JHU. Hence, the President ventured on a strategy of trying to bring the opposition, led by the UNP, into a venue called the All-Party Conference. This gathering of government and opposition outside proper Parliament sessions was to promulgate a political proposal based on some sort of devolution of powers in the north and the east as a base for a negotiated settlement. There were serious doubts on the viability of this approach by all political sides in Sri Lanka. However, important elements of the international community seemed to be fairly optimistic about the process and its Sri Lanka-based ownership rather than direct foreign mediation. The Norwegian facilitator also appeared to be somewhat hopeful that these political manoeuvres of the President could kickstart the faltering peace process.

At the meeting with the SLMM, Mr. Hanssen-Bauer told the somewhat astonished listeners that he had just come from a meeting with Minister Rambukwellah, where he was told that the SLMM had been conducting a very high-profile and negative media policy which had had a damaging effect on the peace process. Considering the sometimes unbelievable rants coming almost daily from Mr. Rambukwellah on the international representation in Sri Lanka and the conflict in general the SLMM monitors could almost not believe their ears. Nevertheless, it was true that after the failed Geneva talks, the then temporarily acting SLMM spokesperson had made some very controversial statements that angered the Foreign Ministry in Colombo to such an extent that it threatened to expel her from the country. These statements had concerned the highly sensitive issue of child recruitment by the Karuna faction in the government-controlled areas in the east and civilian casualties due to SLA artillery attacks. To make matters worse, a Cabinet Minister had claimed that at the venue of the peace talks in Geneva, the Political Advisor to the SLMM HOM had insinuated that GOSL preferred the A9 blocked in order for individual ministers to pocket kickbacks from the companies running the sea transport operation to Jaffna.

That story, which the SLMM tried to downplay without success, had been published as the leading front page item in the *Daily News*, Sri Lanka's largest newspaper. The important issue of the protection of civilians in battle zones unfortunately was obscured by this short-lived clash of words in the media. Now, Mr. Hanssen-Bauer was effectively telling the mission to completely shut up. It was a fate that would fall upon most other international missions in Sri Lanka in the coming months. The SLMM Heads of District assembled were dismayed at this approach and the fact that the Norwegian Special Envoy had first met Minister Rambukwella and then taken his complaints to the SLMM rather than the other way around.

Nevertheless, Mr. Hanssen-Bauer's approach was accepted if somewhat reluctantly. It not only took some heat out of the SLMM temporarily but also diminished the impact of the mission considerably as a conveyor of unpleasant facts. To be sure, the decision on a more subtle SLMM media strategy was undoubtedly based on a sound diplomatic approach by the Norwegian Special Envoy and probably well worth trying. However, it did little to change the course of SLMM's diminishing standing as a body to guard the CFA. In hindsight, it probably speeded up the process of rendering the verdicts of the SLMM irrelevant to both parties. From the end of 2006, the SLMM became a relatively silent international body and fair game for the state media, which continued to undermine the credibility of the mission and its mandate.

The All-Party Conference eventually stalled along the way. Although the two major parties of President Rajapakse's SLFP and Ranil's UNP had signed a memorandum of understanding earlier on how to proceed, the dialogue between the coalition and the opposition unravelled into a travesty. Mr. Rajapakse had sought to strengthen his hand in Parliament and in the last weeks of 2006, droves of UNP MPs crossed the floor to join the government as the leadership of the UNP protested loudly. Many of the so-called turncoats were rewarded with a minister or junior minister position, rendering coveted perks such as cars, assistants and increased remuneration. In early 2007, after the Muslim SLMC and the monks in the JHU had formally joined the government, the UNP publically renounced the MoU with the governing SLFP and concentrated on its role as the main opposition party. Meanwhile, the Cabinet of Sri Lanka had grown to over one hundred full and deputy ministers out of a Parliament of 225. The opposition called it the jumbo cabinet and said that it shamed Sri Lanka internationally. At a time when the country's finances and security were in complete disarray, pictures of the ministers of Sri Lanka could only be taken with a very wide angle camera lens somewhere at a large enough field.

As the attempt at arriving at a bipartisan proposal for ending the ethnic conflict was coming to an end in Colombo, the leader of the LTTE was about to deliver his yearly keynote speech on Heroes' Day. At the end of November Mr. Pirapaharan declared that the CFA had become defunct due to the ongoing military operations on land, at sea and in the air sanctified by GOSL. He bitterly stated that now the only viable solution for the Tamils would be a separate state in the north and east, even though it was becoming increasingly evident that the LTTE was waging a losing battle in the Batticaloa area. The LTTE was also immensely angered by the assassination of one of the most important Tamil Member of Parliament, two weeks earlier. Mr. Nadarajah Raviraj, former mayor of Jaffna and a high-profile member of the Tamil National Alliance, had been an outspoken critic of the government and had been a prolific voice against extra-judicial killings in Sri Lanka. He was gunned down by unknown attackers riding a motorbike near his residence in Colombo.

The suicide attack on Defense Secretary Gothabaya Rajapakse, two weeks later, was yet another important watershed in the development of the conflict in Sri Lanka. The LTTE had been angered by the lack of progress at the peace talks in Geneva, which were to be the last of such meetings between GOSL and LTTE delegations. The assassination of Mr. Raviraj had stirred up great emotions in Jaffna where his body was visited by masses of ordinary citizens as it lay in state. Furthermore, the response to the yearly Heroes' Day speech of the LTTE leader had been received with little more than tacit dismissal in Colombo, both by the GOSL and the international community. And the A9 remained closed in the north, as the SLA was slowly but surely advancing in the east in order to eject the LTTE from its remaining pockets of resistance.

The callous bomb attack on the Defense Secretary in broad daylight was an obvious act of the LTTE. It might have changed events if it had succeeded but Mr. Gothabaya Rajapakse had survived miraculously, just as his immediate military subordinate Army Commander Fonseka half a year earlier. The timing of the attack had come at the worst possible time for the efforts of Norway and Mr. Hanssen-Bauer who appeared to have lost the ability to influence either the LTTE or GOSL to show restraint. His position as a Special Envoy facilitating a peace process had obviously been seriously undermined by the incident. His quest for peace in Sri Lanka was starting to look like a mission impossible.

The suicide attack in Colombo on 1 December 2006 would most likely strengthen both the President and his brother in charge of the Ministry of Defense in their belief that the LTTE could not be contained but must be destroyed militarily. To be sure, the Commander of the Army would concur with that assessment. A few days later, GOSL announced that the Prevention of Terrorism Act, which had been abolished in conjunction with the CFA in 2002, would be reinstated with immediate effect. That in itself was a permanent breach of one of the most important articles of the ceasefire agreement document.

31

# A Decisive War in the Eastern Theatre

Following the SLA success at Mawil Aaru in August, the fighting subsided for a few months as the Army was consolidating control over the newly acquired area stretching from Mutur down towards the town of Verugal. The eminently strategic town of Sampoor had fallen to the SLA and also the coastal towns of Ilakkantai and Ichchilampattai, both considered Sea Tiger strongholds. The LTTE only held a thin stretch of coastline concentrating its rear defense around the town of Vakarai. Thousands of civilians had fled the fighting and the advancing SLA, and a large makeshift camp for them was established in Vakarai close to the hospital. South of Vakarai, the SLA had also advanced up north along the coastline threatening to completely squeeze the LTTE in due course.

The SLA had a main military base within Batticaloa town, the largest on the south-eastern coastline of Sri Lanka. The SLA was also present in other military bases and camps dotted along the A15 and the A11 highways, the main connecting roads towards Colombo and Trincomalee. The A11 was particularly vulnerable as it stretched through sparsely populated jungle areas from the east coast straight to the west towards the ancient city of Polonnaruwa. Batticaloa town was spread over quite a large area, having originally developed out of the delta of the Batticaloa lagoon which stretched almost fifty kilometres from north to south just a narrow tract inland from the coast itself. Batticaloa was always a busy and bustling place being the main commercial centre in the eastern region of the island. There were countless shops and small food outlets, peculiarly called hotels, even though there were no sleeping accommodation to be had. There was a constant stream of fretting three-wheelers and motorcycles moving up and down the main road in the centre of the town where the strategically important bridge connected the coastal highways A15 and A4 over the stretch where the waters of the tranquil lagoon slowly drifted towards the open sea. The bridge was guarded hawkishly by the SLA and so was most of the coastal highway all the way south down to the next major town of Akkaraipattu with its large Muslim component. In the Ampara district south of Batticaloa, the dreaded elite units of the Government's Special Task Force took responsibility for the security. They were respected by the LTTE for their tactical skills but sometimes feared by both Muslim and Tamil civilians for their heavy-handedness in dealing with incidents and alleged insurgents.

To the west of the Batticaloa lagoon, the roads were mere dirt tracks through the jungle and this was LTTE-controlled territory. This area could be reached by a number of very basic ferries on the lagoon, busy transporting civilians on their way to Batticaloa town for commerce and back. In the western hinterland of the lagoon, orientation was very difficult and it was almost impossible for the SLA to pinpoint the whereabouts of the LTTE in the jungle area stretching to the southwest where one could see the beginning formations of a majestic series of hills and mountains stretching towards the uphill interior of Sri Lanka. The region was inhabited by poor farmers and further south towards Ampara the area was almost unspoilt by human settlers. Here and further south towards

Yala National Park, the wildlife was given the necessary breathing space to flourish in a pristine setting of unparalleled beauty.

Since the Karuna split in 2004, the LTTE had been severely weakened in the whole eastern theatre, particularly in and around Batticaloa town where Karuna's cadres had taken over the political work of the LTTE. Following numerous assassinations of leading LTTE cadre including two heads of their local political wing, the LTTE had closed down its political offices and had ended most of their overt presence in the townships in the east. The LTTE was entitled to run political offices in GOSL-controlled areas, according to the CFA, but the CFA could do little to protect against continuous assaults on LTTE premises. The office in Kalmunai, a former LTTE stronghold just south of Batticaloa, seemed a magnet for incoming explosives attacks. The LTTE showed no mercy itself and assassinated and killed Karuna leaders where they could get at them. But in the course of 2005 and 2006, the LTTE continued to lose its covert social grip over the local Tamils as Karuna as a leader grew incrementally in popularity. The 2004 and 2005 assassinations of the highest ranking LTTE leaders in the east had angered the LTTE immensely and it bluntly accused the SLA of assisting the Karuna faction in targeting and killing LTTE personnel. The SLA and on a political level the GOSL routinely denied such allegations. Nevertheless, it became increasingly evident that Karuna cadres could move almost at will through the numerous SLA and police checkpoints, which was impossible for the LTTE. Hence the LTTE was eventually driven out of the towns on the whole eastern coastline and into the jungle to the west of Batticaloa.

Following the military successes in the Trincomalee region, it was a logical step for the SLA to train its eyes on the LTTE presence in the east. At first, the SLA seemed to be targeting the LTTE presence in the jungle west of Batticaloa, firing artillery barrages with increasing regularity towards LTTE positions. Much ammunition was probably wasted in this approach, but the tenacity with which the SLA kept up its show of force by continuously increasing the frequency of devastating multi-barrel salvos towards the LTTE controlled area was bound to soften up resistance there. The scorched earth approach also terrified the civilians in the area which fled in droves, ironically towards GOSL-held territory to escape the SLA bombardment. Thousands of internally displaced people found themselves flowing into a giant refugee camp at Eravur, north of Batticaloa town towards the end of 2006.

Karuna had established a political party for his eastern Tamil platform, the TMVP, and was more willing to operate in the open than before as the threat of the LTTE seemed to be diminishing in the east. He gave interviews ridiculing the Kilinochchi leadership of the LTTE and although the LTTE would have sacrificed almost anything in order to silence him, Karuna was still pulling the strings in subtle but effective ways in the east. His TMVP cadres had become much bolder after the LTTE defeat in Mutur and Sampoor and could now be seen openly patrolling streets in Batticaloa and in adjacent towns, proudly displaying their illegal arms. The CFA clearly stated that GOSL was responsible for disarming any paramilitary groups not party to the agreement, but the SLA claimed that they were doing their best to contain the situation, notwithstanding an understandable glee in the eye observing the fratricidal battle of the LTTE and the TMVP in Batti.

Towards the end of 2006 the alleged SLA and TMVP clandestine cooperation became a sore topic for the GOSL as it found its way into the headlines of the international media courtesy of the international media corps in Colombo. The GOSL was furious and wanted the matter silenced immediately launching a massive campaign of refute of the Karuna story in the state-controlled media. There was, however, an external component to the story which was difficult to contain. Ambassador Allan Rock, Special Advisor to the UN Special Representative for Children in Armed Conflict, had toured the eastern region in November, notably with the assistance and facilitation of the SLMM and other INGOs. He had drawn up an official UN report following his findings and it contained issues which were deeply embarrassing for GOSL and the SLA. The report claimed that the TMVP was conducting child recruitment in a blatantly aggressive way, just as the Sri Lanka authorities had always condemned the LTTE for. However, not only was TMVP snatching child soldiers into their ranks in GOSL-controlled areas, according to the report, but more shockingly, the SLA was accused of assisting the TMVP directly in this highly controversial activity. It further indicated that Karuna cadre's had been given passage through SLA and police checkpoints at will and had even obtained entry to the refugee camps, where they had direct access to youngsters to kidnap into their ranks.

These were shocking allegations, especially for GOSL, which found itself needing to explain a great deal to the international community which in turn had been canvassed for years to condemn the LTTE child recruitment. The Karuna cadres, however, did not seem to be much miffed by the UN findings and they apparently concluded in the same way as the LTTE that they had every right to increase their fighting formations by forced child conscription. Even though the Sri Lanka government angrily rebuked all findings in the UN report, it did leave a stain on a state already heavily criticised for its human rights record by several INGOs. The GOSL responded in a comprehensive smear campaign against Mr. Rock, the hapless UN representative who had drawn immense anger in Colombo. As Mr. Rock was chased out of Sri Lanka, he was depicted as a completely biased sympathiser of the LTTE cause and state controlled media created amazing features varying from trying to connect him to illegal Tamil activities in his home country Canada to regularly consuming narcotic substances. The UN, which had routinely been considered by GOSL as biased towards the Tamil cause became even more unpopular in Colombo and at times demonstrations were staged outside their offices with some politicians seen fuelling the flames rather than trying to defuse the situation. Sri Lanka continued to be a tough place for the UN to operate in.

During December 2006, the SLA appeared to be shifting its tactics in Batticaloa. The bombardment of the LTTE held jungle southwest of the lagoon subsided, but increased fighting in the northern stretch towards Vakarai was reported. There were now strong indications emerging for what had been suspected for some time that the Karuna cadres were actively taking part in SLA offensive ground operations. Most of the eastern seaboard had now been denied to the LTTE and even though they still had access to the sea at the Upaar lagoon by Vakarai, their movements were severely limited as the Sri Lankan Navy was monitoring activity down the coast all the way from Trinco towards Batticaloa. In that sense the LTTE now found itself trapped. However, the lagoon also gave protection towards the western flank. Vakarai would have to be overrun either from a narrow stretch of land in the north or through a vital bridge just south of the lagoon.

The final push for Vakarai started mid-January 2007. Until then the LTTE had bought time by using the approximately 30,000 IDPs in Vakarai as a human shield. The LTTE angrily denied this, but the SLMM could verify that such had been the case, effectively slowing down the SLA offensive somewhat. The SLA had on the other hand lost patience along the way and several artillery attacks on targets close to the main IDP camps were noted resulting in considerable civilian casualties that could have been avoided. Both sides were chastised by INGOs for the way they fought the battle in the east, but it seemed to have a limited effect on the ground.

The SLMM was severely restricted in its operations with both the SLA and the LTTE imposing limitations to its freedom of movement. Furthermore, the SLMM monitors were at times finding themselves in the middle of a battleground with mortars exploding close by, instead of monitoring a ceasefire. SLMM headquarters were forced to impose operational limits on SLMM monitors in the east, who were taking increasing risks in order to be able to see for themselves what was really going on. The ICRC, UN and the SLMM had only been able to escort one convoy with relief goods through to Vakarai at the end of November which had been isolated since. Thousands of the more mobile IDPs had managed to trickle out of the area in the following weeks but in the last days of the battle for Vakarai the LTTE had opened fire on those fleeing bringing the exodus towards GOSL controlled territory to a standstill.

In the final days of the fighting, the hospital in Vakarai took some impacts and the humanitarian situation was desperate. The LTTE had held out as long as they could but now realised that the battle was lost. SLA forces entered Vakarai on 19 January 2007 to find it empty of LTTE fighters who had apparently slipped out the previous night. About eight thousand local residents and IDPs had been trapped in the endgame for Vakarai and there had been several civilian casualties, although in the end the civilian and military casualties were always difficult to assess.

As with the fall of Sampoor and the southern Trinco region in August, the SLA military victory in Vakarai constituted a watershed in the conflict in Sri Lanka. The security forces of Sri Lanka had now gained complete control of all of the eastern coast and main towns and roads in the eastern theatre. The LTTE would now be denied reinforcements by sea and would have to hide in the dense jungle west of Batticaloa. It was not yet a fully spent force however. In a show of defiance, the LTTE attacked several SLA positions on the A11 highway two days later blocking the road for days.

The SLA refocused its attention on the Kokkadichcholai area southwest of Batticaloa in the following weeks, engaging with the LTTE where they could find them. A full victory in the east was declared shortly after the SLA had captured Vakarai or liberated as the term was logically denoted in Colombo. This was somewhat premature and almost cost several foreign Ambassadors their lives. On the invitation of GOSL, a group of Ambassadors, including the outspoken US Ambassador Robert Blake and his German and Italian colleagues, were flown into Batticaloa for a fact-finding trip of the liberated zones. Their aircraft, however, came under mortar attack, whilst on ground by the LTTE, which later cryptically noted that they had not been informed in advance. They delighted in stating that their fighting formations were perfectly capable of threatening military aircraft at the Batticaloa airfield. The LTTE argued that the aircraft had been a legitimate military target in an area where the Sri Lankan security forces had undertaken countless military operations. The Tigers put the blame squarely on GOSL which in a haphazard manner had put the lives of the Ambassadors at great risk. The Ambassadors returned with a government minister and other dignitaries to Colombo, some with slight cut wounds from shrapnel.

It was somewhat ironic that little reference was made to the fact that officially neither GOSL nor the LTTE had taken any steps to abrogate the CFA, even though a conventional war had just been concluded in the Batticaloa region.

The liberation of the east by the Sri Lankan security forces was hailed in Colombo. The LTTE had been soundly defeated militarily in a troubled region, which had suffered enormously from the conflict and only two years earlier devastated by the tsunami. The local population was probably immensely relieved that the fighting was over, although the future seemed uncertain for the Tamil Internally Displaced Persons who had fled their former homes. The GOSL however, proved to be massively capable of extending a comprehensive programme of relief in the east assisted by INGOs such as the ICRC and the UN. Normalcy would gradually increase in the following years.

Sri Lanka President Mahinda Rajapakse hastily flew to inspect Vakarai and the scene of the battle. His trip was triumphant as he saluted the soldiers and told the nation that following this victory, the Sinhalese, the Tamils and the Muslims could all live in peace together in the east. Furthermore, this would be an immensely important step towards reuniting the whole of the island. As the LTTE grudgingly observed, all major television channels showed lengthy reports of the President, apparently being welcomed by jubilant local residents. In what could have been a staged show for the gallery, a prominent local Hindu priest stepped forward and put a garland of flowers on Mr. Rajapakse. This was widely applauded by the Tamil crowd observing this act of accolade for the President, surrounded by heavily armed guards.

The LTTE responded to the spectacle in their cynically swift manner. The Hindu priest was assassinated a few days later in his home in Batticaloa. There was little, however, the LTTE could do about the ground situation in the conflict. The LTTE-controlled areas on the eastern seaboard were lost for good in a stunning defeat at the hands of the SLA.

# 32

# The Sea Corridor to Jaffna

Following the refusal of the GOSL to accommodate the LTTE on the nominally fundamental issue of reopening the A9 to alleviate the humanitarian situation for the Tamil population of Jaffna, GOSL started to search for other alternatives. As Vanni was squarely controlled by the LTTE, an alternative land route would have to wait until the Tigers had been weakened militarily north of Mannar. In the present situation, the most obvious alternative to the now-closed A9 was the sea.

The SLA and SLN had routinely rotated personnel in and out of Jaffna via sea for years and were quite experienced in this. Other, mostly more high-ranking military personnel were flown from the only Jaffna airbase in Palali to Ratmalana military airport half-an-hour drive south of Colombo. There were only a few ferries available large enough for substantial troop transports and they would be escorted by the SLN on the sea voyage between Trincomalee in the east and Kankesanturai, commonly just KKS, on the northern-most shores of Sri Lanka up in Jaffna Peninsula. KKS was a heavily guarded High Security Zone under the command of the Sri Lankan Navy. The troop-carrying vessels were escorted by Navy Fast Gun Boats or Fast Attack Crafts. In the first few years of the CFA, SLMM naval monitors had routinely been stationed on board the Navy vessels to monitor troop transports. The SLMM naval monitors were very welcome passengers on the navy ships as they would fly the SLMM banner, which the Sea Tigers would recognise for what it was and consider it a deterrent for attacks on the Navy. That had been then, now things had changed completely.

As contemplations on alternatives to the transport of people and goods to and from Jaffna were being discussed, with the sea route being the most obvious one, the SLMM was approached by GOSL to play a role in the commercial sea transports. This, however, was not considered feasible in late 2006 as the SLMM had cancelled its naval monitoring months earlier in May due to ever-growing security reasons and the withdrawal of security guarantees for SLMM staff at sea by the LTTE leadership.

Naval monitoring by the SLMM had proven to be the most dangerous task undertaken by the mission with a history of close calls for its Nordic monitors. At times the naval monitors had had to jump into the waters of Sri Lanka from burning or exploding vessels. Following an increase in clashes between the SLN and the Sea Tigers from the beginning of 2006, the then HOM Ulf Henricsson decided as a due diligence to close down the Naval component of the SLMM. It was considered only a matter of time before the SLMM would take casualties as the Sea Tigers had in effect conveyed the message that they would not halt their attacks on the Navy even with SLMM monitors on board. This was demonstrated quite clearly on 11 May when a flotilla of around 15 Sea Tiger boats attacked a formation of 4 SLN Dvoras off the coast of Nagarkovil in Jaffna. The SLN Dvoras tried to evade the attack by sailing towards north-east but the Sea Tiger boats caught up with them sailing parallel with them at speeds over forty knots and firing heavily. They also fired at the Dvora with the SLMM naval monitor on board which was flying a large and clearly marked SLMM flag. One of the Dvoras was sunk by a suicide craft before the Sea Tigers gave up the chase. Many of the Sea Tiger boats were primarily manned by youngsters who may not have given much thought to the significance of the SLMM presence.

Following this incident, the SLMM terminated its naval monitoring and in a letter to Mr. Tamilshelvan, the SLMM Head of Mission suggested to the political wing leader that if the LTTE would not adhere to the CFA, it should simply declare its termination. That was, however, not in the interest of the Tigers.

In late 2006, the prevailing situation at sea was such that GOSL tried to keep open the eastern sea route from Trinco to KKS, sending supplies via cargo vessels escorted by the Navy. The vessels had to take a much longer route than would have been called for under more peaceful conditions as the vessel formations had to stay well out of range moving slowly in deep waters out of the Sea Tiger stronghold at Mullativu in the north-east of Sri Lanka. Nevertheless there would be skirmishes at sea when the Sea Tigers would manage to engage the SLN. However, in deep waters the dreaded high-powered small suicide attack crafts were not as lethal an option as closer to shore.

At the same time as media reports were portraying a situation of isolation, despair and intimidation by the security forces against the Tamil population in Jaffna, GOSL was faced with relentless Sea Tiger activity targeted against the flow of goods towards Jaffna via the eastern sea route. It was tempting for the SLMM to accommodate the explicit wishes of GOSL to reconsider the cessation of naval monitoring to facilitate safe passage for cargo vessels in such dire circumstances. However, given the stance of the LTTE, it was simply not prudent to place naval monitors on board SLN escort ships.

In this current situation GOSL was weighing its options. GOSL had the responsibility for keeping the security and the rule of law in Jaffna. The Sri Lankan Government was also responsible for ensuring a viable economic and social situation for the Tamil population of Jaffna although it could not count on widespread sympathy up there. This was being achieved at a high risk and through sea and air transport. In the long run the only way of sustaining a normal socio-economic situation in Jaffna would be through the reopening of a land route to Jaffna. It was tempting to argue that the only way to achieve that would be to give LTTE a thorough military beating in Vanni proper. And there were indeed substantial indications that that was exactly what Mr. Rajapakse's administration and armed command intended to do.

33

# The Conflict Takes to the Skies

It was indeed a strange scene to behold. At the luxurious Taj airport hotel close to the international airport in Katunayaka, foreign aircrews were resting by the poolside, sipping exotic cocktails apparently oblivious of the warlike situation in the north of Sri Lanka. Clearly visible from the comfortable lounge chairs were the SLAF fighter-bombers taking off from the runway with a deafening noise, racing into the clear blue sky to acquire mach two speed levels on their sorties towards Vanni. Upon returning from their mission, having dropped their deadly load, the aircraft would touch down on the same runway as the gentle giants of the skies, Airbuses and Boeings, loaded with tourists, seeking an affordable tropical holiday at the luxury beach resorts in the south and the west of Sri Lanka.

The Sri Lankan Air Force was mainly operating two types of aircraft in the war against the LTTE, Israeli manufactured Kfir jets and Russian Mig-27 ground attack planes. The Kfir was a legendary workhorse, initially a copycat of the French Dassault Mirage which had been denied to Israel by a French arms embargo in the late sixties. It had been phased out in most parts of the world, but in Sri Lanka it was operating very effectively against a depleted LTTE that had clearly lost its surface-to-air missile capability. The Russian Mig-27s had been quietly added to the SLAF arsenal just before and after the beginning of the CFA period, ironically at a time when GOSL was complaining bitterly to the international community and the Norwegian facilitator particularly, that the LTTE was abusing the ceasefire to stockpile armaments from abroad.

Moreover, the LTTE were convinced that Pakistan Air Force officers were deeply involved in training and assisting the SLAF which was still honing its air campaign skills. It was a view commonly shared by notable Indian military experts and publicised on LTTE-friendly websites. Neither the SLAF nor the GOSL would participate in such discussions. However, it was no secret that Sri Lanka had in the last few years forged increasingly improving contacts with Pakistan from which it was believed to have purchased significant armaments in the past few years. The LTTE would revisit the issue of Pakistan involvement with the SLAF in due course.

The SLAF had only played a relatively minor role in the conflict leading up to the CFA as its fleet of aircraft had been quite limited and an air campaign suited itself poorly for asymmetric warfare against a jungle-based guerilla adversary. In the recent years, the SLAF had acquired a small fleet of Russian Mi-35 and Mi-24 helicopter gunships, which would prove to be immensely effective for close air support in the ground battles that lay ahead.

The LTTE was effectively defenseless against air attacks and pointed out that aerial bombardment had been clearly ruled out in the CFA document, which called for a total cessation of such hostilities in article 1.2. Hence air-mounted operations were usually ruled by the SLMM as gross violations of the CFA.

The SLAFs first flights into Vanni after the commencement of the CFA were actually of a completely different nature than would later become the norm. The SLAF had been very generous in accommodating airborne visits of the SLMM HOM, the Norwegian facilitator and other international dignitaries to Kilinochchi for high-level meetings with the representatives of the LTTE. The modalities were usually such that the peace secretaries with the facilitation of the SLMM liaison officers in Kili coordinated special helicopter flights with VIPs into LTTE's seat of administration in Kilinochchi. A preceding fixed wing flight from Ratmalana military airport south of Colombo would take visitors to the large SLAF base in Anuradhapura where the travelling party would switch to a rotary wing flight taking them further north to Vavuniya airbase. From there it was only a fifteen minutes hop in a helicopter towards Kilinochchi. The helicopters would somewhat nervously touch down at the large sports ground at the southern outskirts of the town, which was secured by the neatly uniformed LTTE police. As soon as the travelling party had left the aircraft the helicopter would immediately return for Vavuniya. After the meetings the helicopter would return upon SLMM request, only to touch down for a few moments picking up the passengers and then swiftly return from LTTE-held Vanni. On a number of occasions, the SLAF had even picked up LTTE delegations bound for peace talks with GOSL at venues abroad, transporting them from Kilinochchi to Katunayaka airport north of Colombo. As the conflict gathered momentum and mutual distrust between the parties increased, these courtesy flights into Kilinochchi proper were abandoned and had ceased by 2006, although the SLAF would continue to fly VIPs up to Vavuniya.

In the first years of the CFA the SLAF only flew sorties over Vanni sparingly, well aware of the symbolic nature of utilising high tech military jets against a fighting organisation that GOSL would like to define as primitive and by no means legitimate as a protector of the Tamil population. That changed dramatically in 2006, most notably in response to the assassination attempt on Army commander Fonseka. Shortly after news broke of the suicide attack within the SLA HQ in Colombo, SLAF fighter-bombers took to the skies and massive airstrikes were reported in the volatile southern Trincomalee area where several LTTE-held towns such as Mutur east and Sampoor were bombarded. What followed seemed to be a clear shift in SLAF doctrine and tactics. From now on, the SLAF would almost invariably fly retaliatory attacks on Vanni following significant incidents attributed to the LTTE.

The roaring SLAF jets instilled panic and fear in Vanni where the civilian population had few places to run and hide. The most frequent SLAF targets were Kilinochchi, Mullativu on the north-east coast and selected sites in the north-west above Mannar.

The CFA notwithstanding, in August 2006 a full-scale war had erupted in Sri Lanka. The SLA successfully carried out its sweeping ground offensive in the Mutur/Sampoor area, several intensive naval clashes were reported and the LTTE had made its futile attempt at breaking through the SLA forward defense localities in Jaffna. Amidst this general mayhem in several theatres in Sri Lanka, a tragedy unfolded on 14 August in Mullaittivu district.

According to eyewitnesses, four Kfir fighter-bombers appeared in the early hours over Sensolaii Children's Home, just west of Puthukkudiyiruppu town, dropping up to sixteen bombs with a devastating effect. The school itself took several direct impacts resulting in an unprecedented carnage from an airstrike during CFA time. At least fifty-five young female students were killed and approximately one hundred and twenty were injured, many of them severely. The LTTE said that around 400 girls from villages in the region, between the ages of 14 and 18, had stayed overnight at the school compound as they were attending a first aid training course. The SLAF target appeared to have been chosen deliberately as the Kfirs had made direct target runs dropping their bombs with internecine effect. The swift and deliberate nature of the air attack on Sensolaii strongly indicated that the SLAF had been in possession of intelligence and coordinates of the site. It was difficult to assess why the SLAF had carried out the attack at this time, but reasons for revenge were bountiful in August. Only two days earlier, the Deputy Secretary-General of the SCOPP had been gunned down in a street in Colombo. At the same time, the LTTE and the SLA were engaged in a bitter clash north of Elephant Pass. Reasons for further bloodletting in Sri Lanka had certainly amassed in the preceding weeks.

The LTTE was outraged at the massacre which received short-lived international media attention. The media reports also focused on a mine blast in Colombo later in the day, targeting the Pakistani High Commissioner to Colombo. Seven soldiers in the convoy were killed and seventeen injured. The mine explosion, which occurred close to the official residence of President Rajapakse, left the Pakistani High Commissioner unscathed. The LTTE refused responsibility, but they had both the means and the motive and the mine attack bore all the hallmarks of their *modus operandi*.

Representatives of GOSL were cautious in their response to the Sensolaii attack appearing somewhat shocked over its lethal effectiveness. However, they sternly insisted that the compound had been a military installation where young female cadres had been receiving military indoctrination. SLMM monitors were quick on the spot and reported that they had not seen any sign of military installations, uniforms, weapons or other indications of military activity. The GOSL refuted these findings and stuck to the line of having struck a military training facility.

As military battles were unfolding rapidly at the time of the air attack on Sensolaii, the horrific strike soon melted in the background of newly occurring reports of clashes and killings in the north and the east. The air attack, however, was clearly a gross violation of the CFA and was ruled as such by the SLMM. The conflict, however, had gathered such a momentum that the SLMM rulings had lost a great deal of significance, particularly for media. In previous years, major rulings had sparked considerable discussions in the island and within the international community. Nevertheless, the head of SCOPP, Dr. Palitha Kohona, understood the moral significance of SLMM that the SLAF had grossly violated the CFA. After having the SLMM HOM wait for three hours in front of his office in one of the World Trade Centre towers in the Fort district of Colombo, Dr. Kohona reluctantly received the ruling, angrily stating that no matter what the SLMM had to say, the Sensolaii compound had indeed been a military facility.

The ceasefire agreement and its most important articles had been violated to such an extent that now both parties seemed to have forgotten its content. The question of the Sensolaii school premises being a military facility or not would have been a question pertaining to the Geneva conventions on warfare, not to the CFA. All airstrikes were obviously gross violations according to that document.

Nevertheless, the SLAF airstrikes would continue and the sight of howling military jets would become a familiar one over Vanni. The SLMM ruled a number of violations against the SLAF due to bombing incidents, particularly ones causing civilian deaths, including an attack causing damage to the General Hospital in Kilinochchi prompting mobile patients to flee in panic.

On 2 November 2007, the LTTE acknowledged that Mr. Tamilshelvan, the head of the political wing and the primary interlocutor for the international community, had been killed in an airstrike by the SLAF. He had apparently been killed by a targeted attack in which the aircraft had released highly sophisticated smart bombs. Mr. Tamilshelvan was killed at a communication centre in the southern part of Kilinochchi close to the headquarters of both the ICRC and the World Food Programme. Several other members of the LTTE political wing were killed in the attack even though they had sought refuge in a nearby bunker facility. It was never fully explained how the SLAF was able to conduct its attack with such lethal precision. Mr. Tamilshelvan had effectively been the front figure of the Tamil Tigers for years and as such his death was a devastating blow to the LTTE.

# 34

## GOSL Abrogates the CFA

In early 2007, it was becoming increasingly difficult to maintain that there still was a ceasefire in effect in Sri Lanka, even though the CFA agreement was officially still valid. The CFA's first two main articles, concerning military operations and the security of the civilian population, were being routinely violated by both parties. In the case of important aspects of the CFA such as the closure of the A9 and the systematic use of air attacks, stipulations of the CFA were being violated permanently. In fact, the only tangible part of the CFA still intact was the presence of the SLMM in Sri Lanka, which both the GOSL and the LTTE claimed they still wanted.

However, the operations of the SLMM were down to a minimum. The SLMM HOM had called most of his field monitors back to a base at the Taj airport hotel from the beginning of 2007, where they remained for more than five months, only deploying into the field for inspections of serious incidents taking place in the conflict. This measure had been taken in order to ensure the safety of the Nordic monitors. However, the district offices had been left to the national staff to run temporarily. The national staff was thus exposed to potential harassment of both the security forces and the Karuna faction and as such the SLMM decision to keep its "white faces" at an arms length from the conflict zones was quite controversial. Some of the SLMM monitors agreed with the measure, others resented being pulled from the field and considered leaving the national staff behind a shameful decision.

The Defense Secretary Mr. Gothabaya Rajapakse was not a man to mince his words about sensitive issues. He had formed a radical opinion on how to solve the ethnic conflict and appeared contemptuous of the value of the CFA and the SLMM. Never a man inclined to hide behind an obscure cloud of diplomatic courtesy, he was now about to share his views with a large audience.

The LTTE had managed to score a considerable propaganda victory in March, as the Tigers launched their first ever airborne bomb-attack on the military part of the international airport in Katunayaka. It had been known for some time that the LTTE was in possession of two to three light wing aircraft. Rumours had it that those were Czech-made training aircraft and as such not real military airplanes. All the same, the LTTE had access to a large airstrip in Vanni, with a runway so wide and long that it was distinctively visible on Google Earth. It had been bombed every now and then by the SLAF, but the LTTE claimed that they had refurbished it with relative ease following such attacks. On 25 March, just after midnight, LTTE aircraft homed in on the international airport and dropped rudimentary bombs on the SLAF hangars. Black Tigers were apparently also involved in the attack as some eyewitnesses claimed they had seen parachutes gliding down over the airport. It was a stunning attack and took SLAF by complete surprise. The damage inflicted by the LTTE on the SLAF was surely overstated by Kilinochchi and downplayed by Colombo, but it was clear that some SLAF aircraft had been damaged and there had been at least three SLAF troopers killed with up to twenty wounded. The SLMM managed to get valuable information in conversations with some of those lightly wounded, but the SLAF denied SLMM access to its airbase and there was no final report on how effective the LTTE attack had been. Nevertheless, it was a surprise attack that the LTTE relished and was reported worldwide. As a result, some major air carriers rescheduled flights away from Katunayaka which had developed into an important international hub in recent years. Other important carriers decided to use the airport only in daytime in the following months.

At a major meeting at the heavily guarded Ministry of Defense in Colombo, all the representatives of the international media based in Sri Lanka were gathered to listen to Defense Secretary Mr. Gothabaya Rajapakse discuss the current situation in the conflict. He was even more candid than the most news-hungry reporters had anticipated and delivered some sensational comments. They were supposed to be for back-briefing only, but that was probably never realistic given the number of journalists present. The reporters had to hand in all their electronic recording equipment including cell phones, so there would be no taped quotes. This was also a measure of the tight security arrangements for Mr. Rajapakse. Asked about the CFA, the Defense Secretary boldly stated that there was no ceasefire agreement with the LTTE. He went on to elaborate that the formal CFA had no real meaning and that GOSL had simply refrained from saying this explicitly in order to keep the international community happy. The Defense Secretary, ever the maverick, then went on to state that the Sri Lanka military would soon push toward the LTTE strongholds in the Vanni and destroy them. He then ridiculed the much repeated claims by several international observers that the conflict in Sri Lanka could not be won by military means. To the surprise of the audience and the amazement of Simon Gardner of Reuters, the head of the association of foreign news representatives in Colombo, who was sitting beside him, Gothabaya grabbed him in a somewhat crude analogy, shook him decisively and said that if he thought he could beat somebody he would grab him like this, and such was the current reality on the ground. It was an impressive show by the Defense Secretary, who when asked about the role of the SLMM, forcefully dismissed any relevance of that organisation following recent development and joked that its staff was lying at the beach doing nothing but earn bountiful remunerations. He furthermore stated that it would take the SLA approximately one to two years to take all of Vanni and annihilate the LTTE.

The so-called off-the-record statements of the Defense Secretary soon found their way into all major headlines and became the main discussion point in diplomatic circles. Some expressed shock over the statements, others argued that although blunt, they were brutally honest and as such gave a much appreciated insight into the real contemplations of GOSL. The impact of the remarkably candid revelations of Mr. Gothabaya Rajapakse did not last long as Sri Lanka was soon overtaken by ever bloodier events. Furthermore, there was perhaps little point in beating around the bush for GOSL, as full war had effectively been resumed.

Mr. Pirapaharan appeared immensely pleased in photographs published on the LTTE friendly TamilNet following the air-attack on Katunayaka airport. However timid his air wing was it was still reported to be the first created by a group of insurgents anywhere in the world. So the training aircraft with their homemade mechanism for releasing bombs also represented a tool to catch the eye of the outside world, which the LTTE felt had left them isolated and betrayed at the hands of the GOSL. By now, the LTTE was willing to increase international focus on the conflict in Sri Lanka by any means. Nevertheless, Mr. Pirapaharan was probably overstating the value of these Tiger endeavours in the air, as militarily they had a very limited impact on the ground situation. It appeared that the Tigers had put disproportional resources into creating its air wing, most likely for pure propaganda reasons. And the LTTE made sure that the existence of its newly formed air wing would not go unnoticed by the public in the south.

28 April 2007, just after midnight, when most of those in Colombo with access to a television were watching the final of the Cricket World Cup played in the far away Caribbean loud explosions were heard across Colombo. The Sri Lanka team had been enjoying an excellent

run in the match and was playing Australia in the final when the Air Tigers struck Colombo. There were loud explosions to be heard in the black of night and from the balcony at Barnes Place in Cinnamon Gardens, the diplomatic quarter of the city, the SLMM monitors sat back and watched the spectacle of tracer bullets shooting into the air as Colombo plunged into an almost complete blackout. There were reports of some impacts to the north of the city where oil storages were said to be hit, but the security forces were reluctant to cede any concrete information on damages sustained by the attack. The major impact of the surprise attack was the fact that the LTTE, through its embryonic air wing, had managed to thoroughly sour a night of celebration of the two best cricket teams in the world for the Sri Lankan cricket fans. This was very embarrassing for the leadership of the military and not the least for the Defense Secretary himself.

At the end of February 2007, the SLMM, in a statement issued to mark its fifth anniversary, said that in the first three years of the CFA less than 130 deaths related to the ethnic conflict had been reported. However, with rapid escalation of hostilities over 4000 had been killed in the last fifteen months. Intended or not, that coincided almost to the day with the reign of Mahinda Rajapakse as President of Sri Lanka. And there were thousands more casualties to be reported in the coming fifteen months.

Following the fall of Vakarai, the SLA had been successful in tracking down LTTE elements in the jungle west of Batticaloa. There were strong indications for the SLA being assisted by the Karuna faction in the jungle fighting a war which the LTTE had mastered so well in the past. This time around, the SLA seemed to advance relatively steadily. The LTTE resistance in its last strongholds around Thoppigala south of Polonnaruwa, deep in the jungle, was crushed by mid-2007. Again, like in the battle for the eastern seaboard, it was very difficult to assess at what cost these military clashes had come to the onward-marching SLA and the defeated LTTE. What was quite evident by now was the fact that the LTTE had been forced to completely abandon the East, where it did not possess significant fighting forces anymore. Surely there would remain some small groups in remote areas such as the sparsely populated Ampara plains, but as a proper military opponent in the East, the LTTE was a spent force.

To mark this, the GOSL held an imposing military parade to celebrate the liberation of the East. On 19 July 2007, the President addressed his military and his people proclaiming a new "Dawn for the East". In his speech there were passages carefully intended for reaching out to both Tamil and Muslim sentiments. It was indeed a historic achievement of the military of Sri Lanka. For the first time since more than a decade the GOSL was in full control of the fragmented and somewhat backward Eastern Province. The people there were among the poorest on the island and had suffered massively through the conflict, the tsunami and general economic hardships. The President outlined plans to pour in aid and improve the infrastructure in the next few years. Moreover, the same day a bill to conduct local government elections in the East was passed in Parliament.

The LTTE could only observe in frustration that for the remainder of the year, the GOSL was busy putting in place structured governance and administration in the East, without the Tigers being consulted in any way. The Karuna faction entered the political mainstream through establishing a formal political party the TVMP, which was quite successful in the local elections held towards the end of the year. The LTTE had long claimed that it would be futile for Tamils to enter into the political system to gain influence and administrative power through democratic means. Tamils would inevitably suffer subjugation at the hands of the Sinhalese if Tamils were foolish enough to put their faith into a biased and corrupt Sinhalese political system. The elections in the East, where several TVMP representatives were elected to important political posts and administrative offices, seemed to run counter to this often repeated mantra of the LTTE.

Just as had been anticipated by most observers and publicly declared by the commanders of the military, at the end of the year the SLA started testing the LTTE on several points at the long demarcation line between the LTTE Vanni and the GOSL-held Northern Central Province. There was a slow but heavy military build-up going on, yet the SLA still seemed to focus primarily on the stabilisation of the East. Nevertheless, it was obviously only a matter of time until the march to Vanni would start. In the meantime the SLA would leave the LTTE guessing where and when it would try to push through to the North.

The last spectacular suicide air-attack by the LTTE came in October 2007 when the LTTE claimed it had launched its most comprehensive assault by Black Tigers in the history of the organisation. In the dark hours of an early Monday morning the LTTA attacked the large airbase in Anuradhapura. It was not clear how the LTTE had managed to penetrate so far south of their controlled area with heavily armed suicide cadres. Vavunia airbase just south of the demarcation line to Vanni was often deemed vulnerable to a surprise attack by the LTTE, but Anuradhapura was more than an hour's drive to the south and heavily guarded by security forces. Nevertheless, it was clear that the attack was quite successful. The Black Tigers appeared to have been able to fight their way into the complex where they had blown up several aircrafts. The attack was assisted by air as the LTTE dropped bombs from what was believed to be two aircraft causing more damage to helicopter gunships and reconnaissance aircraft. The LTTE also said that its Black Tigers had controlled parts of the complex for several hours before being killed by security forces. Their training had been such that they were to stay and do as much damage as they could, as a safe return from such a deep offensive operation was deemed highly unlikely. The GOSL conceded that not only had there been a loss of several lives in the attack, but further, for the first time in years, the LTTE had been able to inflict significant damage to the SLAF fleet of aircraft. The LTTE claimed it had destroyed eight aircrafts.

Twenty-one Black Tigers laid down their lives in a morbid display of dedication to the cause of the LTTE. Breaking with tradition, the LTTE would refrain from blurring the eyes of the cadres in the inevitable group photo taken as a sort of last rites with Mr. Pirapaharan and duly published after the raid on Anuradhpura airbase.

The security forces in Anuradhapura broke with their tradition of treating their fallen enemies with due respect. In a callous way, the corpses of the Black Tigers were stripped completely naked and thrown on a cart, which was pulled to another location, in broad daylight clearly visible to the public. It created a nasty spectacle which would have been avoided by a more disciplined military unit.

The LTTE remained able enough to conduct the odd surprise operations after having conceded the East to the SLA. However, some of these bore the hallmarks of an adversary trying to draw attention from the international community rather than inflicting sustained damage. Some operations seemed to be primarily aimed at embarrassing the GOSL and the military leadership. The suicide attacks and the air attack on Anuradhpura would arguably be the last spectacular military feat in the history of the LTTE.

In Colombo, the GOSL was not only concerned with the consolidation of its power in the East, but was also addressing problems posed by the scrutiny of the international community. The human rights situation in Sri Lanka had gone from bad to worse, as the CFA was completely breaking down. The inhibitions and modest restraints of clandestine forces appeared to evaporate. The media carried a constant stream of news of ably aged men being kidnapped, tortured or simply disappearing. Corpses were found in digs and dumps all over the island with an alarming regularity. Collective brutality seemed to be on the rise and there were countless tales of despairing relatives finding themselves confronted with the horrible task of trying to identify a decapitated and decomposed body left to rot by unknown perpetrators.

Renowned international organisations dispatched their

representatives to Sri Lanka to report on the deteriorating human rights situation, and the GOSL came under sharp criticism from most of them in the wake of their findings. Ministers of GOSL sometimes either snapped back or tried to downplay the criticism, sometimes in such a clumsy way that it led to international incidents. Such was the case during the visit of John Holmes, the UN Under-Secretary-General for Humanitarian Affairs. A distinguished British career diplomat and a former UK Ambassador to Paris, Holmes had visited Sri Lanka and then published a damning report on the human rights situation in general and the security situation for aid workers in particular. According to the UN report, Sri Lanka had one of the worst records in the world for humanitarian aid worker safety, and in the last eighteen months almost thirty aid workers had been killed. Included in that lamentable number were the seventeen ACF workers who had been massacred in Mutur in 2006. In a remarkable response to the report, prominent GOSL Cabinet Minister Jeyaraj Fernandopulle proclaimed UN Under-Secretary-General Holmes to be a terrorist himself and accused him of supporting the LTTE from whom he had received bribes. The UN was not amused and the UN Secretary-General Mr. Ban Ki-Moon made an official rebuke of the Sri Lanka minister's remarks. Although some of Sri Lanka's finest career diplomats had risen to important offices in the UN system, there appeared to be a constant and lingering animosity towards the organisation in Sri Lanka. The issue of Mr. Holmes faded away somewhat and he made a return visit to Sri Lanka in 2009 to assess the situation of Internally Displaced Persons caught in the war zone. Mr. Fernandopulle, the Cabinet Minister, was assassinated by the LTTE while attending a sports event in April 2008.

The SLMM had ruled that the security forces of Sri Lanka were responsible for the massacre of the ACF aid workers who had been shot execution style at the INGOs compound in Mutur, a finding that the GOSL had never accepted. In response to massive criticism from the international community, President Rajapakse, who in the past had prided himself on his record as a politician campaigning for human rights, established a special commission to investigate the ACF massacre and other high-level incidents. The commission, established in February 2007, was called the Sri Lanka Commission of Inquiry and was to investigate fourteen specific high-profile cases of human rights violations in the island. It was to be assisted and mentored by a consortium of international rule of law dignitaries, the so-called International Independent Group of Eminent Persons (IIGEP). The IIGEP soon realised that its advice was not all that appreciated and that it appeared to be an outright nuisance to Sri Lanka's Attorney-General. As 2007 drew to an end, it was evident that little if anything would come out of the work of the Commission of Inquiry and in early 2008, IIGEP threw in the towel and terminated its operations. Most of its suggestions the group finally stated in the course of its year-long existence had been ignored or rejected and aspersions cast on its conduct.

The Ambassadors of Western countries in Colombo were alarmed over the forced ejection of hundreds of Tamils from their meagre dwellings resembling a shanty-town at the outskirts of Colombo in mid-2007. These Tamils were then deported to Vanni by force with the GOSL giving the explanation that they had constituted a threat to the security in Colombo. In response to this and other human rights violations such as the rapid increase in abductions donor countries were subtly letting it be known that further aid would be dependent on an improvement in the human rights situation, but officially the GOSL was mostly defiant.

As the year 2007 drew to a close, it was obvious that there would be no further developments in the now-defunct peace progress. Seniour ministers in the GOSL were claiming that the West was bullying Sri Lanka on human rights issues and trying to tarnish the image of the country internationally at a time when Sri Lanka was fighting a decisive war against one of the deadliest terrorist organisations in the world. The GOSL was further angered by profound criticism from key organisations such as Amnesty International and Human Rights Watch.

The GOSL had fought a war in the east of Sri Lanka in 2006 and finished it in 2007. The Army was obviously going to fight another war to the north in 2008 and both the Army Commander and the Defense Secretary had proclaimed that the military was able and willing to destroy the LTTE. Moreover on the last Saturday of the year, *Daily News* published an exclusive interview with the Defense Secretary where he reiterated that the CFA had become a joke and it should be abrogated.

Both the GOSL and the LTTE had had bountiful opportunities to declare the CFA null and void, but had refrained from doing so. The reasoning for GOSL adhering to a nominal but long defunct ceasefire agreement had already been explained. It was to appease the international community from which useful aid was flowing into Sri Lanka. The LTTE could have terminated the CFA on the grounds of the permanent closure of the A9, the loss of the East through military battle and a regular use of air attacks by the SLAF. However, the LTTE had apparently been massively weakened, with the Karuna split doing the most damage. It had also been almost completely isolated with the EU proscription proving more damaging than most diplomats had anticipated beforehand. At the time, the SLMM HOM Ulf Henricsson had said that the EU proscription would effectively end the peace process and give GOSL a *carte blanche* to abandon negotiations and go for an all-out war to crush the LTTE. Now the LTTE had become increasingly desperate in its isolation and it was not likely to pull the plug on the CFA and thus both the Norwegian facilitator and the SLMM on the ground.

The shift in the ground situation in Sri Lanka had been almost total and complete from the optimistic early days of the CFA in 2002. The island was now embroiled in a war in the north; in the east there were terrible human rights violations being recorded and Colombo had been militarised beyond recognition.

On 2 January, the Cabinet of the GOSL on a recommendation from the President agreed to officially terminate the ceasefire agreement dating back to 22 February 2002. The Norwegian

Ambassador was subsequently handed a letter to that extent from the Sri Lankan Foreign Minister, Mr. Bogollagama. According to the CFA's final article 4.4 a notice of fourteen days should be given by either party to the agreement in advance of the effective date of termination.

The abrogation of the CFA meant that the SLMM would cease operations and it was time to pack up. In a joint declaration, the Foreign Ministers of all five Nordic countries expressed their regret over Colombo's decision to terminate the CFA and pointed out that the early ceasefire period had arguably saved over 10,000 lives in Sri Lanka, given the comparative statistics before and after the CFA functioned properly. The CFA had nominally been in effect for almost six years. Nevertheless, a long anticipated decision had been made by GOSL. On 16 January 2008, the SLMM terminated its operations. On that same date Sri Lanka found itself officially at war again with the LTTE.

# 35

## The Crushing of the Tigers in Vanni

In the first years of the CFA, several very promising opportunities for taking the peace process forward towards a negotiated settlement had been squandered recklessly by both sides. The LTTE had thought it had reached an agreement with GOSL on a federal solution as early as in December 2002 in Oslo. Following those talks the President had backtracked as it became clearer that the LTTE interpreted a federal solution as an almost complete detachment from control by the democratic institutions of Sri Lanka. Moreover, the Interim Self Governing Administration proposals by the LTTE put forward a year later appeared to be a thinly disguised proposal for a *de facto* LTTE-run statelet within the nominally sovereign state of Sri Lanka. Mr. Tamilshelvan's insistence on the ISGA proposal and the almost total lack of flexibility indicated by the LTTE were very unhelpful and made the facilitation role of Norway almost impossible. However, the GOSL had also failed fundamentally in putting forward a sound proposal, clearly defining how far it was willing to go in presenting the LTTE and the Tamil people with a significant and viable package of devolution. After the SLA had taken all LTTE-controlled areas in the East, the likelihood of a negotiated peace became increasingly illusive. In essence, the LTTE had failed to show flexibility on the subject of establishing a Tamil-friendly administration with reasonable powers within the sovereign borders of Sri Lanka. The GOSL, on the other hand, with a democratically elected government and a strong executive President had failed to formulate a realistic offer to the LTTE. The evidently inevitable outcome of six years of fruitless international inducement for a negotiated settlement was at hand. A war, with all its horrendous consequences for the simple people of Vanni, was about to be unleashed.

The GOSL had good grounds to be optimistic in its pursuit of a military victory over the LTTE following the abrogation of the CFA. Defense expenditure had increased markedly or by almost a third year on year between 2006 and 2007 and was to rise even further in 2008 and 2009. The three armed forces of the Sri Lankan military had increased dramatically in strength from the commencement of the CFA. Various external estimates differed, but it was roughly assessed that the Sri Lankan Army personnel had increased from 95,000 to approximately 160,000 in the CFA period. The Air Force and the Navy were both estimated to have doubled their personnel to approximately 20,000 servicemen each. At the outset of the CFA, the fighting strength of the LTTE had been approximated at around 10,000 cadres. With the Karuna split in the east and the continuing depletion of its ranks in 2006 and 2007, it was difficult to assess how many fighters they had left in Vanni, but it could hardly have been more than 6,000-7,000 cadres. This number would drop sharply throughout 2008 as the LTTE suffered immense losses in trying to halt the SLA onslaught.

The Government of Sri Lanka had successfully forged close procurement relations with Pakistan for increasingly sophisticated weapons systems for both the Air Force and the Army. The relationship between the Sri Lankan and Indian navies had been intensified as the SLN had acquired deep-water vessels enhancing its capability to act as a line of first defense for the island. The Navy and the Air Force released several video clips of the destruction of suspected LTTE arms cargo vessels in the deep seas of Sri Lanka. It was suspected that intelligence was being provided by India or the US, or both. Essentially, the LTTE had lost its capability of retaining arms from abroad and its lack of hardware and ammunition would become increasingly apparent in the course of 2008 and into the final battles of 2009.

Economic and political ties with Iran and China had been deepened considerably with President Rajapakse displaying his skills as a statesman securing direct foreign investment from China in building a new harbour on the southernmost tip of Sri Lanka. India, which had expressed some sympathy for the Tamil cause in the past, had refused to re-enter the conflict politically and was faced with its own problems at home with insurgents and terrorist attacks. The gross miscalculation of Mr. Pirapaharan in orchestrating the assassination of Mr. Rajiv Gandhi in 1991 would haunt the LTTE's relationship with India to the organisation's bitter end.

The LTTE had suffered badly after the split with Karuna, which lost them their support in the East, ultimately leading to a finite military defeat in the whole Eastern Province rendering total government control from Trincomalee down through Batticaloa and to the south-eastern Ampara district. The role of Karuna should not be underestimated. He had been the most admired and most important military leader of the LTTE. It was no coincidence that he had been a key member in the LTTE's first delegations to peace talks in Thailand and Oslo. At the memorable only and final press conference of Mr. Pirapaharan in April 2002, he had been one of the few hand-picked members in the podium. The real grounds for his decision to split with the LTTE leadership in Kilinochchi had never been fully explained.

The proscription of the LTTE by the EU had apparently paralysed much of the financing of the LTTE in Europe following earlier measures to the same extent in Northern America. The LTTE had also lost an important source of funds by the closure of the A9, which had put paid to their taxation of goods flowing from the south to the Jaffna peninsula.

In the past, the LTTE had managed to launch spectacular attacks on SLA garrisons seizing large quantities of weapons, a *modus operandi* that had been denied to them by the CFA. During the CFA the GOSL constantly claimed that the LTTE was regrouping and strengthening itself for the battles of the future. The evident lack of means of the LTTE to halt the SLA offensive in the north, and the sheer ferocity of the onslaught indicated that the opposite had been true.

The SLA had transformed itself during the CFA period from a demoralised fighting force lacking political and public support in the south, to a formidable battle hardened unit that had defeated the LTTE decisively in the eastern campaign. Desertion had decreased dramatically and the SLA was now commanded by the tough and determined Lt.-General Fonseka who appeared to enjoy the unconditional support of President Rajapakse and his brother, the Defense Secretary. The LTTE's failed attempts at their lives in 2006 had most likely increased their resolve to pursue an outright and final military victory immensely.

In the first offensives of the SLA into Vanni from the north-western theatre of Mannar, the Army met with relatively stiff resistance from the LTTE. But as the front was widened to several penetration points along the old demarcation line of the CFA, the increased arms technology, material, training and utilisation of military intelligence decisively tipped the balance in the favour of the Sri Lankan armed forces.

The SLA advance to the north was a cumbersome and deadly affair resulting in widespread casualties on both sides. The SLA and LTTE would continue to overstate the losses of the enemy and understate its own casualties. In effect, the SLA stopped releasing casualty figures from mid-2008. This was an indication of the horrible losses the SLA was accepting in its determined march towards

Kilinochchi. The number of casualties suffered by the SLA was interpreted to have reached such levels that it could not be shared with the public in the south, at least for the time being. However, the LTTE was losing ground, slowly but surely. In the course of 2008, the SLA gained inroads into the Vanni and towards the end of the year, the whole western coast had been secured from Mannar all the way up the A32, the old main coastal highway, up to Poonaryn from where there had been a ferry point for boats to cross over the Jaffna lagoon to link the mainland to Jaffna town.

On 2 January 2009, the main seat of the LTTE, Kilinochchi, fell to the SLA. The fierce and bitter fighting for the town left it in rubbles as the heavy SLA artillery pounded the last remaining defense capabilities of the LTTE. Most administrative buildings, from where the LTTE had managed its virtual mini-state within the state, had been levelled to the ground. Kilinochchi, once a bustling city, was now a ghost town as its inhabitants had fled with the retreating LTTE fighters towards Mullativu. Most civilians were simply fleeing the incoming shelling and aerial bombardments, but it was widely believed that the LTTE had also forced thousands of civilians to withdraw with them against their will.

In the early months of 2009 it became increasingly evident that the LTTE was no longer a match for the relentless onslaught of the SLA. The LTTE was obviously running short of arms, fuel, combat cadres and intelligence. In what resembled a replica of the final offensive towards Vakarai in the eastern campaign exactly two years earlier, the LTTE was being boxed in, in a shrinking area around its last bastion at Mullativu on the north-eastern coast. Trapped with the remaining fighting formations of the formerly so formidable Tamil Tigers were as many as three hundred thousand civilians suffering the terrible consequences of a modern war.

The leadership of the LTTE was frantically appealing to the international community to intervene, but there was initially only a lukewarm response to their calls of dire distress. The role of facilitation by the Norwegian Government had been terminated by GOSL a few weeks before the final battles. The Norwegian effort had been one of patience, valour and sincerity, but now it had ended and with it its influence on GOSL. The whereabouts of the LTTE leader Mr. Pirapaharan were not known and nothing was heard from him, but he was believed to be trapped somewhere in his jungle hideout close to Mullativu. The LTTE leader had defied the political system in Sri Lanka where his decree to ban Tamils from voting in the 2005 presidential election had almost certainly robbed the more moderate UNP leader Mr. Ranil Wickremasinghe of a sure victory. It had been an immense tactical gamble by Mr. Pirapaharan, a gamble he had completely lost by overplaying a much weaker hand than anyone had anticipated. In his decision to bar the Tamils from voting for a candidate that had voiced his sympathy for the plight of the common Tamil civilians, rather than focusing on the alleged widespread Sinhalese hatred for the LTTE. Mr. Pirapaharan bore a large responsibility for the suffering of thousands of Tamil civilians who were being killed and maimed in the fighting.

The main voice for the LTTE in the endgame of the civil war in Sri Lanka was Mr. Puleedevan, the head of the old LTTE Peace Secretariat, which had now been completely destroyed. As the last LTTE-held town of Mullativu fell to the Sri Lankan armed forces, the LTTE withdrew with tens of thousands of civilians to a small strip of land on the coastline north of Mullativu, where they remained completely trapped and were at the mercy of the advancing SLA.

A humanitarian catastrophe dwarfing the one in Vakarai two years earlier unfolded in the last weeks of the war in the spring of 2009. The LTTE accused the Army of shelling civilians and hospitals labelling the acts of the SLA as genocidal and constituting to war crimes. The GOSL responded by accusing the LTTE of using the Internally Displaced Persons as human shields, a clear breach of international conventions of warfare. It was hard to verify what actions were actually being taken by the SLA in its determined resolve to annihilate the LTTE.

International misgivings over the scorched earth tactics of the SLA led to an intervention by the French and British Foreign Ministers in Colombo. They were to have been accompanied by the Swedish Foreign Minister of the incoming EU Presidency, but he was denied a visa for entry into Sri Lanka. Mr. Kouchner and Mr. Miliband appealed for a ceasefire in order to seek negotiations to ensure a safe passage for civilians. This suggested halt to the final battle was rejected by GOSL on the account that this would give the LTTE breathing space to regroup. In reality, the LTTE was completely trapped on the narrow coastline north of Mullativu, and in a marked difference from the final defeat in the east two years ago, now the Tamil Tigers had nowhere left to run.

The SLA claimed that it had refrained from using heavy artillery and air attacks in the last days of the humanitarian tragedy in the area of Puttumattalan, but the LTTE said that makeshift hospitals had been hit resulting in an unprecedented carnage of civilians. Independent government doctors trapped within the LTTE controlled area confirmed the use of artillery despite the GOSL pledges to the contrary. As the UN sought to intervene in the last days of the siege, they were told by GOSL that the war effort would be fought to a bitter end until the LTTE had been completely destroyed. The only possible cessation of hostilities could come if the remaining LTTE fighters laid down their weapons unconditionally.

On 16 May 2009, the Tamil Tigers let it be known that they had decided to "silence their guns" as they could not justify more civilians being killed by the incoming artillery shelling by the SLA. The SLA in response said that the LTTE had been shooting civilians desperately trying to flee the battlefield and that the security forces had concentrated on evacuating civilians in a major humanitarian relief operation. The day after the SLA reported that they had killed and identified most of the highest leadership of the LTTE including its enigmatic leader. The body of Mr. Pirapaharan was displayed on the ground apparently killed in a last effort to break out of the final stretch of land during the last battle of the Sri Lankan civil war. Mr. Pirapaharan had embodied the armed uprising of the militant Tamils against the Sinhalese dominated GOSL. As such, the violent insurgence appeared finished and dead, just as the LTTE leader, whose dark and formerly fierce eyes were now frozen in a glazed and morbid stare. The SLA had brought in George, his trusted translator, to identify him along with the man who had inflicted the sorest wound on the LTTE, Mr. Muralitharan, previously Colonel Karuna.

Not only was the LTTE leader dead, but also all of the higher ranking military and political LTTE officers had perished. Credible news reports stated that its last remaining political speakers, the political wing leader Nadeshan and Puleedevan, had been riddled with SLA bullets as they surrendered unarmed waving white flags in the final hour of the conflict.

It had taken Sri Lanka twenty-six years of war to crush the LTTE. The cost of the conflict in Sri Lanka was not only the horrendous figure of nearly ninety thousand dead but also a wide ranging militarisation of the country, a sweeping eradication of most of the basic human rights and an almost total destruction of infrastructure in vast areas in the northern and eastern part of the island. Sri Lanka was economically crippled and its international reputation had suffered immensely in the last years of the conflict. It was a conflict barred from the outside world in its last stages. Half a year before its end, international aid workers were ejected by GOSL out of Vanni. International media reporters were barred from the conflict areas in 2008 and 2009 and only a handful were allowed into Vanni after GOSL had declared a final and complete victory over the LTTE.

A large number of prominent figures had been assassinated in the protracted war, which had gone through four distinct phases, ending with a total military victory for the SLA in 2009. The LTTE leadership had been wiped out completely and with it a battle-hardened organisation that for years appeared to be one of the most resilient non-state fighting forces seen in modern times. The two main protagonists of the GOSL war effort, Lt.-General Fonseka and Defense Secretary Mr. Gothabaya Rajapakse, had both miraculously survived LTTE suicide attacks in Colombo. They had never tried to hide their preference for a military victory over a negotiated settlement. Furthermore, in 2007 they had explicitly pledged to win the war against the LTTE within two years and so they did. The victory had come at a staggering cost. According to the military, it had suffered over six thousand dead and three thousand wounded in the last two years.

The UN Secretary-General Ban Ki-Moon visited Sri Lanka shortly after the final victory of the SLA. He inspected giant camps for displaced persons suffering from the aftermath of war and desperately needing the most basic of humanitarian aid in the form of water, food and shelter. He was also flown over the former no-fire zone on the north-eastern coast. In statements to media he said that he had never before been confronted with such appalling scenes as in Sri Lanka and urged the GOSL to allow immediate, full and unconditioned access to the thousands of internally displaced peoples in several giant camps in Vanni. The GOSL in its response pointed out that it would have to screen the people in the camps for LTTE fighters, a process that could take up to and, maybe, over a year. Mr. Ban Ki-Moon was accompanied by a number of photographers on his flight over the small strip of land where the LTTE had finally been crushed. The pictures appeared to show relatively clearly that the so-called no-fire zone had contrary to the assurances of the GOSL suffered an apocalyptic incoming hail of fire from the SLA artillery. The UN had estimated that around 7.000 civilians had been killed in the battle zone in the first five months of 2009. Following its enquiries and resulting analysis *The Times* in the UK said that over 20.000 civilians had been killed in the crossfire in 2009, most of them due to incoming artillery fire from the SLA.

After the final battle against the rump of the once formidable LTTE, Sri Lanka was faced with a humanitarian crisis resembling in scope that of the post-tsunami year. Aid agencies, still severely restricted in their activities, estimated that around three hundred thousand internally displaced persons were interned in large makeshift camps in Vanni.

Internationally, it was hoped that Sri Lanka would invite and welcome INGOs to help it in resolving the humanitarian crisis in the north of the island. It was obvious that it would take years to bring life back to normalcy in the scorched Vanni.

# Epilogue

Following the horrific final events in the battlefield in northern Sri Lanka and in particular after the alleged heavy artillery shelling of the LTTE and thousands of displaced civilians within the proclaimed no-fire zone, Sri Lanka found itself confronted with serious allegations from various governments and international organisations.

Immediately after the last shots had been fired in the barren stretch of land north of Mullativu, there were several calls for an international enquiry into alleged war crimes committed by both the LTTE and the SLA. At a meeting in Brussels, the Council of the Foreign Ministers of the EU demanded a thorough investigation into this matter.

The US, which appeared to have supported the political and military approach of President Rajapakse from his early days in office, also raised questions over the conduct of the SLA in the final phases of the war. In an unprecedented move, the US administration demanded an urgent and extraordinary special meeting in the UN Human Rights Council where it sought, through its European allies, to table a resolution which called for an official investigation into the alleged war crimes. The motion was countered by Sri Lanka, which received support from the unlikely alliance of China, India, Iran and Pakistan, among other nations that were extremely reluctant to permit international scrutiny into human rights abuses. President Rajapakse had skillfully deepened relations with the governments of these countries which rarely saw eye to eye on matters concerning their direct dealings with each others. Sri Lanka had made a strategic shift internationally, shunning the criticism of the West and intensifying its relationship with the most important regional powers in Asia.

Sri Lanka's defiance towards the US and the West was stunning given the massive amounts of aid that had flowed from those countries. However, the end of the war in Sri Lanka marked more than just the crushing of the epic Tamil Tiger insurgency. It also marked a shift in the external strategy of Sri Lanka. President Rajapakse's government had openly snubbed the most important representatives in the peace process, the so-called co-chairs of the Tokyo donor conference, the EU, the USA, Japan and Norway. Instead Sri Lanka had flirted intensively with both India and China, the two protagonists that were set to become locked in an intense challenge for domination of the Indian Ocean. Sri Lanka would have significant strategic assets to offer in such a contest, which was projected to correspond with a relative decline in the once so formidable might of the US Navy in these waters.

The final and decisive victory of the SLA over the LTTE was celebrated immensely in the south and the popularity of Sri Lanka President Mahinda Rajapakse was elevated to an extent where he was adored like a cult figure. He had been elected on a ticket of keeping Sri Lanka intact and rejecting a federal solution to the ethnic conflict. He had promised to take a determined stance against the LTTE and continue to use force if necessary although a negotiated peace had not been ruled out either. The LTTE, after virtually securing his election by its own tactics, had accused him of pursuing an endstate with war and had never trusted his intentions. But that was history. President Rajapakse was widely believed to be assured re-election on the back of the epic campaign against the LTTE and would thus rule Sri Lanka for years to come.

The whole template of the shifting strategy of Mr. Rajapakse's government, from a stance of reserved pursuit of peace through negotiatons and possible concessions to the LTTE towards an overt push for an outright military victory, would be studied meticulously in other troubled regions of the world. It would surely be noted with great interest by governments facing an ethnic or political uprising and would most likely be emulated by some.

President Mahinda Rajapakse was now faced with the enormous challenge of reconciliating the Tamil people with the south, to rebuild the north and the east and to reunite the beautiful island of Sri Lanka.

In order to achieve that, he would have to reach out sincerely and generously to the Tamil population of the island, which had borne the brunt of fighting for more than a quarter of a century. To be sure, he would have to offer some sort of devolution to the Tamils in Jaffna and Vanni, and most likely also in the east. Barring such concessions, the wounds would take long to heal. Furthermore, given the apocalyptic endgame of the war in the tiny stretch of coastline in the north, he would have to be seen as statesman enough to allow investigation into the conduct of the Sri Lankan Army in the last days of battle, reinstate the rule of law in Sri Lanka, stop the impunity of the rampant death squads and invite international human rights commissions and monitors to bring Sri Lanka back into the fold of civilized democracies in the world.

In an ironic twist of fate, the victorious and supremely popular head of the Sri Lanka Army, Lt. General Fonseka, who had been widely credited with masterminding the military crushing of the LTTE, fell out of favour with President Rajapakse at the end of 2009. Instead of the two mightiest men in Sri Lanka joining hands to exploit the political spoils from the military victory, Lt. General Fonseka stunned his president by stepping down from his position as commander of the army to wage a political battle aiming to unseat his earstwhile supreme commander.

Mr. Fonseka stood as candiate for the UNP, the leading opposition party, which had seen its candidate lose so narrowly in the presidential election in 2005, when the LTTE leader had blocked Tamils from casting their vote. To add insult to injury, the former president Madame Kumaratunga had decided to endorse the candidacy of Mr. Fonseka, hence supporting a candidate from the UNP, which she had fought so bitterly during her long tenure in office. In the January 2010 election, Mr. Rajapakse who had been so widely celebrated following the victory over the LTTE, was threatened with being swept from power in the most unlikely turn of tides in the political history of the indpendent republic of Sri Lanka. However, in this final showdown, Mr. Rajpapakse managed to hold on to power with a comfortable victory. Nevertheless, the political ranks of the elite and the military had been split in the contest for the presidency. Now Mr. Rajapakse would have to overcome internal Sinhalese opposition and find a way to win the peace and bring normalcy, human rights and prosperity back to Sri Lanka.

# Sources and Documentation

Substantial passages of this book are based on the author's diaries from his tours with the Sri Lankan Monitoring Mission in the years 2004, 2006 and 2007. In his capacities of first Public Information Officer and Spokesman, and later Chief of Staff, he gained an intimate first-hand knowledge of the ethnic conflict and the main protagonists in Sri Lanka. He met with key interlocutors of both the GOSL and the Sri Lankan military and the highest ranking representatives of the LTTE. A wealth of information was further made available to the author through discussions with other SLMM staff in Sri Lanka. Meetings with high ranking military commanders took place in several frontline localities and High Security Zones such as Omanthai, Nagarkovil, KKS and Trinco Naval Base.

In a conflict which was marked by severe restrictions for media reporters, the author had the privilege to visit all of Sri Lanka's conflict theatres on numerous occasions including Jaffna, Mannar, Vavuniya, Trincomalee, Batticaloa, Ampara and Kilinochchi. On those visits, the author had the opportunity to discuss the conflict in Sri Lanka with the SLMM local national staff, which over the years turned into real experts on the history and development of the longstanding insurgence in their respective regions. The national staff of the SLMM will not be named here for security reasons. Furthermore, many of the international colleagues in SLMM asked not to be named in this book as some of them feared it might hinder them in returning for visits to the wonderful island of Sri Lanka.

In discussing political events, the author has delved into the great well of contemporary journalism in Sri Lanka, which publishes a range of newspapers printed in English, including the GOSL flagship *Daily News*, the military friendly *The Island*, the intellectual *Daily Mirror*, and the voice of dissent *Sunday Leader*. The senior editor of the *Sunday Leader* was candid and critical in his reporting on the conflict, the GOSL and President Rajapakse. It cost him his life as he was gunned down by unknown killers in Colombo in early 2009. Following his death, a chilling letter from him was made public where he had anticipated his imminent murder and accused President Mahinda Rajapakse for having instigated it.

The ever improving websites of the newspapers mentioned above have made the tracking of exact dates much simpler than it was in the past. To that extent, the LTTE sponsored news site TamilNet has also been useful. In the run-up to the Presidential elections in 2005, the media started to focus intensively on the outgoing President and the two candidates to succeed her. Much of the discussion was at times quite heated in the media, but the wealth of articles by several distinguished journalists simplified and decoded the political labyrinths in Colombo for the author. Very interesting bits of information were regularly shared at briefings for VIPs at the SLMM HQ in Ward Place in Colombo and also picked up at social functions of the international community in Colombo.

The background to the conflict in Sri Lanka has been described in several volumes in local languages. However, the author found limited neutral factual information readily available in English. The nature of the conflict is, of course, such that it is frequently written quite differently by the Sinhalese and the Tamils. Results from elections which indicate the political tendencies and shifts during the six decades of independence are readily available on GOSL websites, some of which include surprisingly candid anecdotal information on Sri Lanka's main politicians.

For a substantial and very vivid description of the early years of the ethnic conflict and the following two decades leading to the CFA agreement, Mr. M.R. Narayan Swamy's *Inside an Elusive Mind* is a supremely rewarding read. Unlike that author, this author has chosen to use the LTTE preferred spelling of its leaders name in English, therefore Mr. Pirapaharan as opposed to the widely used Prabhakaran in the south.

Generally, the author has used the regional and place names in the same manner as they are spelled in the Colombo-based English speaking print media. The spelling and choice of names can be controversial as it can sometimes be seen to imply an intrinsic political connotation in Sri Lanka. If that has been the case in any instance it is totally unintended by the author.

On tsunami-related matters, the websites of the UN family and the Asian Development Bank have been sources of key information.

The author hopes that in a return to normalcy to all of Sri Lanka, writers on political topics and current affairs in the island will find it easier to name their sources without hesitation.

# Index